TORRIDON HIGHLANDS

TORRIDON HIGHLANDS

BRENDA G. MACROW

THIRD EDITION

ROBERT HALE & COMPANY
63 Old Brompton Road London S.W.7

First edition 1953

Reprinted 1962

Second edition 1969

Third edition 1974

ISBN 0 7091 4475 X

Printed in Great Britain by
Lowe and Brydone (Printers) Limited, Thetford, Norfolk

To the Companions of my Climbing
and
My Friends and Neighbours of Torridon

". . . And so from the hills we return refreshed in body, in mind and in spirit, to grapple anew with life's problems. For a while we have lived simply, wisely and happily; we have made good friends; we have adventured well. The hills have taught us to be content in our faith and in the love of God who created them."

(F. S. Smythe, in *The Spirit of the Hills*)

CONTENTS

ILLUSTRATIONS

xi

*The above illustrations are reproduced from photographs
supplied by Robert M. Adam of Kingussie*

Chapter I

APRIL ADVENTURE—THE BEGINNING

WE ran into Edinburgh in the warm light of the spring evening. Jeannie, my Skye terrier, had had more than enough of the train. I was glad that we had arranged to stay a week here before going on to the west.

Coming into that silver city in the mellowing light gave one an odd feeling of nostalgia; and the strange atmosphere lingered. After supper, we left our hotel in Royal Terrace and climbed Calton Hill in the dusk. Below now lay the city, coiled like a great grey dragon about the feet of the hill, breathing smoke into the calm air, winking at us with a million waking eyes. From the top of the hill we gazed across to Arthur's Seat and the Salisbury Crags. We passed the National Monument, and looked down on to the regal sweep of Princes Street. It made a memorable picture, overshadowed by the fantastic Castle, lighted by strings of twinkling lamps, with the bright-eyed cars and trams crawling and interweaving like tireless beetles and the delicate Gothic tracery of the Scott Monument etched on the darkening sky. It is at such moments that one understands the witchery of "Auld Reekie" and her power over the heart.

A week later we were on our way again, running northward through a landscape awakening to life and beauty under the gentle hands of Proserpina. Through the green countryside around Dunfermline—and then Kinross, where the mounting hills were mauve and blue and cocoa-brown under the sun. The ploughed earth was here a pale cinnamon colour, blending softly with grey granite houses and bare brown birch-trees. The tiny haystacks, too, had turned grey under the winter rains. Swarms of sombre "hoodies" followed in the wake of the plough. The warm earth rolled away to meet the whin-dotted moorland which mounted up into sepia hills. Daffodils bloomed on the banks of many a wayside station, and new lambs skipped over the dried grasses of yesteryear.

I

The train began to roar between cliffs of broken rock, emerging to follow the frothing course of a stream.

A hawk swooped over the rising moors. All about us, now, the blue-patched hills lay open to the sky. It was a sight to stir the blood and beguile the mind from the uncertainties of the international situation. I leaned out of the window to look at a tinkers' caravan-camp tucked away among the silver birches—and felt, suddenly, as if I had inherited the earth.

Later came the forest, and we were on the fringe of the mountains. Larches drooped yellow-tasselled boughs to the wet moss. Fir and spruce patched the hills with olive-green. Willows raised their straight, delicate fronds in the sunlight. Young pine-plantation added a touch of vivid emerald. The hills, increasing in stature, were patched with rock and grey scree. The little houses cuddled at their feet, their white walls having the glare of snow in the strengthening sunlight. We ran through long tunnels and along ledges chiselled out of the side of the hill, the engine panting as it climbed. A shallow brown river wound beside us on the west, gurgling over white pebbles. The banks bore signs announcing the Forestry Commission's warning about fires. The sheep—black-faced now—meandered with their lambs over the rough pasturage, their long coats rippling with the flowing motion of unbound hair. The flowerless broom raised olive spikes among the dry grass. The earth had faded to a pale fawn, almost cream in places, like sand. Beside the stream, the pussy-willow catkins were bursting into a shower of sun-coloured foam. By Ballinluig, the dark hills were patched with last year's bracken, rusted by the long rains.

Lunch was served as we passed Pitlochry. Over the entrée, we watched the wonderful pass of Killiecrankie dropping away beyond the window, the tree-clogged gorge lightened by the fret of yellow waters. Blair Atholl then, and Struan—outposts among the forest, beyond which the tarnished moorland, scattered with grey boulders, ran up and up towards the Cairngorms.

There were Highland cattle in Glen Garry—lovely, pale-gold creatures bending massive heads to crop the sparse turf. Gulls flew and cried forlornly over the dry heather. The river was spanned by flimsy bridges flung over the sun-silvered waters. To the east, we saw our first snows, ribs of sparkling white curving down the brown flanks of the high hills. Everywhere was a barrenness and

2

desolation that set a spell upon the wanderer's spirit. Nothing clothed the nakedness of the moors save the silver fretwork of trees, the solemn procession of electricity pylons, the snow-fences, the stone "fanks" sheltering quiet grey sheep.

The river flowed over terraces of rock, and the little grey road with its slim telegraph-poles kept company with the climbing train.

We were coming up to the snowfields now. The crisp air wafted in through the open window, bringing a flush to the cheek and a sparkle to the eye. Dalnaspidal—and the grey lochans lay, remote and unruffled, in the grizzled hollows of the hills. A fine veil of rain descended upon us at the summit of Drumochter, and the white mountains blurred and withdrew into their silences, the Boar of Badenoch hunching his back defiantly against the grey sky. The spears of the rain-faeries struck the carriage windows and glanced off, or stabbed at the brown pools in the peat-moss. But the sun was shining again as we ran down to Dalwhinnie.

Aviemore presented the loveliest sight, so far, of the trip. Snow lay heavy in the Làirig Ghru, and the wide shoulder of Ben Macdhui wore diamond epaulettes under the sun. The great folds of the mountains rolled away and away into sun and cloud. The ancient forest of Rothiemurchus clung like a dark mantle about their knees.

I had been reading a Dorothy L. Sayers "Lord Peter" novel, but closed it now. Much as I enjoy Miss Sayers, I had no choice. The most enthralling book in the world would be no match for the Cairngorms!

It was cloudy when we drew out of Inverness on the following morning, after a comfortable night at our favourite hotel. The sunlight filtered down in broken shafts to bring a sheen to the mud-flats at the edge of Beauly Firth. The water was choppy, foam-crested in the light wind. The hills beyond were dark blue, capped with the grey-white of shadowed snow. The woods to the left of the railway were carpeted with windflowers.

Cloud came down over the hills at Dingwall. Gulls and "hoodies" screamed on the machair, among the grazing sheep. There was little sun now—just a goldish glow out towards the Cromarty Firth.

Beyond Achaneed, the train climbed up into the close-folded brown hills, following the white loops of the road. Ahead, we could see the railway winding away between craggy channels of rock scooped out of the face of the hill. A thin burn threaded its way through a ferny gorge below. Close above us, the grey cliffs gathered and mounted and towered to obliterate the light. Sparse birches clung to the broken buttresses of the cliff. Then the landscape was opening out again, and we looked away across the peat-waste to snow-capped mountains.

Past the woods and the moors and the steel-grey lochans. Under the crags and the precipices, following the winding way to the west. Through the gouged-out tunnels, up and over the braes, past the granite crofts and the stone dykes, the little train puffing and panting through the grey morning.

Garve—and beside us wound the little road over which I had travelled westward by auto-cycle the previous year. On the platform stood three early hikers, loaded down with waterproofs and rucksacks on which hung saucepans, frying-pans and nailed boots. I looked at them—and my heart leapt as the heart of a sailor at sight of the sea. With the window between us, we exchanged a smile and a word of greeting. I was still in my "city-clothes", but they seemed to know that I belonged to their world, that we were brethren of the open road. My mind ranged ahead to the possible Youth Hostel. Romantic Ratagan, on the shores of Loch Duich, looking out upon the wild hills of Kintail? Achnashellach, or North Strome, or Kyle,* at the "Gateway to Skye", within sight of the Cuillin? Even Jeannie was sufficiently interested to prick up her ears as they boarded the train.

Almost too soon, now, we puffed into Achnasheen. A hurried lunch—a greeting from the Alligin bus-driver, who remembered mending my auto-cycle for me last year, and then we were relaxing in the grey shooting-brake, on the last stages of our long journey.

The sun had gone now, and Loch a' Chroisg was slate-grey, streaked thinly with foam. Chatting lightheartedly with "Alec-the-Mail", I looked across to the ethereal curves and corries of Móruisg and the blue mountains of Lochcarron. The brown moors ran down to the winding road. I looked, and loved, and remem-

---

* Strome hostel was closed in 1964, and Achnashellach in 1965. The present hostel at Kyle was formerly a school.

bered. Jeannie slept. In our separate ways we had rediscovered peace. . . .

One of the most striking scenes in the whole of the Western Highlands is the view of Loch Maree from the summit of Glen Dochertie. Familiarity provides no defence against this sudden vision of wild beauty which still, despite hydro-electric development, brings cars and buses to a standstill on the top of the hill. I know of no prospect which offers more perfectly and completely the whole glory of the west—the purple-brown hills soft-folded around the shining loch which lies like a jewel in the deep valley. The dark and ancient islands leading the eye away to the coast, to a fairy horizon filmed by nebulous vapours. Nearer at hand, the long streamer of the road looping down and down to the gleam of white houses, dwarfed by the great sugar-loaf hump of Slioch, rising out of mother-of-pearl cloud.

The bus swoops down towards tossing trees. One has hardly recovered from the impact of Slioch when the pinkish rocks of Meall a' Ghiubhais loom on the left, luring the startled eye upward and westward to the wild white corries of Beinn Eighe.

One can understand why this mountain is so well-beloved of climbers. A pause at the Kinlochewe Hotel, and we are away under the long knife-edge of it, gazing in awe at the shining screes, the white pinnacles of Cambrian quartzite whose age sets the mind reeling back over unimaginable aeons. The name, according to some authorities, means "The Mountain of the File".* Those who have walked the ridge in a mist will appreciate its significance.

On the left, across the purling river, the landscape is for a while dominated by the dark cone of Sgùrr Dubh. Red pines march across the foothills; and, presently, we come to the cool woods surrounding Loch Clair and Loch Coulin, through which the ancient Coulin Pass runs away to Achnashellach. To our right, another mountain is growing up beyond Beinn Eighe—fantastic Liathach, the Grey One, the highest and the most sinister of all the Torridon hills. I am not the only person who has felt that there is something evil about this mountain—and loved her in spite of it. . . . There is a prophecy that Liathach will one day fall and bury Fasaig village. The whole of her south side is covered with loose boulders and the debris of old landslides. Yet the villagers remain and the climbers go on climbing, and the

* See p. 111.

stranger gazes long in awed delight at the sheer sandstone terraces and pinnacles which once, it is said, looked out across the Lost Continent of Atlantis, and brooded over a strange world in the dim ages before the stirring of life on the earth. "Pipe-rock" in the area reveals fossils of worm-casts over 600 million years old.

Almost as fantastic as Liathach is the weird "Valley of a Thousand Hills" which lies in a hollow at the foot of Beinn Liath Mhór. It is here, if anywhere, that the "Wee Folk" must have made their home, for the whole valley is filled with their green cities, the little hillocks piled so close upon each other as to form a maze of miniature mountains to imprison the imagination.

And now we cross the boundary between the estates of Coulin and Torridon, and the bus-driver points out a small herd of deer threading their way daintily across the hill. Ahead, the glen is opening out towards Loch Torridon. A rainbow effect of mist and sunlight dapples the braes. The bright green of young pine-forest paints gay patches on the sombre brown of last year's heather. Wet terraces of rock shine pure silver where the sun kisses the old hills. The following memory is still with me:

"And now comes, at last, a sight of Loch Torridon and a feeling of journey's end. The golden whins are out at Annat, smudges of yellow on the distant green. They dance around the grey skirts of Liathach as we run into Fasaig village. The road is asphalt here instead of gravel, and, for a while, we are spared the interminable jolting which has been our lot since leaving Kinlochewe. In Fasaig we wait an hour for the other bus, from which we must take the mails for Braigh and Diabaig. This vehicle also brings all passengers for Coulin and Fasaig. Only those going on farther might ride in the shooting-brake, which, at the time of our visit, was a fairly recent innovation. Previous to this, there had been no transport at all beyond the village, and travellers to Alligin or Diabaig (the latter some seven miles farther on) had either to hire a private car, or a boat from Corrie,* or walk !"

While we waited for the second bus, I talked to the school-mistress from Diabaig. Ahead, on the far curve of a little bay, I could see a gleam of white which I knew to be the cottage I had taken for the summer. She told me it had once been the school-house at Alligin and had accommodated around seventy pupils. There were now a mere ten, of varying ages, who studied under

* Alternative local name for Coire Mhic Nobuil.

one teacher at the newer building beyond.* Diabaig had its own school; but here the road ended. Visitors to Craig or Opinan, farther up the coast, had to resort to a rough path over the moors. At Craig there was now nothing but the Youth Hostel. Opinan was some nine miles farther on, and one came first to Red Point, an old fishing-station, where the road picked up again. At one time, the people had agitated for a road right through to Gairloch; but certain councillors had opposed the scheme and it had come to nothing. The prior need, at the present, said the schoolmistress, was for a road down to Alligin village, as all heavy luggage had still to be sent by boat from Corrie, and the villagers must climb the brae to meet provision-vans.

(I thought of the substantial packages I had sent on in advance —and my heart sank as I remembered my gramophone records. Whichever way they arrived they would have had a "right good jolting" before reaching the cottage!)

The other bus came in. The mails were sorted and changed over. A postman with a bicycle took those for Corrie, Alligin village and houses along the shore to the end of Wester Alligin.

Away again, now, we left the asphalt and bounced once more over rough gravel, swinging right at the road-junction, up the double hair-pin bend where the road climbed above the forest behind the "big house"—so built, they say, by a laird who wished to keep the traffic as far as possible from his own front door, rather than with an eye to the needs of the villagers. I held my breath as we climbed, remembering how I had stuck here with the auto-cycle the previous year.

Below us the sunlight danced fleetingly on Loch Torridon, as if in promise of fine weather on the morrow. The hills of Beinn Damh Forest were blue-black, lit by patches of emerald where the light touched them and moved on. A puff of pink cloud clung around the proud brow of Creag Sgòrach. Ahead, Beinn Alligin was grey and still, untouched by the sun. The terraces of Beinn Dearg were patched with the silver of precariously lodged snow.

Over the bridge at Corrie, where a waterfall gushed into the dark gorge beneath. Then we were climbing again under the shelter of a semi-circle of wild hills, until the hunched south shoulder of Beinn Alligin rose close above us to shut out the sky, and the white village spread itself out around the little bay below.

* Alligin school was later converted into a private hostel for students of Rutherglen Academy.

"Where will you be getting off?" Alec asked. "At Heather Cliff?"

I nodded. We drew to a standstill on the top of the brae, and my luggage was put out beside the road. A rough track led steeply down beside a cascading stream. There were people waiting to meet the bus, and kindly voices advised me the best way to the village. A lady introduced herself as my next-door neighbour. I was recommended to carry the lighter things and send up for the rest, which would be quite safe beside the road.

I picked up the portable typewriter and a suitcase and started off down the steep hillside, Jeannie slithering delightedly ahead. Small boys appeared to watch us, and laughed at Jeannie's trailing coat and generally bizarre appearance. I gathered that there had never been seen in Alligin a dog like this one. Jeannie pretended to ignore her "audience"—but the glint in her eye said plainly: "Better watch out for your legs, small boys!"

The luggage was getting very heavy when I at length reached the little path running along the shore to the village. Towards me now came three ladies in walking-kit, carrying binoculars and cameras. We exchanged a greeting. I began to feel less of a stranger. Then two men left a coal-heap on the seashore and came towards me. I recognised one as the Postmaster and Warden of the Youth Hostel.* The other was my landlord.

It was from this moment that I began to feel at home. My landlord took the luggage and guided me to his house. His wife, with true Highland hospitality, at once offered me tea. A squad of little boys was sent up the brae for the rest of the baggage. I relaxed and ate home-made scones and shortbread, and luxuriated in the pleasant feeling of having reached the "end of the trail".

After tea, Mrs MacDonald took me along to the cottage on the point. It was long, low and whitewashed, with a corrugated iron roof. There were rows of lichen-crusted scallop-shells along the outside wall. It was fronted by turf on which grew three or four budding rowans and a holly-bush. Beyond this, a crumbling stone "dyke" provided a barrier against the sea. We were almost on the beach; and all day and at night I should hear the crying of gulls and oyster-catchers and the sound of the waves on the pebbles.

A thrill swept over me which was almost a pang at the heart.

* Inver Alligin Youth Hostel was closed in 1964, but the S.Y.H.A. plans to open a new hostel in Torridon when a suitable site and building are approved.

There were white net curtains at the cottage windows—and the chimney was smoking.

Inside, I sat down and gazed around, and knew that I was "home". The room which was to serve as the study-cum-living-room was simple and friendly, with a white ceiling and plain terra-cotta walls. There were a table, two dining-chairs, an arm-chair, a wall-mirror and an excellent oak chest-of-drawers. The floor was covered with blue-and-fawn linoleum. A coal fire burned in the hearth.

Soon, three rosy-cheeked children arrived with the rest of the luggage. I piled it up in the centre of the room and set at once about unpacking. Jeannie popped in from time to time to see how things were going, but refused to stay until I had stopped heaving cases and moving furniture.

Mrs MacDonald insisted on supplying me with eggs and other necessities until I was settled, refusing to take anything but my thanks in return. She came back several times to make sure that I had everything I needed.

Outside, the hills turned to navy-blue, then black, as night came down on the face of the landscape. The sea-loch sang softly over the grey stones. The little rowan-trees stirred in the light wind. I went to the door to call Jeannie—and looked out to the closely folded hills of Beinn Damh and Shieldaig, and the great, brooding, snow-streaked mass of Liathach, at the head of the loch. Behind the cottage, terraces of dark-red rock led up on to a plateau beyond which the first great hump of Beinn Alligin rose against the sky.

The tide was now at the full, lapping around the log "stockade" to which the villagers moored their boats. Later, I learned that this represented the beginning of a pier which had never been completed. The log walls were filled with stones. At low tide, the little boats lay among the pebbles beside them, waiting for the waves to lift them once again to life and the poetry of motion.

It was almost dark now. The scallop-shells were like shadowy flowers growing along the cottage wall. Jeannie and I went in and lit the paraffin-lamp and exchanged expressions of approval concerning our new home.

We had found a large wooden seat in the kitchen, and this, with some canvas cushions from the camping-equipment, served as a settee. The only rug was a horse-blanket originally intended

9

as a bed for Jeannie. But the little room was adequately furnished for our needs. There was now an extra table in the window for writing, and a desk-top from the attic on the chest of drawers, adorned with friendly books. Against the far wall was my camp-bed, on which the irrepressible Jeannie at once settled with a sigh of thankfulness. There had been a stuffed merlin on the mantelpiece, but I relegated him to the kitchen. He was so suggestive of Edgar Allan Poe's sinister Raven that my mind registered a hollow "Nevermore!" every time I looked into the baleful yellow of his eye!

I unpacked the new Primus, purchased at the Post Office, and set to work to make tea. We shared a simple supper beside the fire.

By candlelight, we once more explored the cottage. There were three rooms up a little staircase and three on the ground floor—a long, spacious house in which one could scarcely feel cramped, physically or mentally. All the downstairs rooms had curtains. This was, indeed, civilisation!

Outside, the wind was increasing and its salty freshness drifted through the slightly open window, causing the candle-flame to flicker and throw strange shadows on the wall. The lamp was carefully sheltered to protect the globe. I put more coal on the fire, and Jeannie and I sat together in its warmth. Later, I stretched out on the canvas camp-bed and read myself to sleep.

My canine friend, perhaps remembering Kintail and realising that we had reached our destination, snored contentedly from somewhere near my feet.

CHAPTER II

THE LANDSCAPE UNFOLDS

INVER ALLIGIN is four miles from Torridon or Fasaig village, three from Diabaig and twelve from Kinlochewe. The road is wild all the way. At the time of my visit, one had to go twenty-five miles to the nearest railway station, which was Achnasheen.

Inver Alligin has a Free Church, a Post Office and a cottage converted into a Youth Hostel,* and the village is ideally placed among wild and rugged hills. There is fishing on Loch Torridon (one may hire a boat from local fishermen), but the swimming is not to be recommended because of the swift currents. Loch Torridon is a sea-loch, and from the hilltops one can see the tide coming in in long lines of eddying foam.

Life is hard here for the Highlander. The only means of livelihood are crofting and fishing, with barren ground and uncertain weather to be taken into account. Yet the people are content, the children happy. Some of the villagers grow vegetables, and my landlady had a fine little orchard.

The hills were mainly under deer, and it was important in the stalking season for visitors to see the gamekeeper at Torridon House before planning a climb.

The people of Inver Alligin must surely be among the most hospitable in the world. There is a feeling of intimacy about the village, where, as in many Highland localities, people are known to all by a descriptive name—Màiri Bheag (Little Mary), Dòmhnull Mór (Big Donald), Coinneach Ruadh (Red Kenneth), and so forth. The lady who had previously lived in my cottage had been called Màiri Bhàn, which means Fair-haired Mary.

I spent the first week doing all the essential "odd jobs" pertaining to settling down in a new home. Firewood was collected from the seashore, a teapot and saucepan and various odds and ends of crockery were purchased from the Post Office next door, and it was arranged that the meat ration should be posted each

* A private house now stands on this site.

week from Inverness. The children, passing the cottage on their way to school, did their best to make friends with the "bonnie doggie"—but Jeannie would have none of it.

The weather continued fine, and the landscape was full of life and colour under the warm rays of the sun. At evening, the hills lay quiet beneath a rosy sky, as if studying their reflections in the loch. Sandpipers sped, crying, over the clear waters, and the pied oyster-catchers flitted along the tangle of weed at the edge of the tide.

While busy with household tasks, I found my eyes straying frequently beyond the lace-curtained window. I was beginning to know the hills now. There, just across the loch, lay Creag Sgorach, blue-grey in the soft light. Behind, lightly touched with snow, was rugged Beinn Damh, with An Ruadh-stac peeping over his shoulder. Next came Beinn na h-Eaglaisse, with Maol Chean-dearg behind, the two appearing as one until examined closely. Rosy in the mellowing light, wild Sgùrr Ruadh lived up to her name, displaying her fierce terraces and corries in a vain attempt to rival the silver craters of Fuar Tholl behind. At the head of the loch, the long grey ridge of Beinn Liath Mhór ran down to the grey terraces overlooking Glen Torridon.

Leaning closer to the window, I could just see the vast bulk of Liathach, dwarfing all the others into insignificance, imposing in her grandeur, aloof from the petty doings of man. Her first pinnacle, Sgùrr a' Chadail, was limned with gold; but up the long plateau snow lay glistening on Mullach an Rathain.

Sunrise, too, was a sight to stir the blood. Each morning, Apollo drove his golden chariot over the shoulder of Liathach, lighting little fires all down the dark mountainside, scattering diamonds among the snows, spreading light and colour across the pallid face of the loch. Sometimes, the gold would deepen with the maturing day—at others, it was fleeting as a dream, and, within an hour, the hills would be dead and grey and still among their mists.

The first visitors began to arrive, some carrying rucksacks, looking a little self-conscious, as if aware that there were as yet few of their number present. One or two of them passed the cottage, heading for Diabaig, and Jeannie barked at them so furiously that I had to call her in, lest she should exceed her duties as a watch-dog!

More coal was brought up from the seashore and put into my little shed. The cottage was looking and feeling every day more like home. I had now decorated the terra-cotta walls with enlargements of photographs taken mostly from the "high tops" in Kintail, so that I had the hills indoors as well as out-side. The spring sunlight poured in through the little win-dow, falling warmly upon me as I sat writing at the table, with the gramophone playing Brahms or Beethoven at the other end.

Outside, the wind stirred the shiny leaves of the holly-bush and whispered among the rowans, blending with the hollow sound of the sea to play me a symphony of nature, drawing its inspira-tion from the wild places of the earth.

There were days, it is true, when I thought nostalgically of the south—but there were others when it seemed that Torridon must surely be as close to Heaven as it is possible to get on this earth. On such days everything seemed to have a cosmic significance. A neighbour dropped in for morning coffee—and it was at once as original and delightful an occurrence as if it were the first—or the last—time such a thing might happen. On such occasions my heart went out to these kindly, gentle people, eking out a hard existence with their fishing and their sheep and their few crossbred cattle—yet all the time retaining the freshness of the sea wind in their outlook on life, the gaiety of the hill streams, the warmth of the Torridon sunshine in their welcome to the stranger. The children, often barefooted, passed the cottage on their way to the little schoolhouse under the cliff, and frequently stopped to talk to me and attempt friendship with the uncommunicative Jeannie. I was obliged to warn them that it was no use. Jeannie was what the Scots call "dour". She would make friends in her own time —or not at all if she did not wish to. Meantime, it was best not to approach too near.

During my fifth evening in the cottage, the wind rose to a gale. I went out in the gathering darkness and found some strips of wood to block up a crack around the window. All night, doors banged and windows rattled as the wind buffeted noisily around the little house. Outside, the sea was lashed to wrath, and I could hear the crash of the breakers and the grating of the undertow on the pebbles.

But, inside, I had two lamps, two candles, a glowing fire and a pot of tea. I could therefore listen to the uproar, without (as the Americans so succinctly put it) "caring two hoots"

The first Highland Sunday dawned grey and rough, with white caps on the waters and great billows of black cloud smoking up out of the corries of Liathach. In deference to the custom, I stayed in and spent most of the day resting and reading.

After lunch, the weather brightened a little, though the hills still scowled through their cloud. I called to Jeannie, and we ventured out for a short walk.

The most impressive feature about the Highland Sabbath is its silence. Yesterday, I had watched children playing around the ruins of an old house in the village—and the air had been vibrant with their voices. Today, there was not a sound, nor a soul in sight. There had been no service at the little kirk, for the minister went every third Sunday to Diabaig—but the day had begun in an atmosphere of solemn reverence which was never broken. Fantastic as it may sound, I did not even hear a dog bark—except the irrepressible Jeannie, who looked astonished and hurt when I at once bade her hush. Only the heretic hens went undisturbed about their business, pecking up grit and tea-leaves, cackling and laying their eggs, while the cock crowed truculently from his perch on the little stone wall.

Night came at last to the accompaniment of more rain, the sob of the wind and the sough of the sea.

The next day the cloud had lifted from the hills, and I noticed that some of the snow had been washed away by the rain. It was now possible to appreciate the geological formation of the mountains—the sheer terraces of red Torridonian sandstone climbing up and up like great steps leading on to the desolate roof of the world. I could see that many of the hills are capped with white—the Cambrian quartzite scree which, in sunlight, often has the appearance of snow. I recorded these impressions:

Loch Torridon is thought by many to be the finest sea-loch in Scotland. Its entrance is banked on both sides with Lewisian rock, believed to be the most ancient in Britain. This also occurs at Shieldaig, and underlies all the Torridon hills. The name "Shieldaig" is of Norse derivation, and means "herring bay".

On a clear day, the whole of the landscape presents a most

impressive picture of mountain grandeur. The fierce hills shimmer
in the sun. The blue sea-loch dances in to kiss the grey beaches or
lap under the red rock forming a little headland beyond the
schoolhouse. In the narrows of Shieldaig, Eilean a' Chaoil (The
Isle of the Strait) lies at peace on the calm water. Beyond,
the rocky coastline leads the eye away into shining distance where
the long "backbone" of Trotternish blurs the horizon.

Turning reluctantly from this heart-easing view of hills and
sea, you walk eastward along the shore path towards the bulk of
Liathach. Yellow lizards, basking in the sunshine, scurry under
the rocks at your approach. The "sea-pies" rise from among the
weed and fly, piping shrilly, across the still water.

The budding rowans flicker in the warm breeze. Black-faced
sheep trot away up the hill, their long coats bobbing like a ballet-
dancer's skirt, their snowy new-born lambs capering at their
heels. The shepherds and their faithful dogs keep constant watch.

The "Youth Hostellers" have not yet begun to arrive, and the
little red-roofed bothy waits expectantly among its trees. You
notice that the front door has received a fresh coat of paint.
(Perhaps you can remember happy days here, lamplight and
laughter, and a "céilidh" before the fire.)

Then you halt on the rise and look back towards Inver Alligin.
They are "working at the coals" on the shore—with, of all things,
a lorry, which, at this time, before the advent of the road, has
been brought by sea from Torridon village, borne on two
motor-boats lashed together.

The path winds on—past the white crofts and the ruins of
ancient dwellings. To the left, the peaks of Beinn Alligin emerge
from behind the great hump of the first summit. The fierce gullies
of Beinn Dearg shine temptingly in the sun. Through an iron gate
—and now you are looking down to the little Church of Scotland
and its adjacent manse; and beyond to where waves of dark pine
forest lie about the feet of mighty Liathach.

Just past the manse, a rough track leads up to the brae on to the
road. The grey shooting-brake which does efficient duty as bus is
coming up from Kinlochewe. It stops beside you, and you exchange a cheery greeting with Alec. You are going to photo-
graph the falls above Torridon House? Oh, well, he'll wait for
you, and give you a ride back in the brake. You explain that you
are going to scramble down to a certain cave, that it may take a

long time to find the right spot and set your camera—and go on your way wondering anew at the abundance of kind hearts around Torridon.

It was during my ninth day in Inver Alligin that my landlord showed me a feature of the district which is not known to the casual visitor—the "Smugglers' Cave" just around the headland, hardly ten minutes' walk from my cottage. Here, almost within sight of the schoolhouse, some sixty years ago, illegal whisky-distilling was carried on in a deep cleft in the red rock, protected from the sea by a wall of loose boulders. Mr MacDonald showed me the old track used by the "smugglers", plainly marked twenty years ago, but now overgrown with moss and turf. Beside it used to run the essential hill-burn, but this is now dried up, its course marked only by a depression in the moss. The cleft itself is deep and well concealed—but one has only to peep over the top to look straight down upon the schoolhouse. The Excisemen at that time were stationed just across the loch, at Shieldaig. The "smuggling" was carried on under a piece of sailcloth, and fires were damped down during the day to prevent discovery. The Excisemen periodically visited the school by boat to sign the books—but they never found the smugglers! At night, the spirit was secretly removed by boat, or carried away by the old track to find a ready customer. Mr MacDonald was a boy at school when all this was going on. Now, the cleft is deserted, echoing only the voice of the sea and the whisper of the wind among the bracken.

It appears that this whole district was at one time famous for the illegal distilling of whisky. In his enthralling account of *Smuggling in the Highlands* (Eneas Mackay, Stirling), Mr Ian Macdonald, I.S.O., recounts how the gaugers once discovered a bothy near the base of Beinn Alligin, and another on the margin of a small hill-loch where there was a little island. On the island they found a new copper still buried in the moss. Diabaig was equally active, and distilling was carried on in a seaside cave, among other places. At Upper Diabaig a shelter had been built for the smugglers in an old sheep-fank. An illegal distillery was also discovered in Coulin Forest, between Kinlochewe and Glen Torridon. There was a saying in Diabaig: "Is fada Diabaig bho lagh" (Diabaig is far from law), which seems to sum up the wild

16

nature of the country and the consequent difficulty of discovering the smugglers' haunts.

Returning from the smugglers' cave beyond Alligin schoolhouse, we looked across Loch Torridon to the long ridge of Beinn Shieldaig. There is a loch on the top, and my landlord described how, in rough weather, one may see the spume coming in great white clouds over the edge of the cliffs.

I felt that this had been a particularly interesting day. I had also had a call from the District Nurse, who dropped in for a cup of tea and a pancake. A lively young lady from Glasgow, she had been here nine years now and felt that she really "belonged". Her round extended from Balgy, on the other side of the loch, to Diabaig, a distance of some fourteen miles of very rough going! It was covered either by cycle or on foot. There had been a lot of 'flu recently, and she had been kept very busy. In addition to this she ran a small croft! She had a Shetland collie bitch called "Wily"—which, I am delighted to say, she petted in much the same fashion as I did Jeannie, with similar results!

The weather turned colder. One morning, the hills were grey with a cold rain, the wind sweeping in biting gusts along the foam-flecked surface of the loch. The tide was particularly low, and the villagers were gathering seaweed at its edge, to be dug into the soil for fertiliser. The people of Inver Alligin take a great pride in their gardens. Almost every house has its little patch for vegetables at the back, and gay herbaceous border in front. Seaweed is known to be an excellent fertiliser for potatoes. Any seaweed will do. Kelp (which has to be burned to obtain iodine) is a special kind of weed, usually found far out.

Beyond the grey beaches, a pair of eider-duck skimmed the choppy waters, flying swiftly before the wind. These, apparently, were unknown in Torridon twenty years ago. Close under my cottage window, the sturdy scholars plodded by to the white schoolhouse. The seaweed gatherers bent to their task of tossing the great shiny tangles into heaps out of the reach of the crawling tide, to be collected later with wheelbarrows and creels. A gull soared high over the loch, riding on the gale. The rippling cry of the oyster-catcher rose and fell intermittently from the shore.

I went round to the Post Office to get some rations, and bought tinned soup, carrots and a currant pudding. There was no tinned meat or fish. Apparently, the first was not very popular, and the

Beinn Alligin and Beinn Dearg from Sheildaig

second considered unnecessary when fresh fish may be obtained from the loch. The bread was not in yet. (At that time, it came once a week, from Glasgow!) One could, however, obtain bacon-bones, which, with the addition of the carrots and a few potatoes, made an excellent soup for supper.

Jeannie and I awakened early next morning. It was a golden day with a promise of warmth. The loch was blue under a cloudless sky. We had made the cottage to our liking now, and this was altogether too good a day to waste. I hurriedly cooked breakfast. Nine-thirty saw us tramping along the shore-path towards Fasaig village.

Around us, the new lambs wobbled and cried and nuzzled their black-faced mothers. We passed the picturesque ruin of an old croft, beside whose crumbling walls boats were beached and nets hung over frames to dry. The ebbing tide left behind long trails of shiny brown weed, from among which the oyster-catcher flew up as we passed. A large collie bounded over the wall of a spotless white croft, not pure-bred, but crossed with the English sheep-dog—a type which is known in Alligin as a "beardie".

Down the track we tramped, and through the woods at Corrie, where the gamekeeper's black retriever and brindle Cairns barked furiously as we circumvented the house.

Over the river now, and along the shady lane, emerging from the woods all too soon into the strengthening heat of the sun. Beside us, the loch was scattered with silver prisms, winking and flashing in the brilliant light. Above, the first peak of Liathach, Sgùrr a' Chadail, thrust up its grey snout at the sky. The hot white road ran on towards the village of Fasaig, and we followed it at a smart pace—though I was already beginning to feel as if my boots were full of little stones. By a memorial stone at the roadside, I took them off for examination—and found that nails were coming through both heels! After a vain attempt to flatten them with a stone, I gave it up, and limped on.

The high hills seemed to waver in the sunlight. We came to Fasaig village, but the only shop was closed, and there was no one to "sort" my boots. Two sun-browned visitors gave us greeting. A skirl of pipes followed us as we set off again.

Round the bend of the loch, I stopped for tea and biscuits with a charming lady whose house lay on the fringe of the woods. I mentioned the boots. She at once brought a hammer and a cobbler's last, and I flattened the nails without difficulty.

A shaded walk led on through the woods, where the air was made fragrant by the sweet scent of red pines. The silver birches were coming out around the feet of the hills. Sheep and lambs strayed across the machair. A man was sowing potatoes on a small patch of newly turned ground. Elsewhere, great heaps of seaweed lay ready to be dug in. Primroses, violets and "milk-maids" bloomed in the ditches. Across the loch, the great mauve escarpments of Liathach were marked by yellow veins showing the course of scree-falls or streams. Patches of snow lay among the pinnacles above. Farther westward, Beinn Alligin, also, had on her diamond tiara.

At Annat, there were neat cottages with their blossom-laden gardens. The flowering currant made a splash of rose against grey walls. Hens wandered across the road beside an old bothy covered with mossy thatch. Beyond an iron gate lay the little graveyard, where the old and lichened stones leaned across to the shiny new ones, and the young and old of Torridon whose earthly work was ended slept in peace under their blanket of green turf.

The barking of dogs announced that we were approaching the lodge, where, at that time, only a public footpath led on to Shieldaig. A left branch led away to Strathcarron; but we ignored this and wandered up through lovely woods of larch and spruce and pine around Beinn Damh House. The shadows of the tall trees barred the path. A cool breeze touched and refreshed us. The noises of the village faded, leaving only bird-song and the murmur of hidden waters. The forest closed around, shutting out the blue gleam of Loch Torridon. Wood-sorrel bloomed among a carpet of mosses under the trees. Pale shafts of sunlight filtered down to caress us warmly as we passed. Ahead, Creag Sgòrach was a sombre brown against the sky. To the south, beyond the forest, the bulk of Beinn Damh towered up uncompromisingly. Here follow my impressions of the scene before the road came:

The water-music grew louder. We reached the river, where one might swing left up the tiny track over the moss-crusted pipes which supplied water to Beinn Damh House.

Climbing through the woods, we presently found the first of the falls, spouting down into a horse-shoe of grey rock. It is not high, but the setting is charming and picturesque. From the grassy hillside one looks back along the green gorge to the magnificent terraces and gullies of Liathach, blue and white in the sunlight, with the white houses of Fasaig village at their feet.

The second fall is higher, and pours down into a grey gully littered with scree and fallen boulders. One follows a deer-track through the forest, up and up along the crumbling edge of the gorge.

The trees are thin, and soon you reach a promontory from which you can look down the gorge at the cataract. Wave upon wave of young larches leads the eye away and down to the shining reaches of Loch Torridon. Behind rises the blue mass of Beinn Alligin, serene and remote in the shimmering heat of the afternoon. It is well said that April and May are often the best months as regards weather in the West Highlands.

From Beinn Damh House the track to Balgy was straight and dry, lying over the braes like a yellow ribbon thrown across the heather. One walked through the forest and out into the sunlight— and still the smooth path ran before you, luring you on towards the headland. Across the loch, the grey giants of Torridon rose up coldly to stare at you, or folded the blue robes of their shadows about them and dreamt away the quiet afternoon. Distant snows caught and flung back the fire of the sun. Behind you, the white crofts of Annat and Fasaig hugged the machair, under the ridge of Beinn Liath Mhór, the pinnacle of Sgùrr Ruadh, the dark cleft of Glen Torridon curving away mysteriously in the shadow of Liathach, calling to mind the lines of John Campbell Shairp:

> "Oh marvellous Glen of Torridon
>   With thy flanks of granite wall,
> And noon-silence more than midnight grim
>   To overawe and appal. . . .
>
> On the further flank of the glen,
>   Sweeping in wonderous line,
> Scourdhu, Benlia, Bendamh
>   Their weirdly forms combine.
>
> At every turn new-grouped,
>   Fantastic features and forms,
> Cataract-cloven and corrie-scooped;
>   Homes of the thunder storms.

Mysterious Glen Torridon,
What marvels, night and day
Light, mist, and cloud will be working here
When we are far away! . . ."

There were laurels in the woods, and primroses and violets grew among the rocks beside the Shieldaig path. Perhaps (as we did) one spied a vivid green beetle sailing past on metallic wings, or startled a brown owl from slumber as one sat by a rock-sheltered well. Perhaps one wandered in spirit across the dancing loch, and climbed up and up to the black "Cleft" of Beinn Alligin—or scrambled along the perilous pinnacles of Am Fasarinen, the "Teeth" of Liathach.

. . . Or perhaps one would be content (as we were) to centre one's thoughts on the brown braes and the yellow path running ahead to the rugged fringes of the coast, where, not so long ago, smuggler and Revenue officer outwitted each other among the grey Lewisian rock of Shieldaig and Diabaig, or the red Torridonian slabs of Alligin.

The young butterwort leaves were opening out in the moss beside the track. A few pale-gold clouds drifted across the sky. Beinn Dearg appeared, mistily blue, between Beinn Alligin and Liathach. The whale-back hump of Beinn Shieldaig rose out of the low hills ahead. Looking down to Loch Torridon, one could glimpse the blue inlets cutting into the waves of forest below—Òb Gorm Mór and Òb Gorm Beag, over which gulls fluttered like scraps of white paper. Close to the track, the whins tossed their golden heads in the rising wind. The clouds sailed faster. Through the laurel-copse at Vugie (properly Badan Mhugaidh) one crossed the old road leading towards Creag Sgòrach.

The sun still blazed down upon the heathery moor. Down, now, past grazing cattle to the silver curve of the river at Balgy. Like the sinister sound of drums came the thudding of the falls, echoing back from Beinn Damh and Beinn Shieldaig.

Just before the footbridge, one could turn and tramp up beside the river to where it comes down in a series of uneven steps from the narrowing gorge. A few slender trees added a sylvan touch to the shallow but charming falls. We followed the track up the gorge, and soon Loch Damh opened out before us, a long stretch of silver-green water, blue-shadowed by the surrounding hills.

There were a tiny timber boat-house and a jetty and one rocky islet—but the total affect was one of desolation, probably due to the lack of trees around the loch.

Across Loch Torridon lay a welter of savage mountains, austere and fearful in their beauty. The light was changing as the heat went out of the sun. Beinn Alligin was a chaste blue, Beinn Dearg mauve with a hint of rose, Liathach a wintry grey now, patched with the olive shadows of the clouds.

We returned to the croft of Balgy, and crossed the bridge. The stony road ran on up the brae. It was here that Jeannie decided that she had had enough, and I had to carry her in the rucksack. (As Jeannie was a real Skye terrier, and much heavier than the Cairn that has now taken her place on the "Misty Isle", this arrangement added considerably to my burden!) The nails in my boots were beginning to make themselves felt again as we rounded the head of Camas a' Chlàrsair, the Bay of the Harper, where the flames of sunset danced on the water and a narrow neck of land stood out black against the gold. However, I trudged on, under the dark crags of Beinn Shieldaig, and at last came over the headland to Shieldaig Bay, and looked down upon the village.

Here the houses formed a white procession along the grey beach. Behind, neat gardens and cultivated patches ran up towards the crags of Beinn Shieldaig. On this particular evening, the loch was pure gold in the sunset, the one big tree-clad island black against the amber light. Little boats rocked at anchor in the quiet bay. A bonnie place, where strange craft might take shelter from the storm, and the restless heart feel at home.

Beside the school, the path led up among the grey rocks and over the headland. There were other bays here—tiny green inlets where the sad old sea whispered its secrets to the pebbles, and sheep browsed among the ruins of crofts long deserted and fallen into dereliction. There were two flat islands, chequered with crotal and yellow lichen, resembling two huge turtles floating at ease in the shallows.

Beyond them, the dying sun traced a path of light across the waters of Loch Shieldaig and Upper Loch Torridon, leading north-west to the rocky narrows marking Red Point and the gateway to the open sea.

Over the headland, we came down to the little bay where, already, the motor-launch from Alligin waited to take us home.

We had arranged previously to meet it at Camas an Lèana, to save petrol. The wind had freshened considerably, and the little boat bounced and thumped and wallowed in deep troughs of green water. The outboard stopped, and long strands of weed were disentangled from the propeller. Large waves broke over the prow, soaking us all. Jeannie, who liked to choose her own forms of horseplay, was tense with nerves. I took a good grip of the seat and told myself that it was "great fun". The Postmaster smiled at each wild bound of the boat. His three-year-old son, lost in some delightful day-dream of his own, fixed his eyes nonchalantly on blue distance and spoke not a word.

And so we came across the restless loch to the red rocks of Inver Alligin—and so ended our first long excursion. We had walked round Loch Torridon and visited three waterfalls. More than that, we had gazed across from the woods of Beinn Damh to the snow-streaked mountains sheltering the head of the loch, and had obtained a new vision of the wild and upflung landscape whose age and beauty were already weaving a net of enchantment which still ensnares travellers on the motor-road opened in 1963.

It was as yet early for the arrival of the migratory birds in Torridon. But the wild life intruded upon one at every turn, insinuating its way into casual conversations as if to prove to us how closely integrated was the life of the village with the world of nature.

The "soft" weather was fine for the lambing—and did I hear that the keeper at Corrie had caught a golden eagle this week in a fox-trap? I could go along and see it, if I were interested.

I politely refused this invitation, explaining that I held strong views on present methods of trapping. My informant agreed that they were barbarous. Only recently, a fox had left its paw in a gin-trap. From another source, I learned how some cubs had been trapped near the foxes' earth, and how the distracted vixen had pulled them out by wrenching off the trapped limb at the shoulder. We discussed alternative methods of extermination, and debated as to who was the more cruel—the gamekeeper who destroys beasts of prey with the only means at his disposal, or the smart townswoman who wears a fur coat without either knowing or caring how the skins were obtained. . . .

The fishing had not yet started in Torridon; and the sea-birds went about their daily business undisturbed by passing boats. Often, in the early mornings, a solan goose could be seen dropping like a stone out of the clear sky, to dive with a crash in search of his cold breakfast. The eider-duck sailed in and out of the little bays, crooning softly to each other in the sunlight. Razor-bills and guillemots dived among the sparkling wavelets, and the slim cormorant sped along like a dark arrow, just clear of the water. Occasionally, an eagle circled in the blue heavens, and the swift hawk and merlin pursued their prey over the brown moors.

The young lambs grew and thrived in the warm weather, guarded by the shepherd, with his telescope, and the faithful collies at his heels.

A young crofter discoursed on the training of sheep-dogs, about which there seems to be two schools of thought. He said that he, personally, believed that the secret lay in making friends with them. He would never, if it could possibly be avoided, strike one of his dogs in anger—and they responded to his gentleness with an unstinted affection and willingness to please. When not working, his collies were allowed into the house, petted and made much of, and generally treated as comrades rather than servants— a status of which they were visibly proud.

This was all a revelation and a delight. It is arguable that a dog's finely keyed intelligence responds better to kindness and a little spoiling than it does to what is commonly termed "discipline"—but there are still those who maintain that the best incentive to work is fear. I had lived long enough in remote places to know that there *are* shepherds who ill-treat their dogs, and I lived in constant dread of being an eye-witness to some act of cruelty. It was a joy to find a supporter for the humane view in one whose own highly trained collies were the best possible advertisement for the maxim that "kindness pays".

During the last week in April the wind swung round to the west again, and the good weather came to an end. Heavy rain pattered on the roof, while the fierce gale rattled the windows and slammed gates and doors. Outside, the loch was a cold grey dappled with raindrops. Beyond, the hills were an undulating blur, disappearing into thick folds of low cloud.

It was the time now to visit neighbours, and we sat around the fire and told stories. I learned about the "Golden Cave" at the foot of Liathach, into which two men once disappeared, never to return.

The conversation finally turned on the "Wee Folk". One member of the company knew of a man—and a good religious man at that—who firmly believed in their existence, identifying them with fallen angels whom the spreading of the Gospel had driven out of their haunts in the hills.

There was told a story about the two men from Alligin, who, some years ago, set out to get some whisky from Gairloch for the celebration of the New Year. They were returning on New Year's Eve with the keg of spirit, and were somewhere among the lonely hillocks between Opinan and Diabaig when they heard the "faery music". It was the loveliest and most enchanting sound in all the world, and they followed it eagerly until they came to a cave in the side of a hill. Here, standing at the entrance, they watched the "joyous Shee" dancing and making merry at a faery ball. The little people were about two feet high, dressed in tunics of red or green; and the two beholders were so enthralled that they drew nearer and nearer, until the one carrying the keg of whisky stepped right into the cave. His friend called to him to come back—but, at that moment, the cave closed, leaving no trace on the hillside to mark where it had been.

So the man returned to Alligin without his friend or the whisky—and it was no consolation to him when his story of their disappearance was disbelieved by all!

"Very well," he said, "I will prove to you that I am telling the truth." And on exactly the same hour of the same date, a year later, he returned to the spot with two of the doubters at his heels.

There stood the cave, wide open, with the faeries dancing to the unearthly music—and there, just across the threshold, was the man from Alligin, with the keg still on his shoulder. Swiftly, his friends reached into the cave and pulled him out. In the cold night air, he stood blinking as one awakened from a dream, asking them where was the need to hurry, since he had been away but five minutes.

When they all glanced towards the cave again it was closed, leaving no trace among the rocks to show where it had been. The man had suffered no harm from his experience—but (as is only to be expected when dealing with Highland faeries) the whisky-cask was quite empty!

CHAPTER III

CLOSER ACQUAINTANCE

THE spring planting went on apace. Every day, creels of seaweed were carried up from the beach, to be spread on the newly broken land. At one time, in the heyday of crofting, the organisation was so thorough that even the seaweed pitches were marked out along the beach—so many yards for each croft—and woe betide the crofter who trespassed on a neighbour's pitch! Yet it was not to the laird or his factor that such disputes were referred, but to the Fishery Board, since the laird has no jurisdiction or right to any land below the high-water mark. Thus, today, any dispute regarding, say, the gathering of mussels on the beach, or the laying of sewage-pipes from a house to the sea, would be handled by a Government department.

The spring sowing was made more difficult in Inver Alligin by the fact that there was no plough, and the turning of the soil had to be done by hand, either with an ordinary spade or with the "cas chrom", the "crooked spade" used in the time of Dr Johnson and still employed in the remote corners of the west. There were no horses, and I was told that, in any case, a horse-plough would be impracticable in Inver Alligin owing to the number of rocks and boulders in the soil.

A local crofter expressed the hope that one day he and his friends would purchase between them a small motor-plough to replace the "cas chrom", which he likened to a relic of the Stone Age. Apparently, this implement is extremely difficult to use unless one has learned the trick of it in youth. It is heavy and unwieldy, and no small skill is needed to drive the long blade home in the rough ground with the help of the peg which serves as a step. Once mastered, however, it will turn two feet of soil at a time—certainly an improvement on the ordinary spade when there is perhaps an acre of ground waiting to be broken up and fertilised for early potatoes.

Turnips, cabbages and carrots are also sown in Inver Alligin, and enough hay to keep the livestock through the winter. But, as elsewhere in the Highlands, crofting is not what it was. There are few young people, these days, willing to settle down and wrest a hard living from the soil and the sea, when the cities offer wider opportunities and more money.

However, those who remain in places like Inver Alligin seem to find a peace and fulfilment which the city-dweller seeks in vain. Once the life has taken possession of them, they do not want to leave it. Many of the young crofters had seen the world through the eyes of the Navy or Army. They were glad enough to be home again in their hills, concerned only that the weather should be good for the lambing, making the best of an arduous existence with whatever instruments they had to hand. Sometimes they wondered when the road or the hydro-electric scheme would arrive in Alligin. There was little financial reward for the crofter these days—indeed, most of them grew just sufficient crops for their own use. Eggs, calves and lambs were sold, and, of course. the fish—but here, again, the weather made all the difference. An eight-weeks' heat-wave, though delightful for the holiday-maker, could be a disaster for the farmer or shepherd who saw his crops withering in the field and his lambs dying for lack of moisture on the hill.

Yes—life was hard. There was no doubt about it. Yet here, as elsewhere, it had its compensations, and there was even gaiety for those who needed it. Every fortnight, for one night, the "Highlands and Islands Film Guild" brought their mobile cinema to Fasaig village, and an occasional "céilidh" or dance kept the heart light and the blood young. More than that, the crofters had their peace of mind and an unshakable faith in the goodness of God—two attributes which anyone who has lived in close contact with the life of the cities might well admire and envy.

They had their hills, too. The Torridon landscape, in April, is an ever-changing panorama of delight. Blazing sun one day, dancing and winking over a world of beauty, bringing to life the green and blue and silver of springtime, the red of the ancient rocks, the purple and turquoise of the waters. Then rain, dappling the loch, blurring the forests, folding the quiet hills away behind grey veils of cloud.

The temperature drops, the gale blows, there is snow on the high peaks. One thinks that the sun will never shine again. We huddle around the fire and meditate upon the long winter nights and the "ceilidh". I get out my Gaelic lessonbooks and learn how to ask for provisions and make the appropriate comments on the weather.

One morning the trees are quiet again, the loch as calm as a sheet of smoked glass under a dead sky. But the hills are blue-black beyond, and the pinnacles of Liathach are powdered with fresh snow. The chilly chirping of the oyster-catcher drifts up from the wan beaches, punctuating the dreary keening of the gulls. Across the wintry wastes of Loch Torridon, one can see new waterfalls leaping down the dark flanks of Beinn Damh. To the south-east, Fuar Tholl lives up to its name, the "Cold Hollow" of it gleaming blue-white through a swirl of snow-cloud. It is still snowing on the "high tops", blurring familiar outlines to a new and Impressionist beauty.

An hour later, the cloud lifts and the sun comes out—and the white is pure diamonds against the sable nether garments of the mountains. Liathach presents a fantastic spectacle, with Sgùrr a' Chadail a dead black and Mullach an Rathain behind draped in a robe of dazzling brightness. Mighty Beinn Eighe, peeping over her shoulder, is striped from head to foot with white, the snow clinging in shining bands along her fierce terraces. Across the sparkling loch, Beinn Damh and the Shieldaig hills are a company of pure virgins, each veiled in gossamer and wearing a crystal crown. One could believe it to be winter indeed—save for the green-tasselled rowan-tree nodding in the sunlight before the cottage door.

A black-faced ewe comes delicately into the garden, followed by her sturdy lamb. He is around a week old, with an odd, patched face and black socks. He stands staring, quite unafraid, while his mother nibbles the low shoots of the rowan-tree. (Fortunately, Jeannie is elsewhere, or the pair of them would not be there for five seconds!)

The weather holds good, and, once again, the snow begins to melt off the hills under the warm caresses of the sun.

On the golden morning marking the end of my second week in Inver Alligin I was accorded the rare privilege of being present at a Highland funeral. It was a most moving experience. Conducted jointly by three ministers—the Free Church, the "Wee

Free" and the Church of Scotland—the funeral service was held at the home of the deceased, on the fringe of the loch. We, the women, friends and neighbours, of whom some had come by boat from Diabaig, stood indoors, while the men ranged themselves outside by the sea-wall. Beyond, two fishing-boats rocked on the calm waters. There were three rowboats on the edge of the tide.

The Free Church missionary began with a long Gaelic prayer and the reading of a Psalm. The prayer was for the living—they do not pray for the dead in the Presbyterian churches and kindred denominations. Then the minister of the "Wee Free" Church led the singing—the metrical version of the 103rd Psalm, sung in Gaelic, with such poignancy that the soul was shaken by it. The very cadences, so unexpected to the stranger, so inevitable to the Highlander, were vibrant with a beauty and poetry that bruised the spirit. There was hardly a woman present who did not weep while she sang. It was the music of the strong rivers and the deep snows—of the grey sea lapping endlessly on the crags; of the untamed hills which will endure when "frail man is as the dust".

In the tense pause which followed, the Church of Scotland minister announced that, for the benefit of those present who had no Gaelic, the rest of the service would be conducted in English. He then read from Isaiah and the sublime poetry of Ecclesiastes, and the passage from the Gospel according to St. John which deals with the Resurrection. Beyond the window, the warm spring air wafted a promise of new life, and the boats rocked gently on the ebbing tide.

A prayer concluded the service, and the men outside took charge. The coffin was lifted out of the window and borne down to the beach to be placed in one of the waiting rowboats. Another small craft took the men out to one of the fishing-boats. The boat came astern, bearing its precious burden. The tow-rope was fastened, the soft purr of a motor broke the stillness, and the two boats glided effortlessly away over the still loch to the burial-ground at Annat. One could well have believed them to be setting sail for Avalon, so lovely was the scene, so vibrant the air with the mystical promise of the life after death.

We dispersed soberly, and went to our own houses. Later in the day, the boats returned, and the men disembarked for a meal. Presently, they had all taken their departure, and the fishing-boats had glided away towards Wester Alligin and Diabaig, leaving the loch calmly blue and tranquil under a quiet sky.

Jeannie and I tramped along the shore and scrambled over the red rocks of the point. For a long time we sat in the sun doing nothing. Young thrift and saxifrage were peeping out among the lichened boulders. There was not a sound to break the stillness save the crying of sea-birds, the intermittent "plop" of a sea-trout in the quiet waters of the loch. Nimbus cloud gathered in the blue vault of the heavens. Its shadow made great dark patches on the heaped-up hills. Rain was coming to bring new life to the fruitful earth. The loch was grey now, devoid of colour—but away under the foothills of Beinn na h-Eaglaisse and Seann Mheallan a ray of light fell on the white houses of Annat and filled the machair with gold and the promise of eternal spring.

We went home quietly to tea, and the rain began to fall as we entered the cottage door.

One should choose a golden morning of cloud and sunlight to derive the full benefit from a walk to Diabaig. If there is no need to hurry, you may take the coast-track from Inver Alligin, and the sun will fall warmly upon you as you meander along. Up and over the brae behind the schoolhouse—down now to the bay of Wester Alligin, scattered with a pathetic profusion of ruined cottages and crumbling byres. Here and there, smoke rises in a blue curl from the chimneys of clean, whitewashed houses where those who have remained faithful to the ways of their forefathers live out their tranquil, satisfying lives. A fishing-boat rides at anchor in the blue bay, and the shepherd with his collies goes serenely about his work.

The heather is burning on the foothills, and long strips of land are being planted with potatoes and corn.

One climbs up behind the last red-roofed croft, perhaps following the print of a shepherd's boots in the peat beside a birch-fringed burn. Keeping to the moorland path, the wanderer comes into a wilderness of boulders and heather, where the delicate blue spears of the milkwort and an occasional pale primrose add a touch of colour to the sombre grey and brown of the moors.

To the south, now, the inlet of Òb Mheallaidh is in shadow under the crags of Beinn Shieldaig, but light plays caressingly

over Loch Damh at the back of Balgy. Beyond the desolate headland lies Loch Shieldaig with its tree-covered island. The air
vibrates to the call of sea-birds over the water. A sinister shadow
flits over a nearby hill—and you look up to see a golden eagle
spiralling down out of the clear ether, to fall out of sight behind
the grey crags of the higher hills. The track is mounting now
along the side of the brae, so narrow and overgrown that it is
negotiated with difficulty. Behind, Liathach and Beinn Eighe
are a soft grey-gold, lightly powdered with snow. To the south,
behind Loch Shieldaig, snow-cornices cling to the cliffs of Beinn
Bhàn.

Above, larks trill softly in the warm air. Fritillaries play over
the heather, searching out the sweetness of hidden violets. The
peat-moss is starred with celandines which open their golden
eyes wide at the sun. Ferns uncurl among the tough grass. High
overhead, a few holly bushes cling to the grey rock, their dark
leaves flickering in the pure light. Loch Torridon is wrinkling
and dimpling under wind and sun. Camas an Lèana lies green and
smooth among the brown rocks of the headland. Eilean a' Chaoil
makes a dark smudge in the narrows. Across the arches of the sky,
a buzzard floats in silent vigilance—and, even as we watch, the
gulls and "hoodies" swoop upon it from the grey crags, driving
it away like swift fighter-planes attacking a cumbersome
bomber.

The path climbs more steeply. Loch Torridon falls away
beneath us. Coming over the last headland, we catch our breath
at first sight of the view to the west.

It is like emerging from a wilderness to find all heaven opening
out before you. If it is the right kind of day, the wide expanse of
Outer Loch Torridon will be a Mediterranean blue under the
sun, streaked with pure silver where the wind touches the waters
and moves on. Mingling with the Inner Sound, the sweeping
waters lead the eye away to Trotternish and the cliffs of the
Quiraing, the beginning of the great shadowy plateau running
from Staffin to Portree, the "Backbone of Skye".

Strung out along the far horizon, white layers of strato-
cumulus cloud may hang over North and South Uist and the dim
hills of Harris. Around is no sound but the whisper of hidden
burns, the ecstatic chirring of a lark in the sun-washed firmament
whose pale blue seems to echo on a fainter note the vivid cobalt

of the sea. It is a scene to make the photographer reach for his camera, the singer of Highland songs for his "clàrsach".

One scrambles down the hillside towards a lonely croft in the hollow by the blue sea. This is Port Lair, to which there is no access save by boat or the rough track over the moors. Industrious figures are busy on a small strip of freshly dug land. Sheep browse on the rough hillside. A black cow eyes the visitor suspiciously, seeming in half a mind to bar the path. The collies bark furiously at the unusual advent of a stranger in this remote haven of peace and industry.

One skirts the fence behind Port Lair, and begins to climb once more, following the track to the north now, beside a primrose-fringed burn, to cut off the point. Leaving the wild coast behind, the walker surmounts a rise to find Loch Dubh, where the path literally runs into the water and it is necessary to jump from boulder to boulder along the edge. Westward, beyond the point, one is offered a glimpse of the "Winged Isle". But all around lies the wilderness—grey rocks and crags streaked with the red of the Torridonian sandstone, thrusting up their bald heads at the sky.

Beyond the lochan, the path again rises steeply, almost lost, at times, among the boulders and heather, zigzagging now up the course of a burn, now under a grey shelf of rock which blots out the sun. One emerges on to a desolate waste of naked crags and brown moors, sombre under a blue sky perhaps flecked with cotton-wool cloud. The path leads on to Loch a' Bhealaich Mhóir, or the Loch of the Big Pass, a still pool closed in by the grey hummocks of rock, surrounded by heather and moss wherein flames the cerise candle of the bugloss. Beside the loch, peats have been cut and stacked for the croft below, each neat pile covered with dry turf and held down by the whitened trunks of long-dead trees.

The print of a shepherd's boots leads on over the headland whence the rambler at last looks down to Lower Diabaig. It is a striking picture—the little boats bobbing by the pier, the grey and white houses curving in a crescent along the shingly beach, backed by a wood of budding birches.

Faint sounds drift upward on the warm air—the friendly cackle of hens, the sharp bark of a collie, the quavering bleat of new-born lambs. Beyond the village, the road from Kinlochewe

Loch Torridon and the Beinn Damh (Ben Damph) Forest hills

comes to an end, only a rough track leading on over the moor to Craig.

On most days the bay is calm, and the fishing-boats and dinghies ride at ease on the sheltered waters. Westward, however, the breeze may be whipping up little clots of foam on the Minch, where the scattered islands sweep away into cloudy distance, their colours ranging from the brown and yellow of crotal-crusted rock to an ethereal shade of mauve with violet shadows where the far-away line of the land meets the blue sea.

The path now leads along the rocky hillside above the east curve of the bay. Through a birch-copse—and one emerges by a white house where a watermill clatters busily, harnessing the power of the rushing stream which foams in a series of linns to the sea. A collie bounds up to greet you, and the kindly lady of the house, on learning that you have walked from Inver Alligin, may perhaps offer you a glass of fresh milk to help you on your way.

You emerge from the coolness of her kitchen to follow the sunlit road along the shore through the village. All is quiet and drowsy in the heat of the afternoon. Beyond the curve of the grey houses, the road mounts up the brae between the slender birch-trees which clothe and beautify the whole of Lower Diabaig like a green and silver mantle blown into soft folds by the warm wind.

After exploring the village, you may elect to return to Alligin by the top road which climbs the steep brae to Upper Diabaig. Perhaps the wind is keener now, though the sun still blazes on the sea. At the top of the first rise, you look away down to the bay, where the little boats rock on the incoming tide and the clean houses gleam in the warm light. Beside the road, sheep browse peacefully with their snowy lambs, and men industriously wield spade and "graip" and "cas chrom" in the tiny fields. People emerge from the white houses of Upper Diabaig to bid you good afternoon. Below, to the west, the waters of Loch a' Mhullaich are pure silver in the sunlight.

You climb on, following the white, dusty road beside the loch. Ahead, the weird pinnacles of Beinn Alligin rise above the peat-moss, their grey terraces still powdered with snow.

But the loveliest scene of the day is that from wee Lochan Dearg, looking southward across Loch Torridon to the peaks of Beinn Damh. Indeed, at the first glance, many do not recognise

33

A Highland dwelling by the shore at Diabaig

the scene at all, so altogether wild and precipitous and unreal dc the hills look from this angle. One comes upon the lochan quite suddenly, for it lies on the top of a rise right beside the road. Ahead, the telegraph poles dip over a V-shaped gap through which the eye ranges to the silver flash of Loch Torridon with the ghostly giants of Beinn Damh and Shieldaig looming behind. From this angle, they look incredibly high, their serrated pinnacles sweeping round in a rugged curve to Sgùrr Ruadh and Beinn Liath Mhór.

Down the steep brae now—and you reach home at peace with the world, while evening shadows spread slowly over the still face of Loch Torridon and the bird-song dies with the fading light across the lonely moors.

Among the other features for which Torridon should be famous are its sunsets. The day after my walk to Diabaig, I visited, in the cool of the spring evening, a friend who lived at the back of Inver Alligin village. After tea, we climbed the brae to meet the van which was coming along the top road with the fortnight's supply of hens' food. There was no hurry for such things. If you missed the merchant, he would leave your sacks of meal and corn by the roadside to be collected and transported at your leisure since there was then no road down to the village.

When we reached the road, however, the van was still there, with several people gathered around it. Waiting our turn, Lexie and I stood looking out over the loch.

The waters were silver-grey, with faint splashes of rose. Away out in the centre of the loch, a great commotion and flurry of white wings marked where the gulls had found a shoal of herring. Behind, the hills of Beinn Damh Forest were slowly changing from blue to gold, from gold to amber, from amber to a deep blood-red as the sun dipped lower behind the isles. A girdle of rosy cloud clung halfway down Beinn Liath Mhór, so that the snow-freckled crags rose above it, giving the impression of great height.

Gold light lingered in the shallow pools beside the road, throwing the dark reflections of rock and grass-tuft into sharp relief, every line revealed as clearly as in a mirror. Jeannie sat on a flat boulder while we obtained our provisions, her long coat and tasselled ears sleeked back by the wind.

34

We shouldered our sacks of meal and began the scramble down the hillside towards the red roof of Lexie's house. A lamb, newly marked with blue paint, lay beside our path. We picked it up, but it was already stiff, dead from some unknown cause. A short distance away, the mother bleated sadly as if to tell us that our solicitude was in vain.

The sacks were heavy, and we paused occasionally for a rest. All about us, now, the light was fading from the scarred face of the earth, withdrawing its golden fingers from the wrinkled surface of the loch. The mountains drew a blue veil over their blushes; the pine forests of Annat and Beinn Damh darkened to form a thick blanket around the feet of the hills. The gulls, replete now from their feast of herring, rode lazily on the glassy waters. To our nostrils, borne on the night wind, came the salty fragrance of the seaweed which lay in dark strands on the beaches or made black humps on the fields. Empty creels lay beside the dykes, and lights winked in cottage windows where the hard-working Highlanders sat down to supper and rest.

We deposited the meal, and I said good night to my friend, borrowing a pail to get my coal for the evening from the appropriate heap.

Then Jeannie and I meandered back over the patch of green. Before we reached the cottage on the point it was night, and raining, and the last flicker of sunset had faded over the hills.

Across the loch, the twin peaks north of the saddle of Beinn Damh, known as Sgùrr na Bana Mhoraire, or the Peaks of the Wife of the Lord, were remote and lovely among their clouds.

CHAPTER IV

BEINN ALLIGIN BECKONS

EARLY in May, the first official Youth Hosteller arrived, a young builder from Derbyshire, who had set his heart on climbing Beinn Alligin.

It had poured with rain all day, a steady torrent which swept in grey veils over the loch, with no promise of abating. I was reminded of my own experience the previous year, when I had arrived by auto-cycle from Strathpeffer to make my first acquaintance with the Torridon hills. I had come on the recommendation of George Thomas, a schoolmaster whom I had met at Braemar—and to whom, incidentally, I owe a considerable debt of gratitude.

"Whatever you do," he had said, at the time of the Braemar Gathering, "you mustn't miss seeing Torridon!"

And so—I hadn't; and so, on a stormy day at the beginning of September, this book was born. . . .

I shall not easily forget that ride from Strathpeffer, though. In addition to torrential rains the whole way, there had been a high cross-wind which buffeted the auto-cycle from one side of the road to the other and made any real speed impossible. I was wearing an ex-Army camouflage gas-cape; but even this proved to be small protection against the driving rain. The wind got under it, and I had visions of finishing the journey by parachute! I finally overcame this difficulty by crossing the tapes at the back on the outside and tying them round the waist.

All the same, it was a somewhat chastened and bedraggled auto-cyclist who finally reached Achnasheen and stopped for a cup of tea at the ever-hospitable hotel. The lounge, I recall, was full of local crofters, travellers, a minister and a shepherd with his dogs, all looking nearly as wet as myself. The waitress brought tea promptly, and I sat warming my frozen fingers round the cup. Outside, a bus-driver was examining the auto-cycle with an interest which the rain failed to dampen.

I was already wet to the skin, so dared not sit still for long. On the road once more, I fought my way alongside Loch a' Chroisg, tears from my stinging eyes imparting a salty quality to the rain which ran down my face and dripped off the end of my nose.

The road through Glen Dochertie was like a river, and it was impossible to see the surface. I bounced from one hole to another, skidding occasionally on loose pebbles, climbing now towards the summit.

Even the cloudy vista of Loch Maree—a wonderful spectacle in the deep gash beyond Kinlochewe with its hills running up into rolling vapours—did not move me on this occasion. For once, I was too wet to care!

My dismay increased at my first sight of the road to Torridon. It was far rougher than I had expected, and I was beginning to have doubts about the condition of the auto-cycle tyres. However, it was too late to turn back now, and on I plunged westward under the looming knife-edge of Beinn Eighe, whose white quartzite blended mysteriously with the rolling folds of cloud to create a nightmare mountain of ever-changing shape and size.

The whole of the "last lap" of this journey was like a fantastic dream. The never-ending road—the great, terraced mountains whose steepness took away the breath, scowling close above, pinnacle upon pinnacle, a lost world of darkness and desolation. Apart from the Black Cuillin of Skye, I had never seen such awesome mountains. Sgùrr Dubh, beyond the fretted waters of Loch Clair. Liathach, grey and vast and seemingly inaccessible, overshadowing the road for a full five miles, its western peaks brooding over the headwaters of Upper Loch Torridon.

The rain was running down inside my clothes now. Through Fasaig village the road was made up, and the merciless jolting was momentarily eased. Across the grey loch lay other hills, but I did not then know their names. Ahead, to the north-west, the shoulders of Beinn Alligin were hunched against the fury of the storm.

Of course, being a stranger, I took the wrong road by Corrie pier and went charging up the steep hill behind Torridon House, the engine becoming hotter and hotter, until I was forced to jump off and run, panting, beside the puffing machine. Finally, I came to the S.Y.H.A. sign—and realised, with dismay, that the Hostel must be one of the cottages clustered round the little bay

37

far below! There was at this time no semblance of a road down the brae, and there seemed no possibility of getting the cycle over the rough ground.

While I stood somewhat dismayed, a woman came along the road from the direction of Diabaig.

Oh, yes, she was very sorry, but I had come too far. I must go back to the road-junction and take the shore-path which went right past the Hostel. Yes, it was a gey bad day, but there were people in the Hostel already, and no doubt they would be having a fire on. There was the Hostel—the wee white cottage with the red roof, away down by the path.

I looked. It was a tiny place; but the chimney was smoking! Thanking my kind informant, I bounced off back along the hilly road.

The cycle engine was by now so "warmed up" that it would not stop! We leapt up several inclines with the speed of a gazelle, and roared down the other side, skidding round sharp and shingly curves with more luck than skill. At breakneck speed, we came down the final tortuous incline with its double hair-pin bend which had beaten us on the way up. A sharp swing to the right, and now we were bumping along by the shore, and the fragrant tang of the sea-wrack blended with the unsavoury odour of petrol and hot oil.

Through the policies of Torridon House, where the game-keeper's retriever bounded up in his pen to bark at us. And now the road became a mere straggling track, thick with tree-roots and sharp stones, over which we bounced and jolted on the fringe of the grey sea.

At long last—the Hostel! And, indeed, small though it was, it seemed a veritable haven of refuge to as wet and dirty a traveller as, I believe, ever entered its portals!

It was impossible to stop the cycle simply by switching off the engine, so the desired result was finally achieved by throwing it out of gear and then letting in the clutch so sharply that it choked itself on an indignant snort. Having bestowed the mud-caked contraption in the cycle-shed, I splashed wearily up to the cottage door. It seemed a tiny place for a Youth Hostel, further dwarfed by the bulk of Beinn Alligin behind.

Inside, two earlier arrivals were toasting themselves before a roaring fire. They introduced themselves simply as Malcolm and

Geoffrey, a schoolmaster from Lochcarron and his friend, a history student from Glasgow University. They made room at the fire and offered freshly made tea. Water rolled off me and formed a pool as we talked. Fortunately, the spare clothes in my pack were comparatively dry.

After changing in the tiny "women's dormitory", I rejoined the couple by the fire. A medical student from Glasgow arrived, and fresh tea was made. The line above the range became festooned with wet clothes. We sat and chatted and warmed ourselves, casting an occasional glance at the streaming window. Outside, the rowans bent and wept and tossed their red berries in the wind. At intervals, a great sheet of spindrift was lifted and swept across the grey loch. The rain showed no least sign of abating, so, eventually, the two early arrivals went for the milk, which (so a notice informed us) could be obtained from a croft at Wester Alligin, a mile and a half away.

There were no further arrivals that evening. Over supper we formed ourselves into a "team" and laid plans for the ascent of Liathach on the morrow, weather, of course, permitting.

While we sat eating our corned beef and "Pom" the night came down over Beinn Alligin, and the shadows, sliding down the brown mountainside, engulfed the Hostel before spreading a dark mantle over the face of the sea.

The day dawned bright and clear. The breeze was drawing patterns on the loch as we made ready for our expedition to the hill. About us, all the scarred mountains were basking naked in the sun. For the first time, I was able to see them clearly—to feast my eyes on their wild cliffs and sandstone precipices, all ashine after the long rains. It was good to look across dancing water to Beinn Damh Forest—to discover that here, too, were hills of surpassing beauty and grandeur, a wilderness of upflung crags and scooped-out corries to entice the wanderer's feet.

We were almost ready to set out when the Warden arrived, and advised us to consult the gamekeeper at Corrie first, as there was a stalk in progress that day to obtain venison for the "Sale of Work" to be held in Torridon village on the morrow. We tramped down to Corrie, and made inquiries. Liathach, as we had begun to fear, was not advised. After a short debate we decided upon Beinn Alligin, from whose northern summit may be enjoyed, on a clear day, one of the finest views in the whole of Scotland.

The wind was rising as we left the woods around Torridon House and took to the hill. We walked briskly through the heather. It was wet underfoot, but the sun scattered handfuls of jewels on the bent grasses and tossed golden arrows into the burns. Soon, we were scrambling up the first steep shoulder of this hill which rises like a clenched fist behind Inver Alligin village.

There was cloud coming up now. Behind us, Loch Torridon and the straggling coastline of Diabaig fell away into a grey chasm between dark hills. Fingers of light stroked across black waters, streaking the sombre ripples with thin lines of fire. The sun poured down on us out of a rolling sky. Gold-edged clouds travelled errantly before the strengthening gusts of the wind.

By common consent, we took a short rest; and looked out to the lovely sweep of south-stretching lochs, some black and shiny as ebony, others touched with shafts of gold in the changing light. Beyond, the hills above Loch Carron and Loch Kishorn gleamed through a haze of silvery blue.

Climbing again, we attained a springy plateau; and now came a revelation to the north-east. We looked into a semicircle of serrated peaks formed of layer upon layer of Torridonian sand-stone, capped with shining quartzite and rising fantastically against a sky of ethereal blue. Liathach, Beinn Dearg, Beinn Eighe, the wild "Horns" of Beinn Alligin—they were all there, the grey giants, cruel and immutable, overawing us with their vast age and grandeur.

We were now scrambling on to the bare face of the rise, and a fierce cross-wind roared over from the east, chilling us to the bone, snatching at our clothes, buffeting us flat against the scree. Before us rose the grey hump of Spidean Coire an Laoigh, with the South Summit close behind. Between them, a scree-filled corrie swept up on to a red ridge, slashed by the amber of a burn. Wind howled up out of Coire Mhic Nobuil and the pass between Beinn Alligin and Beinn Dearg, and lifted the spume from the little burn where it plunged over a fall.

To the east, drifting sunlight touched the grey peaks of Liathach, the long white ridge of Beinn Eighe. Before us, a rocky buttress led up towards Tom na Gruagaich, or the Knoll of the Faery-woman.

We began to climb cautiously, conscious of the strength of the wind and its power to throw us off balance. The brief rock-climb afforded good holds, and we had no need to use Michael's rope. Soon we were on moss and turf beside the summit-cairn, where already three climbers were sheltering out of the wind. Ahead of us, the broken ridge swept away and down and steeply up again, over the dark "Cleft" of Alligin to the peak of Sgùrr Mór, 3232 feet, the highest point, sometimes called The Peak of the Axe.

We set off again, after a brief rest. Below us, the wind roared over the debris in Toll a' Mhadaidh, the Hollow of the Wolf. This is believed by the people of Torridon to be the place where the last wolf in Scotland was killed, hence the name. The story told about it runs in this wise:

Many years ago, the Highlanders in this district were worried at the continual disappearance of their sheep, calves and even foals. A man from Shieldaig (Gairloch) discovered, one morning, that his foal was missing, and noticed some strange foot-prints in the snow. He and his son decided to follow the tracks as far as they went. Setting off across the snowy moors they came right over to Beinn Alligin, all the time following the prints of the animal's feet. In the great hollow in the side of the mountain they found the wolf's den with a litter of cubs inside. The son volunteered to go in and slay the young while the old man kept watch outside. As the son was accomplishing his grisly task, something darkened the entrance of the den. He shouted to his father and asked what it was. The old man replied in the Gaelic:

"Mu bhrisidh bun fionn
Bithidh 's a' bhuil air do cheann!"
(If the tail should break
Pity your head!)

The lad's father had caught hold of the wolf by the tail as it was trying to enter the den to save its cubs. He held on until his son came to his assistance, whereupon they slew the savage animal between them. The spot where this took place is now marked by a cairn called Carn Toll a' Mhadaidh, or the Cairn of the Hollow of the Wolf.

There are other localities in the Highlands which lay claim to the distinction of having been the home of the last wolf. The wild hollow of Beinn Alligin, however, seems particularly well suited.

41

Another very striking feature of this fine mountain is the "Cleft", that great gash formed by a landslip on Sgùrr Mór, from the lip of which one may obtain a wonderful view of the eastern landscape, framed in sheer walls of black rock. This is called in the Gaelic "Eag Dhubh na h-Éigheach", or the Black Notch of the Outcry, and a weird story tells how, many years ago, the shepherds used to hear a man's voice shouting there—until, one day, a man fell to his death down the gash. Thereafter, the voice was heard no more.

On the day of our climb, the cold wind forbade long contemplation of this sinister cleft. We scrambled on, therefore, and came to the summit of Sgùrr Mór, the Big Peak. Here we found adequate reason to be thankful that it was a clear day, for it is from this point that one obtains what is considered by many to be one of the finest views in Scotland. I have already written a description of this as a short essay for another book.* I am now giving it again, word for word, as this is exactly how it impressed me at the time, and I cannot describe it more coherently:

"From the cairn, we looked out over the whole heart-shaking landscape of the north-west, patched with sunlight, streaked with the blue of moving shadows.

"To the south, Loch Carron, Loch Kishorn and Loch Alsh were liquid fire flowing out into the blue folds of the Kintail hills. The peaks of Màm Sodhail and Càrn Eige were dark against the haze of distant rain. Beinn Sgriol, above Loch Hourn, wore a mantle of gold under the touch of the sun. Close below us, the peat-moss above Diabaig was bejewelled with countless lochans, all coldly blue under the shadow of the hills. The watery plateau stretched away to Opinan and under the yellow ridge of Baos Bheinn and the hills of Flowerdale. Beyond Gairloch, the gold of Big Sand gleamed on the edge of the sea.

"Eastward, now, our eyes followed the wavering line of the hills round to Beinn Lair, Slioch and the range above Kinlochewe. Away beyond these lay the wonderful An Teallach group above Dundonnell, with the pinnacle-ridge of Sgùrr Fiona etched darkly against an opal sky. On the north-western

* *Hills and Glens*, by arrangement with the Publishers, Messrs Oliver & Boyd, Ltd, Edinburgh.

horizon rose the dim points of the Cóigach mountains, in contrast to the smooth curves of the Ben More Assynt range. East of the heights of Mullach Coire Mhic Fhearchair lay the Fannich group at the head of Loch Broom, with Beinn Liath Mhór Fannaich washed over with gold and the long arms of the shadows stretching down into the glens and corries beneath.

"Rain was blackening the hills to the south as we scrambled down on to the watery plateau to the west. The fickle wind had veered again, and battered the storm into our faces. Behind us, the pinnacles and precipices faded, and Beinn Alligin was once more transformed into a shapeless hump, shutting out the sky.

"Far below, a curl of smoke rising out of a green hollow turned our thoughts to the Hostel and hot tea. . . ."

Such, one hoped, might be the scene afforded to the first Youth Hosteller to attempt Beinn Alligin the following spring—but, on the day after his arrival, the realisation of such high hopes was clearly impossible. The rain had continued all night, and showed no sign of stopping. The entire landscape remained grey and indefinite, swathed in heavy bands of mist. Beinn Alligin was in no mood at all, on this day, for the revelation of her wild beauties.

I was sorry. Had it been otherwise, I might have been tempted to try another ascent myself. Though not so high or so forbidding as Liathach, this fine hill affords an excellent climb, and, for those living or staying in Inver Alligin, is much nearer than the others. There is an easy ascent on the west side of the ridge, behind Tom na Gruagaich and so straight up on to the flank of Sgùrr Mór. The view from any of the peaks makes the climb more than worth while. On the east, the rocky terraces run sheer down to Toll a' Mhadaidh, and on the north to Toll na Béiste (the Hollow of the Beast), where there is a loch. Beyond lie Loch a' Bhealaich and Loch a' Ghobhainn, with Loch na h-Oidhche (The Loch of Night) gleaming darkly between Baos Bheinn and Beinn an Eóin. To the east, the steep escarpments of Beinn Dearg fret the skyline, the wonderful series of sheer gullies making black stripes on the sandstone. Beyond, Beinn Eighe is unbelievably white, the very pallor of it adding to the desolation of the scene.

Beinn a' Chearcaill (The Mountain of the Girdle) is gold under the moving light, the pale circlet which gives her her name turned to diamonds by the sun. Beyond Sgùrr Mór, the serrated ridge of Beinn Alligin drops steeply down, and up again to the weird "Rathain" or "Horns"—a temptation, if you have a steady head and time to spare.

Perhaps most impressive of all, though, is the "Cleft", through which the eye spans an impossible drop to absorb the debris-littered sweep of Coire Mhic Nobuil, where the foaming river winds like a thread of pure silver through a tapestry of grey and green, or cuts a path through the ancient moraine.

If you choose to descend by the corrie between the two southern peaks, you will be rewarded by a view of Upper Loch Torridon which you will long remember. For, leaving the pinnacles and ridges behind, you will come down the last steep shoulder of turf and heather to find the fair expanse of the loch spread out before your dazzled eyes, its blue waters perhaps streaked with thin lines of foam to mark the path of the incoming tide; the Beinn Damh hills, with their fringe of forest, rising quietly against the southern sky to form the first wave in a petrified sea of riven rock which stretches away towards the wilds of Lochaber and Knoydart. You will see the paper-white gulls flashing over the red rock, or swooping into the green shelter of the little bays in pursuit of the life that moves in the waters. Beyond, a sheet of silver reveals itself as Loch Damh, desolate and still under the long, fat hump of Beinn Shieldaig.

The difference between this loch and Loch Torridon is that the latter belongs to the sea, and, when seen from any of the surrounding mountains, this is its most marked characteristic. Your delighted eyes follow it from the green machair of Annat and Fasaig, away down its whole shining length, past green bays and red headlands, to its union with the blue waters of the Sound. It remains ever a part of the sea—sheltered here, it is true, by the towering immensity of the hills—but with its grey beaches new-littered with sea-wrack, its restless tidal waters disturbed by the deep, swift currents which come sweeping in from the Isles.

If you are poetically inclined, you may be reminded of the lines of Principal Shairp, who, writing in 1871, seems to catch so perfectly the sea-born beauty of Loch Torridon, unchanged by the passing of the years:

"Child of the far-off ocean flood!
What wayward mood hath made thee fain
To leave thy wide Atlantic main
For this hill-girdled solitude?
To wind away through kyles and creeks,
Past island, cliff and promontory,
And lose thyself 'mid grisly peaks
And precipices scarred and hoary?

Can it be thou weariest
Of ocean's turbulence and unrest,
Of driving wind and weltering foam,
And, longing for some peaceful home,
Dost hither come in hope to reap
Thy portion of the mountain sleep,
That underneath all changes broods
In these eternal solitudes . . .?

And, far away from plash and roar
Of breaking billows, evermore
Inlapt in hills to lie and dream
Lulled by the sound of inland stream,
And listening the far soothing moan
Of torrents down the bare crags thrown. . . ." *

The finest view of Beinn Alligin herself is, to my mind, that
obtained from the south side of Loch Torridon, looking over the
forests above Òb Gorm Mór and Òb Gorm Beag. From here,
the whole curved ridge can be seen in all its rocky grandeur, from
the broad buttress of the South Summit away round beyond the
"Cleft" and over Sgùrr Mór to the knobbly "Horns" at the north-
east end of the curve. Another wonderful impression may be
obtained from the plateau of Liathach.

But, from Inver Alligin and the shore there is, unfortunately,
no view at all, for the whole semicircular ridge is hidden by the
great bulk of the south shoulder, which rises like an uncom-
promising fist against the sky. Visitors arriving on a cloudy day
are thus often disappointed when the weather clears sufficiently
to allow them their first sight of Beinn Alligin. It looks so tame,
so unlike what they had expected, or had been led to believe by

* "Loch Torridon", from *Glen Dessaray and Other Poems*. Macmillan, 1888.

map and guide-book. It is only when they climb it that they discover the magnificent deception. Only then do they come face to face with untamed and ancient beauty, and hear the laughter of the old gods echoing in the corries, while the wind makes a sound like rushing water as it howls down the dark chimney of the "Cleft" and plays hide-and-seek among the fantastic "Horns".

Those who have not climbed the Torridon hills before would be well advised to start with Beinn Alligin. It is an excellent "training ground" for Liathach and Beinn Eighe. Returning to the little hamlet in the dusk, the visitor will realise that he has had a grand day's scrambling on what proved to be a surprisingly exciting mountain. If he is not tired, he can then turn his attention to something more ambitious.

CHAPTER V

INTRODUCTION TO LIATHACH

THE end of the first week in May presented us with a blazing day which bore out the belief that spring is the best time to visit the west. The morning began innocently enough, with the demurely veiled hills looking at themselves in the clear waters of the loch. There was no breath of wind, and the white clouds hung stationary in the tranquil sky.

Jeannie and I went scrambling over the rocks by the shore, and presently rested on a flat slab of sandstone, where we lay for a while basking in the sun. The sea-pinks had newly donned their frilly bonnets, and peeped at us out of green crevices in the bare rock. Above, a thin film of fresh water ran down a crack thick with young ferns. This fascinated Jeannie, and she spent some time trying to lick the rock dry, until it dawned upon her that the water-supply was inexhaustible.

A rowboat put out from Alligin pier and nosed slowly down the mirror-still loch, one man rowing, the other laying a herring-net from the stern. There was no sound but the "click–clack" of the oars in the rowlocks, the thin fluting of sand-pipers along the desolate beach, the sudden "plop" when a solan goose dropped into clear waters after his silver prey. We were no longer troubled by the inquisitive sheep, for they had all gone away to the hill for the summer.

The sun was dispersing the last shreds of cloud, warming the rock on which we lay. But a light breeze had begun to ruffle the surface of the loch, shattering the reflections of the mountains, and we did not yet anticipate the afternoon's heat.

Soon, we left our slab and scrambled down to the edge of the tide. The rocks here were sharp with yellow limpets and molluscs, dark with the mussels which everwhere hung like bunches of black grapes on a wall. We found red sea-anemones in the shallow pools, among whitened pebbles and empty shells. Strands of shiny brown weed hung like satin ribbons over the

47

rocks, and the short rubbery variety popped juicily under our feet.

From a rough promontory, we looked down into clear, deep water—and it was like looking over steep cliffs into a topsy-turvy world wherein everything assumed new and grotesque proportions and swam dizzily as in a dream. To me, it struck a sudden chord of memory. I realised that I had seen the same fantastic world of perpetual motion when "coming round" from an anaesthetic.

The wind was holding its breath again. We wandered back to the white cottage for lunch—and emerged into a world of shimmering gold with hot brown shadows on the hills and a sparkle dancing in the blue eyes of the loch.

I put up my ex-U.S. Army tent to air it, and Jeannie nosed inside, sniffed at everything, and emerged with a distasteful expression which said plainly that it was far cooler under the rowan-tree.

From the entrance to the tent, I looked away to the wonderful, shining pinnacles of Liathach—to the smooth plateau between Sgurr a' Chadail and Mullach an Rathain. It was on this plateau, during the preceding year, that I had been blown completely off my feet by a gale—but today it was green and still, patched with gold by the hot sun.

Just to look at it caused a lift of the heart. A golden eagle circled over the weird "Horns". Without moving a step, the camper could transport himself in spirit, tent and all, on to that plateau, to spend a night on the breast of the mountain, with only the canvas between him and the stars. He would be little troubled by the knowledge that there is no water on the plateau of Liathach. These things do not matter, in dreams. . . .

The golden day wore on. The shadows changed from brown to blue. The note of the cuckoo rose above the trilling of larks on the hill. The loch remained calm, hardly ruffled by the warm south wind.

I toyed with the idea of swimming. My landlord, passing the cottage, told me that the chaffinches were starting to build in his garden.

The children, playing at their usual game of pirates or smugglers on the rocks behind the house, gazed enviously at the tent. Jeannie, stretched full-length on the threshold now, fixed them

48

The ridge of Beinn Alligin, showing the "Cleft" and "Horns"

with a wicked brown eye which forbade any closer acquaintance.

Then it was tea-time, and the postman arrived with the day's
mail. The sun still beat down powerfully, though the shadows
were lengthening on the hills. The hens, replete with corn,
settled themselves in the dust, ruffling up their soft feathers and
clucking sleepily, while the handsome cock strode watchfully
around, as if to make sure that none of his harem should be
abducted.

The monotonous call of the cuckoo seemed to come from
Beinn Alligin now, and it grew more distinct as the evening
approached. All around in the grass, the yellow-green spears of
the wild iris clove a way boldly between grey stones. The rowan-
leaves were lengthening now, robing the little trees in a mantle
of fringed green. A wild rose-bush was covering her thorns with
tender foliage. A linnet sang ecstatically on the chimney-stack.
The rough ferns uncurled in the wall. Bluebells glowed under the
brambles. Everywhere was life and beauty, brought forth in
abundance by the green fingers of Spring.

The little boats came back from the fishing, moving gently
over the blue-streaked waters. We looked away down to the
woods of Corrie. The pines were dark and mysterious in the
fading light. It was the perfect setting for a queer tale—and here
is the tale itself, once told among the old people of Torridon, but
sinking now into the limbo of things forgotten:

Once upon a time (and not so long ago at that) a man was
living alone at Corrie, with no one to talk to but himself and the
tall trees that sheltered the house. One night, as he was taking his
solitary supper by the fire, what should walk into his house but
three cats, soaking wet. As it was a fine dry night, he guessed that
they must have swum in from the sea. Something told him that
these were no ordinary cats. Looking more closely, he noticed
that one of them was very old and had only one eye.

He was a kind-hearted man, and made his strange visitors
welcome, saying, "Poor pussies—come in to the fire and dry
yourselves. I'm sure you'll be hungry!" And he filled three plates
from a pan of fish on the fire, and kept replenishing them until
the cats were satisfied.

His guests made never a sign of thanks, but rested by the fire

Fasaig village (Torridon) under the screes of Liathach

until the night was well on and they were quite dry and warm. Then, silently, the three of them rose and stalked out into the darkness.

Some considerable time afterwards, there was a dearth of potatoes in the Torridon district, and our friend from Corrie accompanied a party to Skye, to see if any could be obtained there. Leaving his companions to try their luck separately, he presently found his way to a lonely house and knocked at the door. His knock was answered at once by a young damsel, who smilingly told him that he was expected, and invited him in.

Somewhat bewildered, he entered and found that there were two other women in the house, the elder of whom had only one eye. They all made a great fuss over him, and treated him like an old friend. Presently, he told them on what errand he had come. They nodded wisely and said that he could have all the potatoes he wished, adding: "It was yourself that was kind to *us*, the night we called on *you*!"

And thus the man from Corrie got his potatoes, and a fair wind home!

Beyond the woods of Corrie, dying sunlight flickers now on the pallid terraces of Beinn Eighe. Close above the village, Beinn Alligin looms against a purpling sky. Liathach is darkening to a sombre smoke-blue, as if a great shapeless shadow were slowly enfolding the whole ridge. It is an odd phenomenon of the evening in Torridon, that Liathach will become dark and sinister before the shades touch Beinn Alligin or Beinn Eighe, while Fuar Tholl wears a pearly crown and a mantle of silver still lies over Beinn Liath Mhór. It is as if the "Grey One" alone among the Torridon hills raises her face eagerly to welcome the engulfing night. . . .

Even the sunlit plateau is ink-blue now, though the warm light still spreads across the neighbouring hills and dapples Loch Torridon with gold. Again, one visualises a frail tent pitched up there among the shadows—and becomes aware that a night's camp on Liathach would be an experience one could not easily forget. . . .

The Torridon hills are noted for their magnificent mural precipices. The rock—some of the oldest in the British Isles—is believed by some authorities to have been part of the "Lost

Continent of Atlantis" which finally sank beneath the ocean in the volcanic era which threw up the Black Cuillin of Skye.

During the succeeding ice-age, which carved out the west coast of Scotland into the enchanted land of mountains, wild bays, faery isles and secret lochans which we know today, the hills were scarred and riven by the action of the great glaciers whose track of devastation can still be traced by the crumbling moraine. The Cambrian strata are tilted to the east.

In his fascinating book, *British Hills and Mountains*,* Mr Peter Bicknell includes a chapter on "The Shaping of the Hills", the opening paragraph of which (though speaking of the landscape around Lochinver) conveys strikingly the atmosphere of age and beauty which extends southward to the mountains of Torridon. I quote it here, with the author's permission:

> "In the weird and primeval-looking landscape of the extreme north-west corner of Scotland, the geology of the hills is revealed more forcibly than in any other part of Britain. Grotesque peaks composed of red Torridonian sandstone, often terminating in a protective cap of dazzling bright Cambrian quartzite, rise like prehistoric monsters from a treeless bed of rugged impervious Lewisian gneiss, where every hollow holds a tiny lake. . . ."

Without doubt, the most striking characteristic of the Torridon hills is their wildness, the weird fascination of their naked beauty, which draws the wanderer like a charm. Wildest and weirdest of all is Liathach, the "Grey One"—as anyone who has scaled her proud pinnacles will, I think, agree. It is not just the name which strikes a sinister note. I have yet to find a vantage-point from which this great crumbling pile looks anything but stark and awe-inspiring. From Inver Alligin village, the eye is captivated by the dark summit of Sgùrr a' Chadail, the Peak of Sleep, leading up to the knobbly "Horn" of Mullach an Rathain. Seen from Beinn Eighe or Beinn Alligin, the whole, grey, riven mass sprawls clumsily among the desolate waste-land of the peat-moss, her corries littered with the debris of old landslides, her sombre peaks upthrust against the sky.

Most striking of all, perhaps, is the view of the mountain

---

* "Britain in Pictures" Series. Collins, London.

across Loch Clair, for then on a still day, her reflection lies in the weed-fringed water, capped with motionless clouds or white with untrodden snow. She has six peaks, the highest rising to 3456 feet. Like Beinn Eighe, much of her surface-rock is rotten, and care needs to be taken in traversing the ridge, particularly in the tricky crossing of Am Fasarinen, a series of small pinnacles between the highest peak and Mullach an Rathain. There is a track on the south side, just below the pinnacles, which can be taken if preferred though this was crumbling on my last visit.

The names of the peaks seem to have been chosen to bear out the "dark" character of the mountain. Sgùrr a' Chadail, the Peak of Sleep; Mullach an Rathain, the Summit of the Horn†; Am Fasarinen, the Teeth. Then Spidean a' Choire Leith, the Pinnacle of the Grey Corrie; Meall Dearg, the Bare Red Hill; and Stùc a' Choire Dhuibh Bhig, the Point of the Little Black Corrie.

Most desolate of the vistas from the ridge itself is, I feel, that obtained by gazing down the dark cliffs of Coire na Caime† to Loch a' Ghlas Thuill, which lies among a mass of tumbled boulders at the foot. Most sensational is the view of Mullach an Rathain from the shoulder of Spidean a' Choire Leith, with the fierce Teeth rising to a jagged knife-edge in between.

I cannot resist quoting again from Principal Shairp, who, in a few lines of formal verse, draws as clear and authentic a picture of this primeval hill as it has been my good fortune to encounter:

"Liaguch, rising sheer
    From river-bed up to the sky,
Grey courses of masonry, tier on tier,
    And pinnacles splintered on high!

Splintered, contorted and riven
    As though, from the topmost crown
Some giant plougher his share had driven
    In a hundred furrows sheer down. . . ." *

The would-be climber of Liathach needs good weather and an early start if it is hoped to traverse the ridge. It is possible for most average hill-walkers to do all the "Teeth" except one without the aid of a rope—and even that one may be climbed, I think, coming from east to west.

* "Glen Torridon", from *Glen Dessaray and Other Poems*.
† See Glossary.

The ascent from Corrie to the summit of Sgùrr a' Chadail is steep but easy, being over turf and boulders until the short rock-climb at the end. Beyond this lies the long, bare plateau over which the wind sometimes sweeps like a host of howling furies, stabbing intruders with the million silver lances of hail or rain.

For my first ascent, the day dawned warm and sunny, and fluffy golden clouds sailed over us as we tramped from the Hostel down to Corrie. My companions were Michael, the medical student, and a young hosteller from England named Stanley. We took little food and had no conversation, for we were in a business-like mood, our thoughts wholly centred on climbing the hills. Yet, we were by no means over-earnest—just mentally and physically prepared for what might prove to be a fairly arduous expedition.

We made good time to the summit of Sgùrr a' Chadail. Behind us, the shining expanse of Loch Torridon was slowly revealed, sweeping out beyond the white villages of Alligin and Diabaig to the blue sea. We looked south-west, over the hills of Shieldaig, to the jagged ridge of the Black Cuillin on Skye—and beyond these to the dark smudges of the Outer Isles. Below us, the tide was coming in on Loch Torridon, streaking the silver waters with thin furrows of foam. The sun, increasing in power, burned down on us out of the blue sky.

We discovered that what appeared to be the summit of Sgùrr a' Chadail was not so at all—a frequent occurrence on mountains. Before us, another great knob of rock thrust up its nose at the travelling clouds. We climbed on—and looked down the dark precipices on our right to the beginnings of Fasaig village.

Past the cairn now—and a gentle descent led on to the great plateau sweeping up to Mullach an Rathain. The distance between the two points was much greater than one would imagine on seeing them from below. We estimated that it would take about an hour and a half to cover. Today, there was no gale to throw us off balance, and we tramped delightedly over the springy moss and flat stones, while around us the stone-chat flitted among the rocks, and the white clouds sailed dreamily above.

Before us, the summit of Mullach an Rathain was dark and clear against the sky, unadorned by so much as a frail ribbon of vapour. The scree increased as we ascended; but it was an easy climb and we were presently resting on the summit, eating dried apricots and revelling in the glorious panorama of jagged mountains upflung all around. The day was particularly clear, and we spent an intriguing half-hour identifying distant summits.

On again now for what was obviously going to be the trickiest part of the climb. Down a soft slope—and before us the stark and crumbling pinnacles of the "Teeth" crowded one behind the other, guarding the scree-littered heights of Spidean a' Choire Leith. We braced ourselves, and began a careful traverse of this tricky ridge, half-wishing, as it was the first time, that we had brought the rope. It was frequently necessary to test the sandstone for safe holds, as much of it is loose here, and large slabs are apt to shift or come away in the hands.

To our left, the black cliffs dropped away and down to the dark, sand-edged pool of Loch a' Ghlas Thuill. It was the ultimate in desolation, bare and still and unruffled by any wind, lying at the foot of sunless cliffs, among a waste of tumbled boulders which betokened the debris left over from the building of the world.

We scrambled on over the "Teeth"—mere ants on the top of a heaven-high wall. At one point, the tortuous ridge was so narrow that we sat astride it and looked down into nothingness on both sides. To our regret, we had to circumvent one pinnacle by the deer-path, as the descent was too steep for us to accomplish without the rope.

The sandstone continued to move and slide and break away under groping hands and feet. Once we had surmounted the ridge, however, a stretch of safe scree led us steeply upward to the summit of Spidean a' Choire Leith, the real summit of Liathach.

We relaxed here, having attained our object for the day. The traverse of the "Teeth" had delayed us until it was too late to attempt the two remaining peaks. By the cairn, we ate our chocolate and contemplated immeasurable grandeur.

The clouds were thickening now, and mysterious grey shadows ran across the riven landscape, painting strange patterns on the wan faces of the hills. Southward, a lovely curve of mountains sheltered the head of Loch Torridon—Beinn Shieldaig, the green shoulder of Beinn Damh, Beinn na h-Eaglaisse with its shallow rock-terraces, Maol Chean-dearg overshadowing dark Loch an

Eóin. The peak of Sgùrr Ruadh; the rolling grey ridge of Beinn Liath Mhór above the weird Valley of a Thousand Hills. To the south-west, the Cuillin of Skye rose in dark and jagged beauty under the vaporous heavens, and a long shadow on the horizon marked the faery outline of the Outer Hebrides.

North-east, the immense crystal ridge of Beinn Eighe was crusted with diamonds under the sun. The whiteness of the Cambrian quartzite was so striking as to draw the eye again and again to its shimmering beauty, and call to mind a verse of Shairp's vivid lines:

> "Benyea, magnificent alp
> Blanched bare and bald and white
> His forehead like old eagle's scalp
> Seen athwart the sunset's light. . . ."

For a long while we stood and stared at the great, sprawling mass of it. The hollowed-out terraces of Ruadh Stac Mór were like the windows of a Gothic cathedral. We could see a hint of the crags of Sàil Mhór; the sheer cliffs above Coire Mhic Fhearchair; and beyond Cóinneach Mhór (the only patch of green on this grizzled monster) the long, shingly ridge crawling away towards Kinlochewe.

Behind, the great waves of the hills swept away northward into ethereal distance. The cloud was still high enough to reveal them all. We took out compass and map and discovered, to our delight and amazement, that we could see Beinn Laoghal and Ben Hope on the far edge of Sutherland! Swinging southward, we had no difficulty in identifying a flat-topped bulk on the far horizon as Ben Nevis.

But perhaps the loveliest scene of all was that presented by Liathach herself—the sombre ridge we had lately surmounted, with the black "Teeth" rising one behind the other, and, beneath them, the sheer gullies and dark chimneys dropping down and down to the peat-waste far below. Beyond, the jagged pinnacle of Mullach an Rathain, sheltering a great hanging corrie whose walls were littered with precarious drifts of scree.

It is the weird beauty of this ridge which, I think, will remain longest with us, for it summed up the whole primeval fascination of the "Grey One" which crouches, like some dark and sinister monster, among the prehistoric wilderness of the Torridon hills.

CHAPTER VI

LAND OF MANY MOODS

THE heatwave continued. Loch Torridon was a sheet of burning blue beneath a blazing sun, as full of colour as a Van Gogh landscape. It was too hot to climb; though the temperature dropped substantially at night. Jeannie and I spent our afternoons scrambling over the warm rocks by the point, or lazing on the turf outside our tent.

Sometimes, there was the heaviness of thunder in the air, calling to mind an evening during the preceding September, when, with a companion from the Hostel, I had walked to Diabaig in a sultry heat which neither of us had previously experienced in the Western Highlands.

All day, a hot wind had been blowing from the south-west, and the hills were black under waves of sombre cloud. Great humid gusts swept across Loch Torridon, lifting the spindrift in white clouds from the Shieldaig side. Before us, the dry and dusty road mounted away into the mellowing evening, with the scarred braes rising against the hot sky ahead.

We climbed . . . and the little houses of Inver Alligin fell away into the smouldering hollow where light gleamed only over the shot-silk of the sea. Beyond the dark reaches of Annat, we could see the gathering storm pouring down the hills, smothering them in a blanket of cloud. The rowans bent before the damp wind. Waves of rain steamed across the shoulder of Beinn Damh. A rainbow curved over the sultry landscape. Then the vision was gone, and fresh veils of spindrift swept across from Shieldaig.

The narrow road unwound itself over the brae. Soon, we were looking down to Alligin Suas and across to the metallic gleam of Loch Damh, set among blue-black hills. South-west, Eilean a' Chaoil guarded the approach to Loch Shieldaig. Northward and inland now, we tramped on past Lochan Dearg,between the rocky braes lightened by outcrops of quartzite. Behind us, Beinn Alligin crouched like a great scowling giant among wreaths of black vapour.

We came over the last rise—and there, below us, lay the loch of Upper Diabaig, a long stretch of smoke-grey water across which the hot wind traced thin arrowheads of foam, as if a thousand elfin speedboats were streaking shoreward with the dark ripples fantailing in their wake.

It was on this loch that the kelpie, or water-horse, was once seen by an old inhabitant of Alligin, who watched it enter the water just by Eilean a Dà Uillt, or the Isle of the Two Burns—a tiny islet at the junction of two streams on which there is believed to have been a burial, and concerning which weird stories are still told.

Beyond the loch, brown braes rose against piled-up cloud. A waterfall leapt down the hillside to the south, and another—one of the streams beside Eilean a Dà Uillt—was gushing out almost beneath our feet. Suddenly, the clouds rolled apart in the west, revealing a sky of brilliant blue dappled with flame, a glimpse of the glory of the sunset behind the storm. Instantly, the waters beneath caught and gave back the colour. A pathway of azure and rose gleamed among the dark ripples, fading away into the shadows as it neared the shore. This was our last vision of colour, for the clouds swept together again and the threads of gold rusted and darkened and blended into the greying tapestry 'of twilight.

Before us, the blurring road curved away beside the leaden wastes of wind-ruffled water. The sough of the burns blended with the sigh of the flattened grass.

We walked on through a world of lengthening shadows wherein the hills brooded sombrely under the violet dome of the sky. On the edge of night, we came down to Diabaig, where the little windows shone orange through the close-folding dusk.

It was dark when we turned back, a night of no moon and no stars, with rain cooling the torrid wind. The thunder did not come, but the gale increased. We fought our way back along the glimmering road and over the brae, past the shadowy crofts and scarred rock and the lochan where the reeds whispered among themselves as we passed. Far below, two moving eyes gleamed among scattered trees, following the tortuous curves of the road. Presently, the shooting-brake came over the brae, and the driver stopped to greet us and ask if everything were all right. After the little "bus" had gone, it seemed that the last vestige of light had been withdrawn. Only the wet road, shining dimly ahead, showed us our way through the night.

The unexpected meeting with the car (which must have been out on a private hire) started off a strange train of thought. It is rumoured among the villagers that car-lights have been seen several times recently along this road, near to Lochan Dearg, when no car was passing—an omen to those who believe in the Second Sight.

Down the brae now, and over the bridge behind Wester Alligin. Now Beinn Alligin was a vast black shadow to our left. Ahead, the jagged pinnacles of Liathach were dim points of jet against a purple sky.

Below us, the lights of Inver Alligin winked along the shore and danced dimly in the rough waters of Loch Torridon, like puppet pierrots jazzing eerily on a darkened stage. Having no torch, we searched in vain for the Hostel sign which marked a rough track down the face of the hill.

Soon, we realised that we had gone too far. Summoning our courage, we blundered down the brae beside a gushing burn, sliding on wet grass, stumbling over hidden rocks, floundering through knee-high bracken in the darkness. There was no landmark to guide us—only, to our right, the phosphorescent gleam of foaming waters in a deepening gorge. At last we had to cross the burn, and were soaked to the hips in icy water.

But lights rose out of a hollow ahead, and we floundered down to a house. We recognised it as being well beyond the Hostel. But somewhere near this house was a path, the shore-track to the village, which would lead us safely to our destination.

At last, we reached level ground and tramped along by the rugged coast to the Hostel. We arrived to find everyone else had gone to bed, tired by the day's exertions..With as little noise as possible, we cooked eggs and bacon on the still-glowing range.

Outside, the rain tapped on the window. The hot wind still panted through the trees—but no thunder came to relieve the tension in the air.

The following spring, it was the same—a strong, gusty heat which seemed to be bottled up around the head of the loch, as if the demons of the storm were imprisoned by the encircling hills.

The ploughing and sowing were almost at an end, and the

villagers leant on their spades to wipe perspiring brows. Children ran barefooted over the hot pebbles, and the sleepy hens cackled contentedly and ruffled their feathers in the dust. But the cocks crowed indefatigably from dykes and rocks and the tops of garden gates, and the sandpiper flashed untiringly across the sultry waters of the loch.

The fishing-boats went out occasionally after the herring. Visitors were frequently offered a share of the catch.

One day, I had my first experience of trolling, using a rubber eel and fishing off the back of a small motor-boat. I caught one lithe—to the "crew's" amusement, as it is considered unlucky to take a woman on a fishing expedition. After that, the outboard motor failed, and all our energies were bent towards restarting it. This proving impossible, we had to row back to Wester Alligin from Shieldaig. As there were four of us to take turns at the oars, this was not as strenuous as might be expected. The current was with us most of the way, and we were soon back in the little bay where the trim fishing-boat, *Betsy Brodie*, rocked on the incoming tide.

I cooked the solitary lithe for supper. It was very good, and our only regret was that it was not bigger!

The evenings were surprisingly cool, and we still sat around the fire after supper. Sometimes, I visited friends in the village, and we talked of local lore and legend. There was one lady whose mother had seen the "Wee Folk" when, as a young girl, she was sent to bring down the cows from the hill. Many was the time the tale had been told—how she had gone up alone in the gathering dusk, and how she had found a company of little people, dressed all in green, holding hands and dancing in a circle, with the cows browsing near by. How she had run off again down the hill before they noticed her, leaving the cows to come in their own time; and how her mother had commended her for her wisdom in having nothing to do with the "Men of Peace". . . .

Then there had been a man who was one day cutting peats near the burn which runs down by "Heather Cliff". He had wished aloud for a cool drink, and was just about to make his way to the stream when a little lady in green appeared, holding up a bowl of buttermilk. Thanking her, he took a long drink—and from that day he was a changed man, strange in his ways and alien to his family. He did not know, of course, that one must never eat or drink anything offered by the faeries, however tempting it may seem. It is their time-honoured way of bringing mortals under the power of their spells, and once a man has dined with them he is no longer free, but for ever subject to their dark whims and fancies.

In an old book, I had read of a woman who was enticed away by the "Daoine Sìthe" and offered a meal of delicious dainties. Among her captors was one who had once been mortal, and who managed to warn her of her danger. Though tempted, she steadily refused everything offered—and suddenly the veil of enchantment fell from the food and she saw that her hosts were offering her a meal of cow-dung!

There are people around Torridon who can still remember a time when it was customary for a constant watch to be kept over women in childbirth, lest the Wee Folk should steal away the new-born infant and leave a changeling in its place. Once the child was baptised, however, the danger was considered to be past.

I was told the story of a woman hereabouts who, some years ago, went out to help stack the corn. She took her baby with her, and laid him beside a corn-sheaf while she worked. She had hardly stooped to her task, however, when a terrible shrieking came from the place where she had left her child. She started to run towards him—but a man working with her instantly seized her and held her back. The harrowing screams continued for some minutes, during which time the distracted mother struggled vainly to free herself. But the man held her mercilessly, re-marking that whatever was screaming could scream itself out—on no account would he let her go yet. At length, the dreadful noise changed to a soft, normal cry, and the mother was then set at liberty. She rushed to the baby, and found him safe and un-harmed. The man who had forcibly restrained her told her that, had she gone sooner, it would not have been her own child lying there, but a changeling substituted by the faeries as a trap. Once she had picked it up, her own baby would have been claimed by the Wee Folk.

May 10th was so hot that I yielded to the temptation to go swimming from the rocks beyond the schoolhouse. The tide was ebbing, but there were still deep green pools by the point. I scrambled over limpet-crusted slabs and, carrying Jeannie, waded through the clear, cold water, until I reached a tiny "island". Making this my base, I dived and swam until I was tired, while Jeannie basked on the flat rock, eyeing me with a superior expression which implied that anyone who went into the water for pleasure was beyond her understanding. Afterwards, we meandered back over rocks and popping seaweed to bake ourselves among the sea-pinks and saxifrage.

In the afternoon, we walked along the shore towards Corrie. The fishing-boat *Betsy Brodie*, heavily laden, came in on the tide, to anchor just below the Hostel. The S.Y.H.A. had recently decided to enlarge Inver Alligin Hostel by the addition of a timber annexe. In the face of its growing popularity, the time had come for something to be done to accommodate extra visitors. Like everything else of a substantial nature, the timber annexe had then to be brought in by boat. It arrived in sections on the *Betsy*, and we went down at high tide to watch it being landed on the rocks. The men, having edged the boat delicately into the tiny bay, worked with speed and precision. The annexe would be twenty-four feet long when erected, making the Hostel almost twice as big.

The whole hut was soon ashore, and we walked back to the cottage. The throbbing of a motor brought us to the door again to watch the *Betsy Brodie* churning her business-like way back to Wester Alligin, with the dinghy tugging at the leash astern. The job of landing the Hostel annexe on a steep and tricky part of the coast had been accomplished in just over half an hour.

A boisterous wind had sprung up now, and the rowans sighed restlessly, tossing their green hair like mermaids swaying on the fringe of the tide. Across the loch, Beinn Damh was a smoky grey, crowned with a swirl of swansdown cloud. I went out to take down my tent, which was flapping eerily in the wind. The light faded, and the garden was full of strange voices, all somehow echoing the ceaseless plaint of the sea.

Two days later, Jeannie and I set out to find the Golden Cave at the foot of Liathach. It was a cloudy morning, but the sun edged every cloud-bank with gold. Loch Torridon was a luminous sheet of gun-metal grey, streaked here and there with pure silver where the sunlight broke through to touch the calm waters.

We walked along the shore path, past houses in whose gardens the blankets and bedding were airing in preparation for the expected influx of visitors. At one croft, there was a lime-tree in bloom—and before we reached it we could hear it humming, for every bough was alive with bees, droning among the green leaves or suspending furry, striped bodies on the pale tassels of the blossoms. There was a rowan-tree close by, covered with white heads of bloom—but its softer perfume was drowned by the heady fragrance of the lime.

We walked on reluctantly; and the perfume changed to the salty tang of sea and beach and drying nets. The milkwort was out beside the path. Beyond the little Church of Scotland and its adjacent manse, sunlight flashed blindingly on the windows of Fasaig, and the reflected points of fire danced and twinkled in the loch. The sea-birds swooped over the white beaches, and already there were three dinghies out at the fishing. Around the manse, two white goats and some shaggy Highland ponies cropped the rough grass. A golden-haired boy leaned over the fence to eye us solemnly as we passed.

The sun was hot, and we plunged thankfully into the dark woods of Corrie, where bluebells made a cool smoke among the moss. Past the still lochan with its rhododendron-shade—the gamekeeper's house where the dogs rushed out to greet us—and now we were looking beyond the grey roof of Torridon House to the great serrated horse-shoe formed by Beinn Alligin and Beinn Dearg, which rose close behind the house like ghost-mountains dreamed by an Alpine artist homesick for his hills. I have yet to see a more perfect setting for a house, and can conceive of no greater delight than to waken every morning to this vision of green woods and terraced mountains, with the amber river leaping between banks of flowering whins to the sea.

The limes were out here, too, and the whole woodland was redolent of their fragrance, mingled with the hot scent of the pines. Poplars, sycamores and birches fluttered their pale new dresses in the warm breeze. The young copper-beeches blushed a deeper rose at the caress of the sun. The waxen rhododendrons lighted purple candles to the Great God Pan. Underfoot, the moss was starred with primroses, wood-sorrel, bluebells and the shy dog-violet. The tender ferns thrust their curly heads out of the crevices of the rocks, and a queer species of brown fungus like a rubber water-lily had uncurled among last year's leaves.

Emerging from the woods on to the shore road, we found the

field-daisy and tormentil in flower, and the delicate butterwort raising its demure mauve head out of the sticky yellow star of its leaves. Wild-honeysuckle tendrils already attracted the small multi-coloured moths. The dog-rose was in leaf, and the ling was awakening to green life on the lower slopes of the hills. Kingcups filled the ditches with golden sovereigns, and the pussy-willows were veiled in yellow foam. The "lady's slipper" trod with dainty golden feet over the grass by the wayside. The whins had lighted a million tiny lamps—the broom shook out her long golden hair beside the streams. Everywhere bloomed the brazen dandelion. Everywhere was a predominance of yellow, as if this were the colour especially chosen by the gods to light the world after the pallor of the winter snows. On the fringe of Fasaig, the bugloss added a touch of delicate rose to the glowing tapestry of spring.

The village, too, had its flowers. Narcissi, velvet wallflowers, the white hawthorn, the cultivated honeysuckle on the wall. One house had wistaria over the door, and a rock-garden riotous with primulas, saxifrage, laburnum, rock-roses, lobelia and a brilliant blaze of azaleas.

We passed Torridon schoolhouse and the turning to Annat. Close above us brooded the desolate crags of Liathach, layer upon layer of splintered rock towering up into the blue air. A wilderness of tumbled boulders lay about her feet. In their wild recesses, we sought vainly for our cave. Finally, we gave up what seemed an impossible task, and walked on around the bend into lonely Glen Torridon. Here, I sat down under fragrant pines to eat my lunch of chocolate and oranges. And here, for an unmeasured interlude snatched out of time, I gave myself up to day-dreaming.

It was the sort of day wherein life and death seem very close together, each a necessary part of the same eternal beauty. One thought of the light which draws the persistent grass through the soil—the darkness which casts a blue shadow over the unresisting hills and weaves long fingers through the amber waters of the stream. The life-giving warmth—and the creeping cold. The rustle of new life in the nest—and the bleached bones on the moor. Everywhere the fertile womb of Earth brought forth beauty in abundance—and everywhere some earlier beauty rusted and crumbled and was received back into the clay from which it had come.

About us, tiny insects danced on warm breaths of air. The chirring of the lark rose to a paean of ecstasy. The cuckoo reiterated its two lorn notes until the heart was torn by their infinite melody. High above, the ageless mountains lifted their grizzled heads to the sun. Vast shelves and terraces laid down by ancient rivers in the youth of the world. Cambrian quartzite strewn by the Great Architect long before He thought of creating the first man to raise dazzled eyes unto the hills. Older than all, the hard core of Lewisian rock underneath. Was it only yesterday, in the eyes of God, that the first cuckoo awoke strange echoes among these mountains of pre-history, and the savage cave-dweller discovered that he could weep? . . .

One looked away over the dark escarpments of Liathach to the white pinnacles of Beinn Eighe. The two great mountains formed a baroque contrast of light and shade, each, through comparison with the other, being seen in her full glory.

The harsh cry of an eagle vibrated down the heights of Liathach. Somewhere, in the clear ether above me, Death flew with outstretched talons, his ghost-heart beating strongly in the wing-rhythm of a bird. Now his shadow falls across the young lamb, symbol of the innocent life for ever sacrificed that the pattern might go on.

We turned at last and retraced our steps along the glen. We had not found our cave. Yet who, in the face of so much that was inspiring and beautiful, could say that the day had been wasted?

View to the south over the woods of Torridon

CHAPTER VII

OF FISH AND FISHING

IF you want variety in diet at Inver Alligin, you must fish. But it is advisable to go with someone who "knows the ropes".

The evening was warm when Lexie and I set out for Wester Alligin; but we had put on thick overcoats in anticipation of the cooler atmosphere on the water. There was a south wind blowing —good, so my friend informed me, for the lithe, so long as it did not get too strong.

The boat was waiting in the bay beyond "Bellavista", manned by Roy from the croft, and Big Sandy, the retired game-keeper who bred Cairn terriers. The four of us pushed off and rowed towards the narrows. The evening shadows were creeping over Liathach, but, over her shoulder, Beinn Eighe gleamed gold and rose in the sunset, while the hills of Beinn Damh Forest flamed blood-red, as if on fire.

We kept close in to the rocks, trolling over the back of the boat with rubber eels, one red and one green. Above us, the delicate harebells danced in the face of the cliff. A buzzard's nest lay on a wide shelf of rock overhanging the sea. The game-keeper pointed it out to us, and remarked that he had occasionally see the peregrine falcon hunting here.

The tide was on the turn. Roy told us that it sometimes runs through the narrows at a speed of eight miles per hour. A slack tide is bad, though; and, for a while, we caught nothing.

Then the red eel began to get busy. We caught four fair-sized lithe, which were landed with the aid of a gaff.

Presently, Lexie caught a "cuddie", or small saith. The larger ones are known in this locality as "coal-fish", and are caught farther out, in the middle of the narrows, usually where the gulls are feeding. They are good eating, though reckoned below the lithe in quality.

I had the green eel, and caught nothing. However, acting on a "hunch", I refused to change. Green is my lucky colour—besides being the colour said to be favoured by the "Wee Folk"!

65

Fishing on Loch Torridon, under ancient Lewisian rock

The tide was coming in now. The wind caught us as we bounced round the point. Across the loch, Shieldaig village was flooded over with gold. Big Sandy pointed out the ruin of an old inn on a rocky headland close by, once a favourite port of call among the fishermen. We drifted in to the tiny beach at Port Lair, where we had a message to deliver, and disembarked by a shed in which salted haddocks were hanging up to dry. The solitary white house, backed by gnarled brown hills, awaited our coming. We had a late tea with the hospitable people who run this croft in the back of beyond, to which the only access is by sea or over the open hill. They gave us home-made cream cheese, with bread and biscuits, and we took it to the accompaniment of eager conversation in Gaelic—too fast for me to follow, though I amused them by trying a few sentences on my own. While we ate, the room darkened until the flame from the peat-fire threw tall shadows on the walls. One of the collies, unused to seeing visitors, growled at us without ceasing from under the table.

We went out into the gathering twilight—and it was a cool night with nimbus cloud scurrying across the sky. According to Big Sandy, "the kerry was running fast", and we might find it rough going later. We might even have to beach the boat and walk back over the cliff-path. But there was one more place that was worth trying for a fish.

We rowed westward, away from the bay of Port Lair—and looked up to see a new moon sailing into the cloudy vault of the sky.

"In the South," I said, "we spit and wish and turn our money over."

I spat with as much delicacy as I could manage, wished the same wish three times, and surreptitiously turned the purse in my pocket. My wish was that the green eel would at last be lucky. It was no sooner made than I caught my first fish, a fine lithe! Going back to Alligin, I caught four more, two of which staggered me by their size. Sandy allowed that they were "good enough fish" —but not so big as the one he caught the time before the last, etc., etc.

He began to tell us some of his experiences as a gamekeeper— how, only the other morning, he had seen a grey seal come up just below his house at Wester Alligin, and how he had run for his rifle, but it was gone when he returned. Lexie said that she had often watched the grey Atlantic seals basking on the red rocks of Mull.

I remembered the old legend—that they are the daughters of the king of Lochlinn,* under a spell, and that one can tell their royal blood from their beautiful eyes and the sad songs they sing on the far beaches of the Hebrides. I was glad Big Sandy had not managed to shoot the one that was so rash as to come up near his house. . . .

The wind was freshening now, and we bounced along, the men taking turns at the oars. Soon, a light rain drew a mist of silver across the fast-darkening hills. We began to sing, softly at first, then gaining courage as the magic of the hour crept upon us.

Soon it was quite dark. Above us, the looming rocks made a deeper shadow on the blackness. The sea hissed mysteriously around the little boat. Great drops of phosphorescent water flew off the oars, like a thousand glowing matches tossed into a molten whirlpool. We were all dim shapes, white-faced and huddled in the enchanted gloom. Periodically, someone pulled a fiery fish out of the luminous waters and laid it with the glowing company in the bottom of the boat. The whole adventure had long ago taken on an atmosphere of unreality. Even our voices and laughter had the somehow hollow quality of an echo from the coral caves. . . .

Ahead, now, the lights of "Bellavista" called us across swirling water. We drew in the sodden lines and "called it a day". Singing "Will ye no' come back again", we guided the little boat into the bay, edging up to the beach between an anchored dinghy and the big bulk of the trawler *Betsy Brodie*.

We were cold now—but the warmth of the little house and the hospitality of Annabella MacLennan acted like a charm. Though it was now midnight, we all sat down to a supper of Scotch broth, followed by curds and cream. Afterwards, warmed and refreshed, Lexie and I borrowed a torch and took the rough homeward path to Inver Alligin, carrying our share of the fish.

At the week-end, two campers arrived, and erected their little green tent beside the Hostel. Their Tricouni-nailed boots revealed that they "meant business" as regards the hills. One was telling me that it was his first visit to Torridon. I did not think that he would regret it. The weather being somewhat doubtful, I lent them my U.S. Army tent for their stores.

* Scandinavia.

67

Long after darkness had fallen, the cuckoo continued to call from the woods of Corrie. The rain held off, and I began to envy the mountaineers, alone with their camp-fire and the soft noises of the night, with only the canvas between them and the stars. . . .

The next morning—the beginning of the hottest day so far—I met the two climbers on their way to Beinn Alligin. We stood out in the increasing sun for a while, talking about hills. As I had thought, they were hardened mountaineers who meant business. One of them talked of doing the Beinn Eighe and Liathach ridges in the same day. Being only a hill-walker myself, I sadly refused their kind invitation to make a third on an expedition to Beinn Alligin.

Instead, I sat in the sun and read Highland history. One hundred men, under the handsome John Mackenzie 3rd of Torridon, fought for the Stuart cause at Culloden, in 1746. "Young Torridon" was later pardoned—it is said, because of his popularity with the ladies!

The climbers returned from Beinn Alligin, but I saw nothing of them until the following day. Then, to my delight, they invited me to a camp-supper. We had soup, corned beef, black pudding and "Pom", poached eggs, bread, honey and tea(!) on the grass outside the tent, served and eaten with commendable speed considering that plates and cutlery had to be washed in the burn between each course. Afterwards, we stretched out with cigarettes and more tea and discussed modern poetry. I returned to the cottage in the dark, stimulated by the conversation, at peace with the world.

Having brought among my luggage a portable gramophone and six albums of classical records, I had recently started a series of gramophone recitals for anyone at the Youth Hostel who might be interested. At the second meeting of the "Inver Alligin Music Club", the two campers formed an appreciative audience. We played Bach, Chopin and the Seventh Symphony of Beethoven. Conversation, over coffee in the "interval", touched upon a variety of topics, from the poetry of T. S. Eliot and the Imagist School, to happy memories of Kingshouse, Glencoe, in the days of the inimitable Mrs Malloch. The visitors left me a string of fine brown trout for breakfast, caught from the Alligin Burn that morning.

There are many of the opinion that the "wee broon trootie" is

the best of all Highland fish, both for looks and flavour. Personally, I even rank him superior to the silver salmon, for the
delicately sweet flesh of him, and his colour, which is as the hue
of sun-dappled waters.

He has the added advantage that he is not reserved for the *élite*,
or those who elect to spend their holidays at some hotel holding
the "fishing rights" on a particular river. True, there are some hill-
lochs where one may not fish for the brown trout without
permission from the landowner—but there are also the yellow
mountain-burns, his natural habitat, along which, in many localities, anyone may wander with rod and line to "try his luck".

The fascination of trout-fishing grows upon one—perhaps because there is more to it than just catching the fish. Anyone who
has tried, for the first time, "the gentle art of casting" will
appreciate this point. You watch your friend, noting the expert
way he flicks his line, so that the fly—perhaps an "Alder" or a
"March Brown"—describes a figure-eight in mid-air, to land with
the lightness of thistledown over a peat-brown pool. It looks so
easy—until you try it for yourself! . . .

After you have spent a harrowing ten minutes trying to dis-
entangle the fish-hook from your hair or the back of your collar,
you try again. Gradually, there grows upon you a deeper respect
for fishermen than you would ever have deemed possible—and a
determination to catch at least one fish, even if you have to spend
the rest of the evening freeing your clothes and person from the
unwelcome attentions of the now rather bedraggled fly.

At last, you make a passably good cast. The fly sails out, and
lands (it seems to you) with the force of a small explosion in the
centre of the pool. A greedy young trout is fool enough to rise to
it—and before you know where you are, you have hooked your
first fish!

Of course, you lose it—and spend the rest of the evening
blaming everything but your own inexperience for your ill-luck.
Presently, your friend joins you, carrying a fine string of spotted
denizens whose little serpentine heads seem to avert themselves
in scorn at your grudging admiration. You feel the veriest tyro—
but you know in your heart that "the game has got you" and you
will do better tomorrow.

It is then that you realise anew that there is more to this trout-
fishing than meets the eye. Your friend is a tried and tested

disciple of Pisces, well versed in the rites which attend the capture of his sun-dappled children. He arranges boulders to form a shelter from the breeze, and fills the shielded space with dry heather. A match, then, and a billy-can full of burn-water suspended on a "cromag" over the fire. It is your job to collect fresh heather to feed the crackling flames. You are kept busy, too, for the dry scrub burns swiftly.

The fragrant smoke of it fills all the air—and soon the water in the billy-can begins to bubble invitingly. Into it goes a tobacco-tin full of tea, and it is stirred with a rowan-twig to impart a special charm. Sugar is added (if you have it) and the whole boiled rapidly for some five minutes. Then a mugful of cold water is put in "to cool it", and the magic potion is ready.

Such tea should be drunk strong and sweet, without milk, or the ceremonial loses some of its character. If it has been made correctly, the colour of it will be deepest amber, and the taste will hold the smoky fragrance of burnt heather—a "tinkers' tea" worth writing a poem about, if one can find the right words. You can eat what you like with it—my own choice is dried bananas and a plain biscuit, but Abernethys and cheese are a pleasing alternative.

Afterwards, you will lie back with a cigarette, watching the heather-fire smoulder down to a grey ash among the scorched boulders—and you will know that life is good, and that tomorrow, yes, tomorrow, you will catch a fish!

It is in fishing for the brown trout that the angler seems to come closest to the untamed heart of Nature—to touch hands, as it were, with the Spirit of the Hills. Perhaps that is why I enjoy trout, rolled in oatmeal and fried to a crisp and crinkly brownness over the campfire, more than any other dish I can name—why, for those of us who love solitude and the song of a mountain burn, there is no fish quite like them. . . .

Some two weeks later I was able to try a third type of fishing. The lobster-pots, it seemed, had little attraction that year, the price for live lobsters having gone down—but there was still the trolling, chiefly for home-consumption, though some saith (or rock-salmon) were sent south on the overnight lorries from Gairloch.

Trolling for saith, or "coal-fish", offers a greater thrill, perhaps, than for lithe. The saith come up in shoals to play on the surface, and the gulls, which have been keeping watch from afar, sweep down in a great flurry of white wings on to the boiling waters, adding their harsh screams to the general commotion.

I have rowed through calm waters in the dusk when the coal-fish were almost jumping into the boat. But they were not "taking" that night, and only one small "cuddie" fell a victim to the rubber eel. Near the shore, the waters were alive with "small fry" and squabbling gulls. Above them, the grey Lewisian rock was veined with pink, blackened here and there as if by primeval fires. Beyond Port Lair, we drifted past the dark Cliff of the Intestines—so called, I was told, because of the pinkish streaks of quartzite which coil like entrails along the face of the rock. An alternative explanation for the rather grisly name is that it is due to the number of sheep which have dashed themselves to death over the precipice.

We came round now into a little bay, and rowed under a black buttress of rock patched with splashes of startling white. A flock of cormorants dived out of the crannies at our approach. One young bird, more curious than cautious, sat still and eyed us from a little shelf, twisting its snaky neck back and forth and wriggling its willowy body like a Hawaiian dancer. A male member of the expedition audibly wished for a gun. I would have been more than content if I had remembered to bring my camera.

Leaving "Cormorants' Rock" astern, we cruised on beyond Diabaig and circled twice round the rocky islands off the west curve of the bay. Here, we caught another fish, a smallish lithe. Apart from this, there was nothing doing, so we gave up and started the outboard. Back near Wester Alligin, the water was still alive with coal-fish, and the wee cuddies nibbled tantalisingly at our lines. At intervals, we stopped the engine and tried again— but our catch for the evening remained at two.

Later in the same week, we tried a different type of fishing— the deep-sea or drop-line variety. For this, one goes over to "the banks", about two-thirds of the way across the loch. Only those who have been at the business for some time know just the right spot to anchor the boat. The bait used is a mussel or cockle attached to a paternoster which is then lowered to the sea-bed and raised again to a height of barely one foot from the bottom. The depth here is between twenty and twenty-five fathoms. One catches—if the fish are "taking"—haddock, whiting and codling, with an occasional gurnet. The fishing is better with a light breeze and a hint of rain in the sky.

On the afternoon chosen for this excursion, we were favoured with what appeared to be perfect weather. We had hired the new motor-launch from "Bellavista", taken a large hamper of tea and sandwiches, and were prepared for a whole afternoon and evening of activity.

There were two other boats out, and they were obviously taking in fish. Our crew of two took a careful bearing from certain landmarks on the shore, and we put the lines down. The water was just choppy enough to rock the boat pleasantly as she swung at anchor. In the first hour, we caught two fair-sized haddocks. Then the anchor dragged, and we drifted a little. Thereafter, luck deserted us, and we decided to change our pitch.

Re-starting the engine, we chugged across towards Beinn Shieldaig, to drop anchor and lines again on the fringe of the Òb Mheallaidh. It was deeper here, but we must have struck a shoal for three of the party instantly had a "bite". One line, when it came up, had a whiting on each hook !

The wind was dropping now. We caught one more haddock—and then came a lull so prolonged that we eventually decided to move to the narrows.

By this time, it was evening, and we had eaten most of the sandwiches. The tide was running in so fast at the narrows that our lines would not sink to the bottom. The sea was now dead flat, swirling in oily coils and whirlpools around the boat, piling up gobbets of foam where the currents met. Occasionally, a flower-like tendril of weed circled slowly up from the green depths, swaying and pirouetting like a languid ballerina until it flattened into shapelessness on the surface.

A porpoise suddenly rolled close by the boat, then another, then one that leapt in a black curve right out of the water and crashed down again amid a shower of flying spume. Their hoarse breathing filled the air with a weird rasping noise like the puffing of rusty bellows.

The strong tide swung the boat. We drew up the anchor again and puttered back among the floating weed towards Alligin. It was eight o'clock when we put in at the rocks by the schoolhouse to collect extra sweaters and refill the flasks with hot soup.

Out again, then, into a softly gathering night of violet sky and still water from which the light was slowly being withdrawn, and with it all the colour which had brought life and glory to the earth. The sea was so calm now that it reflected everything with the faithfulness of a mirror—the blue-shadowed lift of the hills; the fading twinkle of white houses along the shore; the masts and furled sails of a visiting yacht which had anchored over the banks. One of the smaller boats was still at the fishing; but soon we heard the putter of the outboard and saw the ripples spread smoothly as the little craft sped towards the shore.

Then the yacht hummed softly into life, using her Diesel engines as there was no wind. Slowly, like a great sea-bird, she glided away towards the head of the loch—and the blue shadows swallowed her up, leaving no trace of her going.

We put down our lines again, but caught nothing. Away at the narrows, the gulls quarrelled over an incoming shoal of herring. Soon, the surface of the waters around us was broken by the little ripples of their passing. Then, harsh and laboured again, came the regular breaths of the porpoises. We made no sound, and they passed close by the boat, so close that we could see the long, lithe shapes of them weaving just under the surface. When not "rolling", they moved with shark-like swiftness, their slender, greenish bodies having the appearance of phantom-fish created out of the cold currents.

Soon, darkness closed softly over the face of the loch. Colour was wholly withdrawn—and, it seemed, life also, for we heard no ripple now, and there was not so much as a twitch at our lines.

Only, away at the narrows, the tireless gulls keened plaintively, their voices vibrant with hunger and the desolation of night falling on the wan wastes of the sea.

If one might think of sound in terms of colour, one would surely describe the crying of gulls as the "greyest" sound on earth. One does not need to be a poet to associate it with the million inarticulate voices of "the poorest, the loneliest and the lost", for ever crying along the shores of the wide and unheeding world.

We came back to Inver Alligin through a close-gathered darkness which was warm and soft as velvet. The tide was ebbing now, and a faint perfume of sea-wrack tingled in our nostrils as we neared the shadowy beach. Lights winked along the shore, and an undulating blur behind marked the rise and fall of the hills.

Our engine off now, we drifted noiselessly in on the current. The barnacle-crusted rocks which served as a pier were yet wet to the touch.

We gathered up raincoats and the hamper, and bade goodnight to our "crew". Our fish traced arcs of silver as they were thrown out on to the rock. As distinct from lithe, they exuded a strong odour of the sea. We had four haddocks and three whiting—not a big catch, by any means, but enough to give us each a meal.

And, for this, we had rested, for the best part of a day, in the lap of the

> ". . . great, sweet mother,—
> Mother and lover of men, the Sea"

—and her age-old beauty was still with us. Many moons would pass before we should lose the memory of her loveliness when, at early evening, she had raced and made merry in the narrows, with the green tendrils of weed tangled in her long grey hair. . . .

Like the poet, Swinburne, we had found that Loch Torridon is, indeed, "no mountain-moulded lake", but the untamed sea:
> "The sea, that harbours in her heart
> sublime,
> The supreme heart of music deep as
> time,
> And in her spirit strong
> The spirit of all imaginable song."

Chapter VIII

ROUND ABOUT THE VILLAGE

I HAD elected to take care of my neighbour's hens while she was away visiting relatives in England. Hens, I discovered, are a race apart, and there is no end to their vagaries. They will leave six nests standing empty, and fight jealously over the one, into which as many as possible will pack all together, seemingly oblivious of the resulting discomfort. Any small object placed in the nest will put them in the right frame of mind for laying there. China eggs, apparently unobtainable in Torridon, are a luxury. Jessie Mathieson's flock were quite content with small pepper-pots!

In three weeks, I grew quite attached to them—and, for their own part, they followed me about with a touching air of devotion, particularly at meal-times. Often, they would come right into the cottage—to Jeannie's wrathful disgust.

One does not usually credit hens with individuality—but this is a mistake. When allowed to wander about freely, they become highly "canny", and each one seems to develop a personality of her own. Those closed up in hygienic "batteries" may be another matter. Acquaintances of mine who keep them in this way say that a hen is an adaptable creature who worries little so long as she has her food regularly. She will not lay well if she is unhappy. But I am unconvinced and unreconciled to the idea of treating living creatures as machines.

During my brief acquaintanceship with Jessie Mathieson's little colony, I found the greatest pleasure in watching them flutter towards me down the cliff at meal-times, making almost as much noise about it as a flock of capercailzie. Apparently, hens have very little sense of direction or balance, for they would often land in the most undignified attitudes, flat on their faces and nowhere near the food! But the flurry of wings was a lovely sound, and it was pleasant to watch them scratching delightedly in the dust.

Before long, some of them had names. The speckled cock,

75

whom I dubbed Charles, was a handsome fellow with a sweeping tail strikingly plumed with white, and a gentle and fatherly way with his harem. His head and neck were a burnished copper-colour, reminding one of a golden pheasant. Then there was Pollyanna, a white leghorn who went away by herself under a rock and hatched out six handsome chicks.

Two of the colony went broody; and, as an experiment, I gave them some eggs. It was soon obvious that the ways of a "clocking hen" are obscure, and beyond the comprehension of mere human beings. One calmly settled herself in the most popular nest and refused to move. The others simply laid their eggs on the top of her. "All were safely gathered in", and she would have hatched a hundred chicks if something had not been done about it. I finally solved the problem by covering her with an inverted box and supplying an extra nest for the morning rush.

The other broody lady, whom I had christened Lizzie, I placed on thirteen choice eggs in a deep seaman's chest lined with straw, and battened down the hatch with a brick. She grumbled some-what, and made one or two determined assaults on my fingers each time I went near, but finally settled down. The trouble came at meal-times. As in duty bound, I would lift her off and put her out with the others for food. For some five minutes, she would stagger around as if in a trance, "casting a jaundiced eye" on the world from beneath her flopping red comb. Then, when all the food was eaten, she would suddenly wake up, peck furiously at nothing, and settle down for a prolonged sunbath in the dust. Useless to try to persuade her to return to the eggs—she simply cackled indignantly and dodged all attempts at capture. Finally, I would give up the struggle and go indoors. Creeping stealthily into the hen-house some half-hour later, I would find the eggs cold and Lizzie in a different nest, crooning lullabies to a pepper-pot! Once safely installed on the eggs again, she was good for another twenty-four hours—but if any of them hatch, I thought, it will be no thanks to her!

My neighbours told me what to do if any more hens started "clocking". It seemed that the only way to get the "clock" off them was to make them really uncomfortable. Suggested remedies included ducking them in the burn, leaving them for three days under a creel without food or water, and pegging them up on the clothes-line in a sack, to swing in the wind. There was one formidable lady among Miss Mathieson's flock whom I had named Spiteful Susan. After several painful encounters in the hen-house, our relations had become decidedly strained. But Susan had enough sense to refrain from going broody!

Elsewhere in the district, life increased and multiplied. Nellie, the collie bitch at Braigh, had eight puppies. Four were drowned, but the others, two dogs and two bitches, flourished apace.

One morning, I went over to see them. The mother was black-and-tan, the father, Bruce, black with a white collar and paws. Two of the puppies were mostly black, the other two white,, with little patches of black or brown. They were two weeks old, and their watery blue eyes looked out uncomprehendingly at the dark world of the byre.

It was a mistake on my part to see them. I can never resist puppies. Duncan put the little white bitch into my arms, and she nuzzled my face. Already, he said, he had found homes for three of them. But there was a chance that nobody would take to the white bitch, as light-coloured dogs were not popular among the shepherds. In that case, she would have to be destroyed.

(I remembered a story I once heard about a shepherd who had a white collie which the sheep seemed to dislike—until he blacked her with shoe-polish! But, for a pet, the colour would not matter. It would be an experience to own a Highland collie . . . or would Jeannie be jealous?)

The puppy whimpered appealingly in my arms.

"Save her for me," I said, rashly, "and if Jeannie doesn't like her, I can probably find someone who will."

Duncan smiled; and I went home, the proud owner (or almost) of my first sheep-dog. After a lot of toying with names, I chose "Brighde", Gaelic for "Bridget", which was simplified to "Bridie" for ease in calling.

Now all I wanted was a few sheep and a cow and I could set up as a crofter! It was amusing to entertain visions of winter "céilidhs" over the tatties and salt herring!

Saturday came, bringing the van with the hen's food. In company with my neighbours, I climbed the long, steep brae to the top road and shouldered my three stone of meal. Cautiously, we began our descent, resting several times before reaching sea-level. Then back up the brae again, this time for household provisions.

Year in, year out, this procedure had gone on for the people of Inver Alligin. In winter, it was sometimes dark when the van arrived, and one had to descend through deep snow, holding the heavy sack of meal and corn with one hand and gripping a torch with the other. There was no proper path down—just a rough track by "Heather Cliff". The hillside was slippery and full of holes, and the gradient steep enough to require care under normal conditions. With a film of ice, it was perilous. The people of Inver Alligin had been agitating for a road down to the village for forty years. In desperation, during the summer of my visit, some held back their rates for a while to draw public attention to their plight. Correspondence on the subject appeared in newspapers of nation-wide circulation; but, at that time, little else was done, and Inver Alligin remained, to all intents and purposes, the "Forgotten Village".

During the last few days of May, the weather turned icy cold. Rain swept in dense veils over the loch. Snow fell overnight, and lay heavy on Liathach and Beinn Alligin. But the pattern of late spring went on. The campion, crimson and white, made cushions of colour beside the shore path. The delicate orchis bloomed among the peat-bog above the clean white houses. The yellow iris raised its half-unfurled banners against crumbling dykes. The purple foxglove towered up among grey rocks, nodding its heavy bells in the light breeze. The ditches were full of marsh-marigolds, and frail windflowers tossed their white skirts in the shelter of a tiny birch-copse.

The crops were growing apace, coaxed up by the recent hot weather. The thin grass-blades rose in restless ranks over the patch of cultivated land in the centre of the village. The thick, furry shoots of the new potatoes broke through the furrowed earth. Spring cabbages were planted out, and the yellow-green of young lettuces made gay stripes across the kitchen-gardens. The lime-trees, their exotic perfume forgotten, rattled their bunches of keys to remind the passer-by of their new and sober status as wardresses of the meadow-land. Already, the rhododendrons were withering, the rowans scattering their crinkled blossoms on the grass. Already, the golden sovereigns of spring were tarnishing a little at the edges.

The following week, Jessie Mathieson returned from London

and took over the hens. For several days, however, they still queued up expectantly at my cottage-door, and clucked indignantly when no meal was forthcoming. Pollyanna's shy chicks were still living in their cave under the rock, long-legged and wild, but noticeably robust as a result of their open-air existence. One of the broody hens had hatched seven eggs.

We were on the edge of summer now. The clover, purple and white, brought a sweet fragrance to the meadow. The vetch entwined its curly tendrils among the fast-growing hay. The ragged robin flaunted a crimson cloak on many a dark patch of the wilderness, and birdseyes blinked in the short grass.

The evenings were still cool, but there was plenty of driftwood on the beaches for fires, baked brittle by the sun. Most days, now, the loch was windless under high cloud, reflecting the green contours of the Beinn Damh hills. The eider-duck played and courted on the calm waters, and once a seal swam under the cliffs below the Hostel.

The mountains had cast off their snows and repaired their threadbare winter garments with patches of new green, stitched on with the bright threads of the bell-heather. Climbers and walkers came and went at the Hostel, but there were few visitors, as yet, staying in the village itself. Work progressed apace, however, and interested groups gathered daily around the boat-builder's little shop, where freshly painted dinghies lay drying in the sun.

Conversation turned once more on the illegal whisky-distilling, and I was informed that there was a still, or "pot dubh" in my coalshed. It was like a studded metal tub, and much larger than I had imagined. It had been unearthed some years before by a shepherd at Coulin; but the most important piece of the equipment, the lid with its copper "worm", was still buried somewhere in the hills.

Taking advantage of the good weather, a Cambridge friend and I packed up sandwiches and cameras and set out one morning for Coire Mhic Fhearchair. I had already visited this wild place once while descending Beinn Eighe in the previous year; but it had been dusk when we entered the corrie, and one could obtain only a hazy impression of its magnificence.

Now, tramping the other way, on a day of cloud and sunlight, we found at first no hint of the stark beauty to come. Leaving the road at Corrie bridge, above stately Torridon House, we wandered along a sun-dappled path, through fragrant woods beside the cascading stream, between the great ridges of Liathach and Beinn Alligin. The bell-heather painted vivid splashes of colour on either side of the track. Everywhere drifted the elusive fragrance of the bog-myrtle, the warm perfume of sun-touched pines. Black shadows barred the path and dappled our shoulders as we strode along. The air was made melodious by the trilling of mavis and lark, the echo of the cataracts in the gorge below.

Emerging from the woods, we tramped along beside the frothing river. On either hand, the hills were palely green, streaked with the mauve of moving shadows. A wisp of cloud clung in the "Cleft" of Beinn Alligin and wreathed itself around the brow of Sgùrr Mór. Across the gorge, the forked Allt Toll a' Mhadaidh flowed out of the hollows, foaming down the scarred mountainside to leap into the main stream of Coire Mhic Nobuil. Sunlight danced on the tumult of white waters, and set shafts of amber fire trembling in the peat-brown pools. We passed the horseshoe ridge of Beinn Alligin, and now we could see the Allt a' Bhealaich coming in from the pass between Beinn Alligin and Beinn Dearg.

We crossed the bridge and followed the right fork of the path beside the river. To our right, now, the dark pinnacles of Liathach were beginning to take shape over the shoulder of the brae. Ahead, stately Beinn Eighe was grey and cold, capped with the shining silver of her quartzite screes. Cloud flowed down over her cliffs, and clung about the diamond terraces of Ruadh Stac Mór.

Our path became rougher, meandering along through boulders and peat. Above us, the sinister ridge of Liathach towered black against a pale-gold sky, littered with crumbling debris, slashed by the flickering rapiers of her waterfalls. The whole series of perilous escarpments lay open to the eye. There were the two humps at the east-end, the grey peak of Spidean a' Choire Leith, on whose summit we could see the tiny pimple of the cairn where, three days before, we had rested for tea and heard the hill-gods chuckling in the mist. A series of gullies slashed the peak on the north side. We paused to reflect that it was up one of these that we had made a memorable climb. There were the fantastic "Teeth", black and broken and crooked, apparently of knife-edge sharpness in the withered gums of the hill—and there, west of

Coire Mhic Fhearchair (Beinn Eighe), showing rock-buttresses and loch

these, the ridge rose in a series of great steps (whose steepness we well knew) over the top of Meall Dearg to the summit of Mullach an Rathain. The whole ridge seemed a fantastic length; and, seeing it from this angle, we were not surprised that we had spent eleven hours on the hill in cloud a few days before.

We had now lost the path altogether, and were tramping over peat-bog and heather towards Sàil Mhór. Lochans began to gleam among the waste land: Loch a' Chaoruinn at the foot of Liathach, and, farther on, Loch Grobaig and the string of dark pools at the entrance to Coire Dubh Mór, the dark pass between Liathach and Beinn Eighe.

We topped the last rise—and, suddenly, the whole scene had changed. We were above Loch nan Cabar—and before us stretched the glorious landscape of Flowerdale and Kinlochewe, a water-jewelled plateau surrounded by wild and solitary hills. Beinn a' Chearcaill, with her girdle of cliffs and cloud-crowned brow. Beinn an Eóin at the back of a string of wild hill-lochs. Near at hand, the crags of Càrn na Feòla, the grey scree-slopes of Sàil Mhór, the western summit of Beinn Eighe. Farther north-west, Baos Bheinn was veiled in blue haze.

We descended the hillside and crossed the valley at the head of Loch nan Cabar, between the loch proper and the two tiny pools whose still waters mirrored the dark grass-tufts and the blurred reflection of Liathach. Climbing again now, we traversed the rough slopes of Sàil Mhór, scrambling over boulders and heather while the water-laden plateau twinkled below. Northward, now, through the wild pass of Glen Grudie, we could see the blue gleam of Loch Maree, with a welter of golden hills behind.

A cool wind fanned our faces as we came round the northern flank of Sàil Mhór. Above us towered black, overhanging cliffs, slashed by the steep gully of loose sandstone scree known among climbers as Morrison's Gully. Here, we were surprised to see a patch of unmelted snow. Still climbing, we crossed another yellow scree-shoot and scrambled up the rocks beside the foaming fall which tumbles out of the corrie. Over the lip at last—and there we were, in what the guide-books call "one of the wildest corries in the Highlands", displaying striking evidence of glaciation.

Before us, sheltered from the wind, the lochan lapped softly on the grey stones. Our awed eyes ranged from the black crags of Sàil Mhór, along perilous scree-drifts to the towering cliffs whose

81

Snow-capped Slioch, above Loch Maree

three great buttresses are famous among rock-climbers. Cloud was pouring down into the gullies, outlining fantastic ledges and chimneys, enhancing the impression of height and the wildness of the whole desolate scene.

We had lunch at the edge of the loch, in the shelter of a large boulder. The cloud went away again, and sunlight touched a ledge of green moss and bejewelled the scree-shoot at the far end of the corrie. It is this shingly gully which affords an easy glissade from the ridge above.

Patches of colour moved and changed across the scree below Ruadh Stac Mór. The loch was brown and gold and luminous green, with black shadows where the brooding cliffs looked at their scarred faces in the water.

These cliffs, to the uninitiated, look insurmountable; but, in fact, all three buttresses have been climbed, as have also the cliffs of Sàil Mhór, on the east side of Morrison's Gully. Details of these ascents are given in the Scottish Mountaineering Club's guide—*The Northern Highlands*.

For our own part, however, it was enough to see Coire Mhic Fhearchair in all its fierce beauty—and, for this, we could not have had a more perfect day.

The light was going out of the landscape when we began the descent to the shadowy plateau. Soon, beyond the string of shining lochans, the great, sharp edge of Liathach grew tall amid the grey-gold mists of the evening. The river murmured softly over stones washed smooth by the passing of many waters.

Tramping briskly, we left the dark pools and the peat-waste behind, and came once more down the green expanse of Coire Mhic Nobuil, under the shadow of Beinn Dearg, among whose knobbly summits we saw deer etched delicately on the sky-line beneath a film of cloud.

Finding the path again, we stopped for tea, then swung briskly along beneath the darkening ridge of Beinn Alligin. On the fringe of the woods, the warm air was heavy with the scent of bog-myrtle, and the bell-heather was a crimson flame against the quiet colours of the evening.

So, happy and not at all tired, we came back to supper at Inver Alligin, bringing a memory of wild crags and cloud-brushed precipices, holding fast to a sense of peace gathered from the quiet places of the hills.

CHAPTER IX

LOVELY LOCH MAREE

TOWARDS the end of June, Jeannie and I made our first excursion beyond Glen Torridon. Rising early to catch the mail-bus from the top road, we jolted into Achnasheen to meet a fishing-party. Thence, by another bus, we journeyed to the "Loch Maree Hotel", to spend a fortnight trying our luck with the sea-trout.

At least, that was the intention of the rest of the party. For myself, I would be content to establish closer acquaintance with the loch itself, believed to have been named after St Maelrubha, who came from Bangor, Ireland, to found a monastery at Applecross in the year A.D. 671, and who is counted second only to St Columba in the history of the early Celtic saints. There are many stories and legends told about lovely Loch Maree and its islands—and I confess that these attracted me a great deal more than the fish.

The day of our journey was a grey one, with great banks of low cloud hanging over the hills. *En route* from Achnasheen, we had only the briefest glimpse of Móruisg, looming over bare braes to the south. At Kinlochewe, Beinn Eighe was a dream-mountain, shining palely through rolling vapours.

We swept on through the twinkling woods beside Loch Maree. The bracken was thick beneath the maturing pines, lying like a green quilt over the feet of the slender birches.

I thought of Alligin with its few frail trees—how summer would change it in the short time that I was away. Lizzie's chicks had been mere fluffy balls when I left. Even in a fortnight, they would have grown tall and unfamiliar. . . .

We ran on towards the hotel. It was a Saturday, and the train from Inverness had been two hours late. It was teatime when we at length reached our destination—but, apparently, the hotel staff were accustomed to that sort of thing, for we were at once provided with an excellent lunch.

83

Despite my general preference for "the simple life", I found much that was pleasant at the Loch Maree Hotel. The building itself, with its pink stuccoed walls and high hedge of rhododendrons, made a charming picture. It was not large, and one absorbed very quickly its restful and homelike atmosphere, its air of quiet distinction which was further enhanced by the freshly gilded coat of arms on the outside wall.

Across the road was an explanation of its connections with Royalty—a simple memorial-stone bearing this inscription:

"Air an dara latha-deug deth mhìos meadhonach an fhochair
1877
Thàinig
Bàn-Rìgh Bhictoria
a dh'fhaicinn Loch Mariubhe agus nan crìoch-an mu'n cuairt.
Dh'fhan i sèa oidhche s'an Tigh-òsda so thall, agus 'na caomhda-
lachd, dheònaich i gu'm biodh a' chlach so 'na cuimhneachan
air an tlachd a fhuair i 'na teachd do'n chèarn so de Ros."

The following translation was framed in the front porch of the hotel:

"On the 12th day of September, 1877, Queen Victoria came to see Loch Maree and the surrounding district. She remained Six Nights at the Inn over there, and in her Gracious Condescension willed that this STONE should be a remembrance of the pleasure she found in coming to this part of ROSS-SHIRE."

The front lounge of the Loch Maree Hotel was decorated with enormous stuffed sea-trout and salmon mounted in glass cases—all wearing expressions sufficiently fierce to deter any inexperienced fisherman. On the day we arrived, roses bloomed along the outside walls, and every table bore a vase of rhododendrons.

The next day, being Sunday, we did nothing. On the Monday, feeling that it was high time to "get down to business", we took a motor-boat and fishing-tackle on to the loch.

But either the water was too still, or somebody had told the sea-trout that their season had not yet started, for we did not have so much as one tiny "strike". However, we were more than compensated, to my mind, by the scenery.

We chugged between thickly forested islands, one-time haunt

of the rare osprey, where sandy bays invited us to land and explore. It needed no very great imagination to believe oneself in
the South Seas. All about us, the brown water lapped over white
rocks or traced a path of silver into the secret coves. Mallard
flew low over the ripples, to vanish among the trunks of whitened
trees. The reeds pattered out a message as we cruised near to the
desolate shores, and long heather blew in the light wind. We
steered cautiously through the narrows between Eilean Sùbhainn
and Garbh Eilean. The water in this narrow channel was black
with depth. Splashes of white paint on the rocks marked out the
various "fishing-beats". Before us, on the Letterewe side, brown
braes ran up against a blue sky. A high waterfall caught the light
before the stream plunged into a gorge thick with waving trees.
To the east, mighty Slioch towered up in stark and sombre
beauty, with blue shadows outlining her turrets and her pinnacles wreathed in golden cloud. Looking westward across the
loch, we could see the wild ridge of Liathach looming at the back
of blue-washed hills, black and naked and forbidding under
gathering rain cloud. Near the head of the loch, a series of pale-
grey hummocks marked the beginnings of Beinn Eighe. Un-
furling mist revealed a hint of the great quartzite ridge above.

The geology of the Loch Maree country is as interesting as that
of Torridon, being an admixture of Lewisian and pre-Lewisian
rock, together with the Torridonian sandstone of Slioch and the
islands. The hotel stands on Lewisian gneiss, but the sandstone
begins again nearby. Many of the houses are built on the old
river-terraces left behind at the subsiding of the waters which
once surged across the valley and lapped around the flanks of the
hills.

No visitor to this fair district should omit a trip to Isle Maree,
most charming and most historic of the twenty-four lovely
islands. It was here that St Maelrubha had his cell, and, before him,
the Druids used the island for a place of sacrifice.

Choosing a clear day with just the faintest ripple on the loch,
we set out for this romantic tree-clad shore, towed behind the
fishing-party—as the ghillie refused to trust me alone with the
outboard. (When I became better acquainted with the rocks and
sandbanks scattered among the isles, I had nothing but praise for
his caution.)

Behind us, the hills were clear under a calm sky. We cruised over sparkling water, bobbing in the wake of the leading boat. Ahead and to our left, Garbh Eilean was grey and wild behind the olive-green woods of Eilean Dubh na Sròine. To the east, Slioch was remote and still against a pearl-grey heaven.

We cruised past the half-submerged rocks off the point of Aird na h-Eighamh, and into the channel. To our right rose the green-topped braes of Eilean Eachainn, or Hector's Isle, believed to have been named after a warrior of local lore. Eilean Sùbhainn was a mass of grey crags and heathery wasteland, scattered with the bleached bones of fallen trees. We looked across to the golden curve of a sandy bay, where a little herd of goats basked in the sun. Their colours ranged from coal-black to snowy white. Like little statues, they stood rigid to eye us as we chugged past. Behind them, the ancient rock rose against blue sky and blue water. It was like a vision of the Isles of Greece, and one half expected to see a sun-tanned goatherd with his pipe come wandering barefoot across the warm sand.

The narrows were full of rocks and sandbanks, some marked with a warning stake. Before us now lay Isle Maree, small and cool, inviting us with its shingly shores and canopy of green trees.

We parted company with the other boat, and I rowed round into a pebble-strewn bay. The sun had come right out now, dancing on the amber water, scorching us as we beached the boat and secured her to a boulder.

Jeannie leapt ashore with the eagerness of the true explorer. The warm stones crunched under our feet. Before us lay the dark forest, full of bird-song and shadows, a faery kingdom into which one peered in delighted awe, mentally absorbing the grace of a tendril of creeper, the gnarled shape of a Disney-esque tree.

A leaf-scattered track enticed us into the deep-green shade. The trees closed thickly around, until the little beach was a golden glimmer behind, the loch a flash of blue through the close-gathered green. Fallen branches of larch scattered the path, and the air was fragrant with the scent of their drying cones. Everywhere, the holly-trees shone dark and glossy among a wilderness of oak, pine and rowan. Worm-riddled trunks of silver birch lay rotting among the moss, light and unsubstantial, like old bones that crumbled to dust at the touch.

We followed the path to where a low wall of moss-grown stones encircled the old burial-ground. Here, for a while, the wanderer may browse among the simple memorials erected over the years to those who rest on this enchanted isle, where ancient and modern are united for ever in their last long sleep.

If you know where to look, you may quickly find the great stone slabs, lying side by side, that mark the ancient graves of the Lovers of Isle Maree, about which local lore tells a beautiful story.

In the old days of the Vikings, a certain Prince Olaf of Norway used to visit the Western Isles in his galley in search of plunder. In winter, his boat was drawn across the land from Loch Ewe to camp beside Loch Maree.

One evening, as he was walking alone by the shore, he met the beautiful Princess Deora, daughter of the King of Dalriada, the old kingdom of Argyll and the adjacent isles. She had a refuge on Isle Maree, and was returning there, attended by a young warrior and an old man. It was "love at first sight" for the fair damsel and the handsome stranger. As Prince Olaf did not see her again, he sailed over to the island to ask her to become his wife. She accepted, and the Prince returned joyfully to the mainland to make preparation for receiving her.

Before he reached his camp, however, he was waylaid by the young warrior who had been in attendance on the Princess. This young Highlander, known as Hector Ruadh or Red Hector, was also in love with Deora, and he insisted that Prince Olaf fight him for her. In the ensuing conflict, Olaf was seriously wounded and left for dead. He was found later by a hunter, and was taken once more to Isle Maree. Here, the Princess Deora, with the help of the old hermit, nursed him back to health.

When he was convalescing, however, the Princess was called away to visit her sick father. For some time, there was no news of her; and, at last, the old hermit went to seek her, promising Olaf that he would show a red signal from the shore if she were coming, but a black one if tragedy had overtaken her.

Daily, from the island, the Prince watched the further shore— and, presently, the signal came. It was black! In overwhelming grief, he drew his dagger and plunged it into his heart.

Returning safely to the island, Princess Deora found her lover dead. She turned to accuse the old hermit—but he at once drew his dirk and slew her. Then, casting off his false wig and beard, he revealed himself as Hector Ruadh, whose jealousy had driven him to accomplish the death of the two lovers. Deora's followers at once fell upon him, but he escaped them and dived into Loch Maree. Though they watched for a long time, he did not reappear. The legend recounts that he was changed into a kelpie, or water-horse, which even to this day raises storms on the loch, and sinks boats by "Hector's Isle", or seizes people at night to drown them in the dark waters.

This version of the old story is given in *Tales from the Moors and Mountains** by Donald A. Mackenzie. Another recounts how the Princess was persuaded to feign death to test Olaf's love for her. Whatever happened, the two of them now sleep side by side on Isle Maree, united in death.

Beyond the graves of these ill-fated lovers, light flickers through the woods, limning the stony mounds which are all that is left of the chapel which St Maelrubha built and dedicated to the Virgin Mary. The name of this chapel is sometimes offered as an alternative explanation of "Maree". The ruins lie all around the ancient burial-ground.

Walking on over the moss-cushions and through the long grasses, one comes to the little hollow where once gurgled the Holy Well, famed far and wide for its miraculous powers of healing. Some remarkable cures are said to have been effected here, chiefly the restoring to health of the insane. In the old accounts, one reads that the customary prelude to immersion in the spring included towing the sick person three times round the island at the back of a boat! For many generations people visited the well to avail themselves of its healing properties—but it is said that eventually a farmer brought a mad dog for treatment. The dog was cured—but the healing spirit was so offended that it departed, never to return. Shortly afterwards, the well dried up. Today, there is no trace of moisture in the little hollow, and it is difficult to determine the exact location of the spring.

Beside the Holy Well stands the famous "Wishing Tree", at one time a sturdy holly whose branches were covered with strips of bright cloth and rags as gifts to the saint, as well as being thick with hammered-in coins. The tree is now dead, and propped up by a stake. Much of the "tribute-money" has fallen out on to the ground; but fresh coins are contributed by visitors of today, who also hammer them into the stake and the bark of surrounding

* Stories from this book retold by permission of Messrs Blackie & Son, Ltd, Glasgow.

trees—presumably because there is so little space left on the traditional one.

It is on record that Queen Victoria, when she visited the island in 1877, was pleased to place her offering in the dead trunk of the old tree. It is now without doubt as tarnished and bent as the rest —it may even be one of those which have fallen on to the ground beneath. So Time, the great leveller, treats alike the gifts of princes and paupers.

With some little difficulty, I hammered in my own small tribute to the memory of the healing spirit of the well. Then I wandered on down to a little bay on the south side of the island, where I sat on a flat rock to rest in the sun.

Before me, the brown waters lapped over a rocky bank just off the shore. Beyond rose Eilean Sùbhainn with its golden sand and grey crags littered with fallen trees. Near my boulder, the butter-cups bloomed among grey stones, and a thrush sang ecstatically from the topmost branch of an oak-tree overhead.

Jeannie lay flat in the long grass, among blooming bell-heather and trails of wild honeysuckle. We looked down the shining length of Loch Maree towards sun-gilded Slioch and the mauve hills behind Kinlochewe, and across Eilean Sùbhainn to Beinn an Eóin, Baos Bheinn and the mountains of Flowerdale, with the ridge of Beinn Dearg looming behind. To the south-east, beyond the grassy knolls of Hector's Isle, waving ribbons of light fluttered over dark Meall a' Ghiubhais and touched the first shining summits of Beinn Eighe.

The larches moved above us in the warm wind. The bell-heather lit crimson fires among the rocks. After a while, we rose and wandered along the shingly shore, around the west end of the island. The beaches here, when examined closely, are a mass of variegated stones, all washed smooth by the lapping waters, some formed in layers of curious colours, with a predominance of pink quartzite and conglomerate granite and a delicate sprink-ling of micaceous gneiss. Among them, the milkwort— exceptionally tall and strong here—flaunts her royal-blue banners in the breeze. The broom is going to seed—but a few golden flowers yet linger among the pods of silver-green. The prickly whins bloom gaily, their roots set deep in the insecure anchorage of the shingle. You find a dead birch-tree, out of whose brittle trunk grows a weird white fungus hardened to the consistency of wood. Tufts of yellow-green larch thrust their rough heads out of the pale drifts of scree on the fringe of the forest.

Presently, you come round again to the little bay where you have beached the boat. A few minutes of strenuous pushing, a splashing of ice-cold water over your bare feet, a last-minute leap, and you are away again, drifting over the sunlit waters of Loch Maree. Into the narrows now—and perhaps a rasping scrape off a submerged sandbank. Then you are rowing strongly back towards the hotel, into blazing sun and a sharp wind.

It takes much longer than you had bargained for to reach the mainland, and the chances are that you will be late for lunch. You may also collect some outsize blisters from your struggle with current and wind. But the enchanted atmosphere of Isle Maree will follow you over the water; and, already, you will be planning the next excursion to the islands.

In olden times, the isles on Loch Maree provided a stronghold for many a warlike chieftain, and we learn that the MacLeods of Skye made one of them a "base" from which to conduct marauding expeditions against the MacKenzies of Kintail. This island is known as Eilean Gruididh, and lies by itself in a little bay towards the eastern end of the loch.

On a calm afternoon, we hired a motor-launch and a most obliging ghillie named Charlie and set out to pay it a visit. Passing Eilean Sùbhainn, we swung into the narrows beyond Hector's Isle. The water is particularly shallow here, the surface broken by treacherous rocks. Several times, our boat "touched bottom" before we floated once more into deep water.

We cruised eastward along Loch Maree, leaving behind the picturesque cluster of islands at the widest part of the loch. Before us, Slioch was crowned with cloud. Light moved over the dark-blue hills beyond Kinlochewe and brought to life the vibrant green of the braes to the south. Opposite Letterewe, we passed Fools' Rocks with their little, stunted trees. From here, one could see the site of the old Letterewe Iron Works, established in the seventeenth century by Sir George Hay but long since fallen into disuse.

There was no beach on "Grudie Island", but Charlie guided the boat to a landing-place among the rocks. A lizard darted off a flat stone as we stepped ashore. As distinct from Isle Maree, this island is completely overgrown with birch-trees. A carpet of long, thick heather underfoot greatly impedes the walker. The old fortress of the MacLeods is now a crumbling circular wall, almost hidden by the undergrowth. One looks down into the deep hollow which once served as a dungeon for captured MacKenzies. It is like a big well, the bottom thick with long grass —a perfect refuge, we thought, for snakes. Charlie showed us where staples had at one time been driven into the walls, to secure the chains of the hapless prisoners. It was a dark and melancholy place, and we were pleased to scramble back again on to the warm, creeper-covered rocks where waited our boat.

Pushing off, we glided round the island into the little bay. Here, just below the surface of the water, one may find the "Giant's Stepping-Stones"—three great stone blocks, lying some fifteen feet apart, which local legend says were used by a giant who once lived on the island as a means of getting to the mainland.

The light wind dropped completely as we swung once more into the narrows. Cloud dropped lower over the hills. We cruised through black, still water dotted with sombre islands. Beyond the shallow channel, we looked back to see that the waters in our wake were an oily blue-green, backed by the indigo hills. Slioch was swallowed up by swirling vapours. I pitied the climbers who had left the hotel that morning to attempt an ascent.

Largest of the isles of Loch Maree is Eilean Sùbhainn, the Isle of Berries, on which we had seen the wild goats. It has three lochs; and the fallen timber strewn from end to end of the island would provide enough fires to keep a modern "Swiss Family Robinson" in comparative comfort for as long as they wished to stay.

We had hoped to see Eilean Ruaraidh Mór, or Big Rory's Isle, the farthermost island at the west end of the group, named after a chieftain who had a stronghold there. There are said still to be traces of the foundations and gardens, but the visitor finds little else—apart from the unexpected and treacherous rocks in the channels around, guarding, as it were, the approaches to the isle. We had seen these already on one of our trout-fishing excursions, but had hoped to land and make closer acquaintance with the island itself.

This, however, we were denied. The weather turned cold and gusty, and Loch Maree was suddenly a mass of leaping billows capped with hissing foam. Once, we tried to take a boat out for some fishing in one of the more sheltered bays; but the strong waves swept us relentlessly back to the shore. We therefore abandoned the loch altogether, and spent the day fishing for brown trout on Loch na Fideil, a small oval of peat-brown water set in the waste land to the east of Talladale. Avoiding the fringe of reeds near the shore, the semicircle of water-lilies beyond, we cast on to the ruffled water, while sun and rain and the great gusts of the north-west wind afforded us a day of infinite variety.

We were fated, however, as regards the fishing, catching only one tiny brown trout which we put back. I walked around the loch in search of a better place—and found myself floundering through black peat-hag stagnant with the bodies of drowned cattle. Crossing the two streams at the eastern end of the lochan, I came round over steep crags thickly patched with precarious birch-trees. There was no better place for fishing, so I waded the burn which flows down to Loch Maree and returned to our original spot.

With a boat, we might have caught larger trout beyond the water-lilies. As it was, we tramped back to the hotel with nothing but a memory of the little windswept pool backed by a shining waterfall and the beginnings of wild hills. Though comparatively near to "civilisation", Loch na Fideil had, on this day of sun and storm, all the desolate beauty of the true hill-loch.

I have, so far, dealt little with the other side of Loch Maree, the Letterewe country. There is, however, a charming old story set on this side of the loch which is well worth re-telling. In Mr Donald Mackenzie's *Tales from the Moors and Mountains* it is called "The Story of the Lost Prince"; but it is also known as the Tale of Ewen MacGabhar, or Ewen, Son of the Goat.

In the days of the Lordships, a widow and her son, Kenneth, lived at Letterewe; and they kept a pet goat. Like most goats, the little creature was possessed of an adventurous spirit, and was addicted to wandering off on its own when in the mood. One day, it set off in the direction of Àrdlair. Kenneth followed it— and, presently, found that it had taken refuge in a cave,* where were also a lovely maiden and a young boy.

On being discovered by Kenneth, the maiden gave her name as Fewnvola, and explained that she was the aunt of the boy, Ewen, and that they had fled to the cave to escape the man who

* The cave is still known as "The Cave of the King's Son".

had slain Ewen's father. That was all she could tell him, for their real identity was secret, and they lived in fear of their lives.

Filled with compassion, Kenneth took the two fugitives home to his mother at Letterewe. The kindly woman made them welcome, and they were introduced to neighbours as relatives from a distant part. The boy, Ewen, grew up, and was called Ewen MacGabhar, or Ewen, Son of the Goat.

One day, the Earl of Ross visited the neighbourhood. Someone told him the story of Kenneth's "relatives", and he became suspicious. When he went away, he left his kinsman, Hector Dubh, to make further inquiries about the strangers. Questions were asked—discreetly enough, no doubt—but before long Fewnvola and Ewen heard about Black Hector's curiosity, and returned in alarm to the cave.

Here, Kenneth and his mother presently joined them, and the four of them went to Poolewe to await an opportunity of crossing the Minch to Lewis, where Fewnvola said that she had friends.

Before they could escape, however, a galley manned by the Earl's men sailed up Loch Ewe. The little group parted, and Kenneth and Fewnvola, who had now fallen in love, fled together. They were captured, however, and taken to Kintail. Meanwhile, Ewen and Kenneth's mother got across to Stornoway, where the chief, Colin Mór, was so impressed with Ewen's bearing that he took him to be trained with his own sons.

Before long, Kenneth and Fewnvola escaped from Kintail and landed in Skye, where they were married. One day, a boat brought them news of Ewen, and, joyfully, they went to Lewis. Here, they found Kenneth's mother alone, for Ewen had gone away for training with the Chief's sons. Kenneth at once entered Colin Mór's service, while Fewnvola disguised herself as a man, found Ewen, and was accepted as his ghillie. Secretly, she concealed among his belongings a box she had carried with her through all her adventures. It contained a purple robe and a gold-hilted sword.

A while later, it was known that Colin Mór was planning a great expedition against the Queen of Mull and Argyll. Ships from Skye and Kintail arrived to join his fleet of galleys, and, as a beginning, they plundered Tobermory. Colin Mór went on to Oban, and landed men on Kerrera.

However, the Queen's fleet were concealed in Loch Etive; and there they stayed in hiding until it was dark. Then, launching a surprise attack, they sailed out and wrought havoc among the enemy. Caught unawares, Colin Mór's armies were overthrown and he and his men taken prisoner. The Queen sat in judgment on them amid great pomp and splendour, and all were condemned to die, the young men first. Among these was Ewen MacGabhar, who at once courageously stepped forward. The Queen, recognising his likeness to her dead husband, fell to the floor in a faint. When her astonished courtiers had revived her, Ewen's "ghillie", Fewnvola, approached, bearing the box containing the purple robe and the gold-hilted sword. The Queen embraced her with great emotion, for they were sisters.

Ewen was hailed as King by the assembled Court; and his first act was to pardon Colin Mór and his men and to welcome them as friends.

So, amid great rejoicing, the story of Ewen, the Son of the Goat, came to a happy end.

. . . And so, with this and other charming legends in mind, I said good-bye to the gracious and historic landscape around "lovely Loch Maree". From the fisherman's point of view, no doubt, we would be counted as unfortunate, for we had been too early for the sea-trout. (In July, I learned later, they had a record season!) Yet, it would have been hard to convince any of us that our sojourn in this picturesque corner of the West was wasted. We had seen much, felt much—and the magic lingered. . . . For myself, I was already planning how and when I might return another year.

A new double-carriageway road alongside Loch Maree will provide better parking and viewing facilities for the growing number of visitors to the Beinn Eighe Nature Reserve, which I have described more fully in the Chapter on Beinn Eighe.

CHAPTER X

RETURN TO THE HILLS

BACK at Alligin, the hay had grown tall, the "tatties" were earthed up and almost ready to flower. The "wild" chicks had waxed in strength, and hopped briskly about among the rocks behind the hen-house.

The bracken was covering the braes with a mantle of waving green, and the bog-asphodel lifted its brazen spears among the spotted orchis in the peat-bog. The hay-field was a riot of colour, with clover, yellow rattle, vetch and dog-daisies tilting their heads at the sun. These "weeds", apart from the clover, would have to be picked out by hand after the hay was cut and spread out to dry, and this one field would have to keep all the livestock in Alligin during the coming winter. It was easily understood why hostellers and other visitors were particularly requested to keep to the marked path.

Returning to the cottage was like coming home. With joy, I pulled up the dandelions beside the front door and opened the windows to let in the sweet, salt air.

The visitors continued to arrive, by bus, boat and on foot or cycle. One day, an artist lay sprawled on the grass outside my cottage, painting Liathach while waiting for the ferry over to Shieldaig.

The hot weather returned, and almost every day the boats were out on the loch. Two holiday-makers brought a collapsible canvas canoe fitted with a little sail. It had the grace of a seagull, and was a delight to watch as it bobbed over the calm ripples. The "locals", however, shook their heads dubiously and remarked on the risk of taking such a light craft on such treacherous waters.

A motor-launch came in to the rocks by the schoolhouse, bringing the Medical Officer, the doctor, and two uniformed nurses. In the schoolroom, the children received injections to immunise them against diphtheria. The medical party then re-embarked and set off across the loch for Shieldaig. The visit, one learned, was repeated four times a year. In winter, the boat often had to fight its way in against heavy seas.

Watching it push off again, one thought of the old days when the Revenue officers used to land on these same rocks to inspect the records at the little school. There was the crevice in the rocks, not ten minutes' walk away, where, it was said, the distillers of illegal whisky would be busy under their canopy of sail-cloth while the Revenue boat cruised up and down the loch, often within easy hailing-distance. No doubt several pairs of wary eyes would be keeping watch until the "gaugers" were safely away again.

The bus-driver told a smuggling story which confirmed an account of an old haunt at the foot of Beinn Alligin. There had been a bothy, it seemed, beside the Alligin Burn where it flows through a deep gorge to the north of the bridge. Here, during the last century, lived a solitary man renowned in the district for his physical strength and his habit of wearing little clothing—as well as for another pursuit of which he had long been suspected by the Revenue officers. One day, a party of gaugers crept up on the lonely bothy and broke in. The man was caught red-handed at the still, and at once seized—but he, being clad only in "trews", slipped out of his captors' hands like an eel and made for the door. They pursued him hotly to the lip of the fearsome gorge; but, little daunted, he made a tremendous leap across the yawning chasm. "See if you can do that!" he shouted, gaily; and, with a parting wave, he disappeared up the flank of Beinn Alligin, leaving his baffled pursuers speechless on the brink of the abyss.

Another smuggling story concerned a great local distiller who once found himself in conversation with a minister of religion. He asked what it meant to live a good life, and the minister replied that one of the essentials was, on all occasions, to speak the truth and take the consequences.

A few days later, the Excise-man called at the man's house and inquired if he had any whisky.

"Och, aye," he rejoined, frankly, "and plenty, at that. It's upstairs in a cask, under the bed."

"You're a liar!" rejoined the gaugers' leader, promptly, "If you really had any, you would never have been such a fool as to tell us!" And he led his men away, doubtless congratulating himself on his profound knowledge of human nature!

96

Heather in bloom on Loch Maree hills

At Wester Alligin, the fields burst into a yellow froth of mustard-bloom, and summer surged over the land. The village prepared itself to deal with a fresh influx of visitors. Most nights now, the Youth Hostel was so crowded that people were sleeping on the floor. Extra beds had been put up in the cycle-shed, as the annexe was not yet erected.

The rowan-berries reddened, and the world became filled with the gold of July. The Free Church missionary put up a sign announcing that he sold hand-woven tweed. The interested, calling in to see his loom, would be shown two bales of new material, hand spun and woven and dyed with the soft natural .colours of the hills. With his wife, one might discuss dyeing, and the relative merits of tansies, black currants, soot, crotal, heather and the various herbs which have been used by the Highlander for hundreds of years to achieve the misty blues and browns and mauves and greens of the famous "Harris" tweed. The missionary would make material up to order, if none of that in stock appealed.

The wise old hills were gnarled under the sun, wearing their vast age gracefully. On a day of blazing heat and no wind, in company with my friend Jill from Sussex, I once more climbed Liathach. To our surprise, we met no less than seven people that day, by the cairn of Mullach an Rathain, members of three different parties who had climbed the mountain by their separate ways. Hardly a one of us but had "caught the sun". Yet, despite the dust and the sweat and the aura of horse-flies which surrounded each one of us, it would be difficult to imagine happier faces.

On another brilliant day, we trailed over the shimmering peat-bog for a return visit to Coire Mhic Fhearchair. The snow had at last melted from Morrison's Gully, and the three great buttresses at the head of the loch were clear against a burning sky. Panting with the effort of the climb, we rested for a while in the shade of the dark wall of Sàil Mhór—but the merciless sun crept over the ridge and drove us to seek fresh shelter from her searing rays. After we had cooled down, we spread our sweat-soaked clothes on the rocks and slipped into the loch. The water was clear and breathtakingly cold. I swam out to a tiny rock-island, and lay like a seal basking on the sun-warmed slab, looking down into the green and gold caverns below. The waters lapped idly, distorting the vision. The shadow of the rock lay black on the moving green.

Hay-making at Diabaig

One could stare into a dream-world of perpetual motion, thinking of nothing, while the sun burned the water's ice out of one's limbs.

We had tea by the lip of the waterfall where the loch overflows and leaps down towards the jewelled plateau far below. Afterwards, we lay flat again on the sun-baked slabs in a blissful state of half-slumber, while a black monster of a shadow crept slowly towards us from the cliffs of Sàil Mhór. At half-past four we dressed and began the descent beside the fall—and all the long way back the sun continued to burn us, until we finally reached the blessed shelter of Corrie woods. Even here, the air came in hot, sudden breaths, heavy with the scent of bog-myrtle and sizzling pines. It was only when we reached the road that the red sun finally dipped behind Beinn Alligin and the cool breeze of evening fanned our scorched cheeks.

A few days later, they began to cut the hay in Alligin, and the scent of it filled the whole village with sweetness. It was laid out to dry, and the weeds were laboriously picked out and thrown on to a great pile by the dyke. Soon, a row of tiny stacks dotted the field, exuding a soft fragrance under the sun. Having no horse, the villagers carried the hay on their backs, and the women bore as heavy a load as the men.

The baby sparrows had flown away from under the eaves of my cottage. Sometimes, while out "at the fishing", one might see a brood of young razor-bills following their pied mother across the loch, their tiny feet working as industriously as the wheels of little paddle-steamers. My landlord spoke of two male golden eagles which had been found locked in a death-grip in Toll a' Mhadaidh at the back of Beinn Alligin. A dead hen-bird had been discovered the week before, and it was assumed that one of the cocks had been guarding the nest when attacked by the other.

The eider-duck no longer awoke trembling echoes with their strange love-call. Only the hungry crying of the gulls seemed endless, having no season. The chicks which had hatched under the rock were now almost full-grown, with snowy plumage and bright-yellow legs, as fair a sight as one could wish to see.

The hot weather continued; but we refused to yield to the temptation to rest. Before Jill returned to Sussex, there was yet one climb which we must do—the obvious one from Alligin village.

And so, on a morning of blue and gold, we set off for Beinn Alligin. It was my second ascent, and as sufficiently different from the first as to merit description.

We had originally planned to climb up behind the Youth Hostel to the west of the ridge, avoiding the South Summit and striking straight up on to Sgùrr Mór. Outside the Post Office, however, we met "the Miller", who told us that the best way was straight up a gully in the steep south face. I had often looked at these crags and wondered if they were practicable, and rejoiced at the kind advice, as it would enable us to do the ridge from south to north, taking in all the main peaks.

We mounted slowly above "Heather Cliff", in blue heat-haze pierced by the long spears of the massing legions of the sun. We were in no hurry, for Beinn Alligin is the nearest of the Torridon hills and we had the whole day before us. Up among the peaty foothills, over the high fence which kept the sheep up on the hill all summer, and now we were heading for a pimple-like boulder on the skyline which had been pointed out to us from below. Beyond this, the cliffs of the south face rose steeply above us into blue sky, gashed by sandy scree-runs and patched with tufts of blooming ling. We could not see the summit, but a fantastic, toppling pencil of rock loomed over one of the gullies—as if someone had balanced a stone on its point to signify a cairn.

We took a deep breath, and began to climb. Up slippery heather-slopes first, scattered with boulders and tumbled scree. Then we came on to the first pitch of rock, and scrambled up towards a great horseshoe which opened in the cliff face to reveal the sky.

The valley dwindled and misted below. On either side of our chosen gully, the sandstone crags loomed in wild beauty, darkened here and there by thin trickles of peat-brown water. Some of the rocks were formed in smooth layers, having the appearance of great heaps of pancake-mixture poured out and left to harden. We had noticed the same formation on the plateau of Liathach; but the strata of Beinn Alligin seemed safer and harder and far less liable to break away under the weight of hand or foot.

The rock ended again, and we slipped and slid on loose rubble dotted with a few parched tufts of heather. Soon, we came level with the grotesque obelisk of rock which we had seen from below. It stood quite alone, away from the main face, and was so delicately balanced that it seemed about to crash down at any moment on to the debris far below.

Up and up now in sunlight, to where sheep were etched on the skyline. At last, we came on to mossy, gentle slopes—and suddenly we were looking away and down over sheer crags to the great rubble-filled valley of Coire Mhic Nobuil. Beyond this vale of desolation loomed the blue spires of Liathach, rising closely one behind the other at the back of the pale plateau sweeping upwards from the Peak of Sleep. Following the curve of the corrie with our eyes, we saw the tiny path winding along beside the river towards the dark lochans in the pass between Liathach and Beinn Eighe. To the east rose the diamond-white terraces and Gothic windows of Ruadh Stac Mór, and between these and sombre Sàil Mhór we could see the beginnings of the three great buttresses of rock which tower over the head of Coire Mhic Fhearchair.

Underfoot was springy moss over which we ascended to the cairn marking the South Summit, Meall an Laoigh. From here, we looked away north-west to lonely Craig and the golden sands on the curve of Gairloch bay. South-west, the "far Coolins" thrust up their weird heads through pearly drifts of heat-haze.

We began to follow the ridge to the north, and presently the moss gave place to loose rubble where a great, shallow basin indicated the path of a glacier. We walked in silence, sobered by fresh realisation of the fabulous age of these magnificent hills.

Picking our way across the scree, we began now the ascent of Tom na Gruagaich. Here, we met two more climbers, resting in the sun by the cairn. We chose a shaded spot on the north side of the summit, and had lunch. Then we took off boots and socks and stretched our toes in the sun.

Below us, the sheer cliffs dropped down to a waste of debris, grey and lifeless, the ultimate in ruin and desolation. We gazed along the narrowing ridge as it dipped away down to a boulder-strewn depression, to climb and climb again towards the dark pinnacle of Sgùrr Mór. All down the rock-terraces on the east side of this peak, sheep browsed as nonchalantly as if they were on a grassy plateau, though the dizzy shelves of grass-grown rock seemed hardly wide enough to afford a foothold. From here, one could see only a hint of the fearsome "Cleft".

After a rest, we set off again, down the rocky ledges to the ridge. Over a pile of boulders and past a tiny, dried-up lochan; then we were climbing again, over moss, turf and loose stones. Looking back, we were awed by the perilous cliffs on the eastern face of Tom na Gruagaich, falling dizzily to a waste land of reddish-coloured rubble. We marked the wonderful formation of the terraces, which formed black and green stripes along all the sheer, dark, scooped-out face of the hill. Across the wide expanse of Coire Mhic Nobuil, Liathach was spreading herself out to fret the skyline with pinnacles of pale grey-green, touched by moving fingers of light and patched with vast rolling shadows which poured down into the valley as the ruffled clouds sailed like swans before the wind.

The ascent of the last pitch was a weary "slog" up to the spectacular "Cleft", from which we gazed between sheer walls of rock to the headwaters of Loch Torridon, backed by massed blue hills. The gully itself was filled with loose scree at the top, but beyond the lip of this we could see nothing. I once heard two climbers discussing its possibilities under snow and ice conditions, but looking down from the top one would judge it to be tricky, to put it mildly.

North-west, the landscape was pale gold under fleeting sunlight, with the thousand peat-dark lochans catching the light and reflecting in their ebony waters the blue and green of the hills behind Diabaig. The long, rocky ridge of Baos Bheinn was shadowed with indigo. At its feet, between Loch a' Bhealaich and Loch a' Ghobhainn, sprawled a weird pile of hummocks which most strikingly resembled a giantess asleep in the hollow of the hills. Here, a careless curve suggested the languid arm thrown out across the moss. There, a smoothly rounded rise marked the hunched shoulder or the graceful arc of the hip. She was lying on her side, with one foot drawn up a little, as if to avoid putting her toes into the loch. Every contour of her was so softly rounded that one might judge her to have been moulded out of the mountain by the inspired chisel of Henry Moore. Or she might have been a woman of the fabulous race of the Finga-lians, who fell into a charmed slumber in the days before the Firbolg. Did she dream, one wondered, of the golden age when, as Malvina the daughter of Toscar, or fair Bragela, beloved of the great Cuthullin, she had sent the heroes out to battle warm from her embraces, and welcomed them home with joy to the feast of shells? . . .

After the "Cleft", the summit came surprisingly soon. We had decided not to go on to the "Horns", so rested here and had tea. The cloud was thickening now, and hanging in a dark pall over the hills. The vast, sprawling range of Beinn Eighe was blue-black, save for the shining screes of Ruadh Stac Mór. We could see the summit-cairn now, a squat pimple above the "church-window" terraces, turned to silver by a shaft of moving light.

Jill rested by the cairn. I took off boots and socks again, and walked barefoot over the warm moss to the edge of the cliffs overlooking Toll na Béiste. I made no sound—and suddenly (a rare sight in Torridon these days) a mountain hare emerged from under a rock close by. He was wearing his summer robe of brown and beige velvet; and, caught unawares, he sat up on his hind legs and stared at me for almost a minute—until I furtively moved my camera, whereat his long legs took him off at an amazing speed down the hillside. For a while, I lay flat on the moss, re-picturing the grace of him. Then I rejoined Jill on Sgùrr Mór, and we began the descent.

We came down the easiest way—straight off the main summit to the west. Following the southward sweep of the plateau we descended easily to Alligin village beside the dried-up course of a burn. On a ledge, we found the ruin of an old bothy, surely at one time the haunt of smugglers, for it lies beside the stream and is most cunningly concealed by the surrounding braes, being visible neither from ridge nor road.

We reached the village in the early evening, after a pleasant day during which, without unduly tiring ourselves, we had discovered a new way up the south face of Beinn Alligin to make fresh acquaintance with the mountain in her summer dress. One need hardly add that we had found the experience worth remembering.

CHAPTER XI

DOGS AND DIVERSIONS

THE collie puppy arrived, and quickly proved herself to be an endless source of delight and amusement. The local children loved her, and she (as distinct from Jeannie) enthusiastically returned all affection regardless of its source. At the age of nine weeks, she was already showing signs of a remarkable intelligence.

Jeannie's attitude to the newcomer gave cause, at first, for some anxiety. It was soon obvious that she was wildly jealous, and considered that I had broken the sacred bond of our long friendship by introducing a boisterous third member into the household. Bridie, blissfully unaware of all this, continued to tease and romp and cajole and make a general nuisance of herself—and, surprisingly, this proved to be the right line of approach. After two days, Jeannie's iron reserve began to melt a little. She no longer bristled when the puppy approached, being content merely to avert her head in lofty scorn. On the third day, she forgot herself sufficiently to play with it a little—with a warning snarl every time the game showed signs of getting too rough. With delight, I watched the friendship bud, and blossom.

Having heard much concerning the intelligence of sheep-dogs, I resolved to try an experiment. Bridie would never be used to herd sheep. She was energetic and, already, full of mischief. I planned, therefore, to keep her out of trouble and develop her fine brain by teaching her, by kindness, as many simple tricks as she could comfortably assimilate.

She was already learning to sit down and offer a paw on request. Starting from there, I taught her, in three weeks, to "speak" for a titbit, to carry my gloves on walks, to come to heel when called, and to lie flat at the word "die". We perfected one trick before going on to the next—and she took to her training, with its inevitable titbits and praise, with astonishing enthusiasm. Her anxiety to please was in itself an encouragement—but there were also moments when, puppy-like, she refused to concentrate upon the business in hand; and it was at such times that I realised my own shortcomings as a teacher. I soon discovered that it did no good at all to scold her or speak sharply—she would simply give up altogether and go and sulk in her box. A quiet voice with a hint of suspense in it was the thing to arouse her interest and curiosity. Jeannie, who had never learned a trick in her life, watched tolerantly as our mutual education progressed. She was no longer at all jealous, and had accepted Bridie without reservation as a part of the scheme of things.

I learned, gradually and painfully, that there are two main points to be observed when training an intelligent puppy. Be firm—but be prodigal with your praise and your reward. Bridie would do almost anything to gain the coveted titbit. When she failed, it was almost invariably my fault in that I had not made plain what was required. Occasionally, she would try to get away with something—as, when I said "box", she would sometimes edge cautiously towards the door. I then promptly brought her back and repeated the command in a sterner tone, with perhaps a light slap by way of admonition. She would thereupon dive into the box as if pursued by devils! She was amazingly sensitive and easy to handle, and observers said she would have made a first-class working dog.

She had a prodigious appetite, which I did my best to satisfy. From Duncan, her previous owner, I learned that sheep-dogs, if well fed when young, become dainty and fastidious at about nine months. If they receive insufficient nourishment as puppies, they will be gaunt and hungry all their lives.

During the month of August, Bridie learned several new tricks. I would produce a handkerchief and, bidding her "Watch", would hide it in the outside pocket of my rucksack. At the word "Find", she would go and get it, to exchange it willingly for a piece of biscuit. Later, she learned to close the door, fetch a news-paper or slippers, and, finally, to lay a small table with cup and plate and sit up as if ready for a meal—a trick which always provoked delighted mirth from spectators.

It was nearly the end of August now, and the hay was stacked in neat little pyramids on the fields, held in place by encircling ropes. Its fragrance was everywhere, and the visitors enjoyed nothing more than walking back to the Hostel at night, when the harvest moon hung like a big lantern in the roof of heaven and the lights of strange yachts spilled fragments of gold on to the quiet waters of the loch. On such a night, the dreaming, fragrant earth seemed very close to paradise, and one walked at peace through a bat-haunted dusk, silenced by the beauty of sky and water and sweet-smelling fields, in tune with the Infinite.

The hot weather was back again, ripening the haystacks. The strange yachts continued to sail in like swans and rest for a few days off the little pier before spreading white wings to float away again into the unknown. One day, a business-like grey corvette nosed into the loch and dropped anchor off the Alligin pier. Two men came ashore in a dinghy, and spent a long time examining the steep track leading down from the high road by "Heather Cliff". I was told that the ship was "the Government Boat", and the men an advance party to survey the ground with a view to planning the longed-for road down to Alligin village. The Secretary of State for Scotland was coming himself during September, so it looked as if something was being done at last. The village as a whole, however, showed pleasure but little excitement. One had the feeling that they would believe it when the project was actually started. Perhaps one becomes philosophical about such things, after agitating for forty years with no appreciable response. . . .

For a few days after the departure of the Government vessel, the loch was quiet save for the local red-sailed fishing boats. The schoolchildren had a picnic over at Camas an Lèana, and the *Betsy Brodie* was conscripted to take them over. In all, there were some fifty people, for the children came from miles around to join in the fun. They returned to the accompaniment of merry music from a harmonica and bagpipes. The *Betsy* was crowded to capacity, and the whole loch seemed to echo to the lilt of music and youthful voices.

More visitors arrived, and more strange craft came to Loch Torridon—collapsible canoes, rubber dinghies and the air-sea-rescue rafts, a vivid reminder of recent conflict. A big clipper came in, graceful as a solan goose, her white sails half-furled in the light breeze. For several nights, her lights scattered gold-dust on to the still waters by the little pier.

The shepherds and crofters had finished their clipping, and the sheep's wool was packed into large sacks, covered by a tarpaulin and towed away in a rowboat behind the Post Office launch. The fleeces were making a good price that year, two shillings and twopence per pound. The average weight of a blackface fleece is around six pounds. The crofter must send his wool to a chosen factory, but each croft was allowed to reserve forty pounds for its own use. After the wool had been dyed and spun up ready for knitting, the crofter purchased it back from the factory at a cheap rate. I was shown some garments knitted during the winter from Alligin wool. They seemed rather harsh to the touch, but I was told that the wool softens considerably with washing. Some of it is treated with oil, and this is used for knitting seamen's socks. Each season, the factory sends patterns of the colours for which dyes are available. All winter, most women have something "on the wires". Blankets, also, are made of local wool. Though not particularly soft, they are beautifully light and warm.

The city-dweller would, perhaps, wonder what the inhabitants of a remote Highland village do for entertainment, apart from the time-honoured "céilidh". The advent of the "Highlands and Islands Film Guild" has, however, done much to bring the outside world to such isolated corners of the west, and the Highlander knows much more than one would imagine about the life of the "big city". True, there is still some opposition to films, on principle, among the stricter religious sects. (I have heard of children being forbidden to watch educational films put on at the schools); but, in Torridon, the mobile cinema commanded a good audience, with a fair percentage of children occupying the front row at the fortnightly performance in the village hall.

One Thursday evening, I cycled down from Alligin in the blue dusk to take my place in the audience. Along the undulating shore-path, the cycle leapt and bounced over ruts and sharp stones, diving down the steep brae picturesquely named Creag a' Ghrianan, or the Crag of the Sun. Day was fading over the purple woods of Corrie, the indigo sky merging into a translucent green, with shreds of flame in the west. I met the school-teacher, and we sped together along the darkening lane towards the awakening lights of Fasaig village. The little houses were cuddled at the feet of mighty Liathach, like sleepy cats whose orange eyes blinked in the dusk. A cow loomed up out of the shadows. The district nurse's geese stood motionless by the wayside, like a company of strange statues carved out of pure-white alabaster. Twin arc-lights flooded the darkness behind us, and we dismounted to let the mobile cinema pass. The big van filled the road.

People were slowly converging on the village hall. We parked our cycles by the dyke, and went in to the "theatre". It was expertly blacked-out, being lighted by only one paraffin lamp at the table which served as a cash-desk. We paid our two shillings and took our seats at the back. Though filled with neat rows of chairs, the hall looked much bigger than I had expected. The screen was quite large, and clearly visible to all. The door closed, and the sound-track whirred. The first film started, a British-made documentary on the marvels of engineering, with an inspiring musical score to give it romance. Then followed an American cartoon, and, lastly, the "feature", which was *Great Expectations*. Throughout the whole performance, the audience sat attentive and still, completely absorbed in the happenings on the screen. There was not so much as a whisper, the rustle of a chocolate-paper, or a giggle from the front row. Those accustomed to fidgeting city audiences would find such a degree of attention a refreshing change.

Going home, we pushed our cycles, for the darkness was too profound to permit us to ride the rough road to Corrie, or the narrow shore path beyond, with any degree of safety. A cold breeze had sprung up, and chilled us after the warm atmosphere of the "cinema". Soon, a pale moon glowed in the velvet blackness of the sky. The woods closed around us, dark and murmurous, and full of strange shadows where the black branches moved across the face of the moon.

I remember remarking that it was a perfect setting for the Wee Folk, and was taken to task by the school-teacher for believing in such things. . . .

I had hoped, during my summer in Alligin, to attend a Highland dance—but, somehow, I never managed to "fit it in". I was fortunate, however, in being present at many an intimate little "céilidh", during which we talked of Highland customs and exchanged opinions regarding psychic phenomena and the Second Sight. I learned more about the "ghost" of Lochan Dearg, on the road to Diabaig—the kilted chieftain who is said to appear periodically to a Murdo Mackenzie, and how one man of that name had seen the ghost within living memory, though the man himself was now dead. It was said that he had spoken first to the ghost without realising its supernatural nature, and, afterwards, had drawn a ring round himself with his stick and blessed it, by way of protection. The phantom had tried to entice him outside the ring, and he had agreed to come, if the ghost would recite the 23rd Psalm. The apparition had been unable to do this, but had recounted how he, a Mackenzie of Gairloch, had been slain by a Macdonald of Torridon and buried on this spot, with his sword nearby. One of his clansmen, he said, was buried on the slopes of Ruadh Mheallan. He eventually disappeared in a puff of smoke, cautioning Murdo not to look behind him for a while, as all the legions of hell would be at his heels.

It was some time after Murdo Mackenzie's experience that a man cutting peats unearthed some large bones near the spot where the ghost had been seen. Rumour went around that they were horses' bones, but this was never proved. The sword was never found, and the ghost came no more.

And so the tales went on. And so I learned that there is an ancient burial-ground at the back of Seann Mheallan, just west of the Valley of a Thousand Hills. Here, it is said, are buried the bodies of MacLeods slain by the Macdonalds in one of the old clan battles. The graves may still be seen if one knows where to look. The rock of Seann Mheallan is believed locally to be some of the oldest in the world.

Among the old tales which used to be told in Torridon is the story of the cairn in the "bealach" between Beinn Alligin and Beinn Dearg. The version I am giving here was told to me beside a friendly fireside at Wester Alligin, during an evening of song and laughter and story-telling which will long be remembered with a stir of the heart. I learned how the Gaelic name for this crumbling pile of stones means "Diana's Cairn", and that it was so called after a woman from Lochcarron who lies buried there. The tale of how she met her death on the hill runs in this wise:

At one time, during a festive season, twelve men from Gairloch came over the pass on their way to Lochcarron, to see what they could get from the laird to supplement the victuals. At the same time, twelve men from Lochcarron went to Gairloch—taking with them one woman, Diana by name.

The first party got nothing; but the Lochcarron men were given a bull by the laird of Gairloch. They proceeded to drive it back through the pass, and stopped to rest at a big knoll beside Loch a' Bhealaich, nowadays called Meall an Tairbh, or the Knoll of the Bull. Here, they met the party from Gairloch, returning empty-handed. After a discussion, they decided to divide the bull between them, so that each party would have something for the festivities. The animal was thereupon slain at the knoll, and they set about the business of carving it up. It was not long, however, before they discovered that the fat, or suet, was missing, and had obviously been stolen and concealed by someone in the company. An argument started, swiftly developing into a serious quarrel as each party accused the other of the theft. Soon, the men came to blows, and, before long, a fierce battle was raging. Finally, the ground around the bull's carcase was strewn with the bodies of the slain, and only one man, a native of Gairloch, was left alive! Dazed and wearied by the battle, he stood gazing around him, assuming everyone else to be dead. As his eyes cleared, however, he saw a solitary figure running away into the distance, towards the gap between Beinn Alligin and Beinn Dearg. Despite his weariness, he started at once in hot pursuit—and, finally, at the summit of the pass, he caught up with the woman, Diana, who had been with the Lochcarron party. As he thought, it was she who had stolen the suet and precipitated the battle. Without compunction, he slew her, and she lies buried on the spot where she fell, under the crumbling cairn which is known by her name. Another version recounts that the portion of the bull stolen by Diana was the liver.

One of the best "queer tales" I heard in Alligin is the story of the old man at Diabaig who had a sick cow. This story, in particular, delights me, because, though it occurred within living memory, it has the authentic flavour of the Gaelic legends.

The tale recounts how the old man, being unable to decide for himself the nature of the animal's illness, sent for an elderly friend from Alligin. To his amazement, the second old man arrived with a gun! On examining the cow, he declared that, as he had suspected, she was suffering from "marcach Sìthe", or the Wee Folk riding on her. But he would soon cure that! With great vigour, he raised his rifle and fired a volley of shots over the startled creature's back, at the same time shouting, "Shoo! Shoo! Am monadh oirbh, a' bhéistean!" ("Shoo! Shoo! Away to the hill, you rascals!")

... And—whether from fright or otherwise—the sick cow recovered!

CHAPTER XII

BEINN EIGHE

IF Liathach is the most sinister of the hills of Torridon, then Beinn Eighe is certainly the most desolate. The first sight of it from Kinlochewe—the great, frosted pile mounting up to a fierce pinnacle above a scooped-out corrie—strikes awe and emptiness into the heart of the would-be climber.

The feeling increases upon closer acquaintance. As you ride along Glen Torridon, the long, sprawling ridge looms above you for mile after mile, littered from end to end with white rubble which turns to silver at the touch of the sun. Here are the naked and crumbling bones of the Old World, worn down to a fine dust by the centuries, bleached to a dead and dismal whiteness which strikes with cold mockery at the living flame of adventure in your soul. You gaze and gaze—and it seems that the dust is in your nostrils, stifling the even rhythm of your breath, silencing, subduing, submerging all things under the lost moraine of the primeval earth, which contains fossils of the oldest known animals.

If you have studied your Scottish Mountaineering Club guide, *The Northern Highlands*, you will already have found mention of the screes of Beinn Eighe, together with a little Gaelic verse:

> "Si mo rùn Beinn Eighe,—
> Dh'fhalbhadh i leam is dh'thalbhainn leatha."

or,

> "My love is Beinn Eighe,—
> She with me and I with her would go."

It is a poetic thought which well expresses their dangerous fascination. You may also have found, in your Youth Hostels handbook, a warning against attempting the ridge at all if you happen to lack experience as a climber; and, again, the reason given is the treacherous instability of the screes which, in places, slide at a touch.

According to some authorities, Beinn Eighe means "The Mountain of the File", and it is an apt title, for the top of the ridge rises to knife-like sharpness. It also means "The Mountain of Ice"— no doubt so called for the shining Cambrian quartzite screes.

The eastern peaks, notably Sgùrr an Fhir Duibhe, are particularly unstable, being composed of broken Cambrian quartzite. The western and northern summits are of Torridonian sandstone with quartzite caps. There are seven peaks, the highest being Ruadh Stac Mór, 3309 feet, whose northern and north-eastern sides fall steeply down in perilous rock-terraces to the watery plateau below, and are definitely dangerous, except for a properly equipped and experienced climbing-party. Between Ruadh Stac Mór and Sàil Mhór lie the great cliffs of Coire Mhic Fhearchair, three terrific buttresses dropping dizzily down to the loch. These cliffs are 1250 feet high, and are divided by two great gashes. The middle buttress was climbed by the celebrated Prof. Norman Collie, who gave his name to one of the Cuillin peaks in Skye, Sgùrr Thormaid, or Norman's Peak. North of the buttresses is a gully of loose scree which affords an easy glissade from the ridge into the boulder-strewn corrie. There is another gully—Morrison's Gully, in the cliffs of Sàil Mhór—which I have dealt with in a previous chapter.

The loch in Coire Mhic Fhearchair has a bed of green and pink rock-slabs, and is ideal for swimming, though, even on the hottest day, the water is like newly melted ice. High above it on three sides towers the ridge, shutting out sun and sky. There is a fine echo from the mouth of the loch, where, if you shout or laugh, your voice is caught up and tossed to and fro among the crags and corries, so that one might imagine the summits themselves to be calling to each other across the bald wastes of the scree.

Visitors to Inver Alligin will find that the chief obstacle to climbing Beinn Eighe is its distance from the village. At my own first attempt, I was staying in the Hostel, and had a rush to finish breakfast and my allotted task in time to catch the mail-bus from the high road at five minutes to nine. For company, I had a medical student from Glasgow. Beinn Eighe, like Liathach, is the sort of hill that one should never climb alone.

We took the bus along Glen Torridon to just beyond the Valley of a Thousand Hills. It was a fine morning, with sunlight dappling the changeless yet ever-changing faces of the mountains.

III

We began the ascent beneath Coire nan Clach, a basin-like depression of white stones slung high under the ridge. The going was steep, but presented no difficulty. We took our time, pausing now and then to glance back at the diminishing glen with its thin thread of road and, beyond, the bare blue lochans rising out of the hollows of the hills. Soon, we could see Loch Clair, with its tiny island—Loch Coulin, with its fringe of dark pines, and the blue gash marking the Coulin Pass to Achnashellach. We rounded the curve of the corrie and began the scramble over the rocks of the last pitch. Suddenly, we stopped. Above us, quite close, a herd of deer were threading their way daintily along the ridge. We did not move, and they did not see us. Slowly, with indescribable grace, they tiptoed along the crumbling quartzite edge of the "file"—and, on the heels of one of the hinds, followed a tiny fawn, with all the gold of the late spring somehow shining out of his dappled coat and luminous eyes.

Remembering him now, I am reminded of a story told to me by a Torridon gamekeeper—how he had once taken an American lady deer-stalking, and how, when at long last within range of the stag, she had refused to fire on it because it was so beautiful. "And a fine shot she was, too," said the keeper, regretfully. "But there. You can never tell with the ladies."

I had smiled. It was a reason after my own heart.

The deer moved off, still unaware of our presence just below the ridge of Beinn Eighe. We looked down then, exchanging a vision of infinite grace for one of infinite majesty.

All around and below us now lay the lovely serrated landscape of Torridon and Kinlochewe—riven crags, mist-blue glens, amber lochs and burns catching the light among pale grey hills. We gazed across Coire Dubh Mór to the wild peaks of Liathach, all sombre save for quartzite-crowned Spidean a' Choire Leith. Below us, to the south-east, Loch Clair and Loch Coulin gleamed in sunlight; but the scarred whaleback of Beinn Liath Mhór was shiny with rain. Shafts of gold touched the bronze hill-lochs at the feet of Maol Chean-dearg and Sgùrr Ruàdh.

We tramped along the shingly ridge and scrambled up on to the summit of Spidean Coire nan Clach. Before us, a soft scree-slope led the eye along an undulating ridge towards the crumbling white peak of Sgùrr Bàn. Away beyond, across a four-hundred-foot gulf, the sombre cliffs of Sgùrr an Fhir Duibhe towered

A ruined croft at Wester Alligin

against the blue sky, falling down and down to a waste land of debris, the bone-yard of an era lost in the vapours of time.

A brief glance south-west showed us transparent veils of rain drifting across the hills of Beinn Damh and Shieldaig. We began the descent into the gulf, taking it fairly fast, for the hill was soft and our heels dug in here and held. The ensuing climb, however, was a different story. Sgùrr an Fhir Duibhe, or The Peak of the Black Man, is noted for its dangerous scree, and it seemed that one false movement might start an avalanche which would sweep us down into the abomination of desolation below.

To the north, the black crags fell sheerly beyond the sight. A gash appeared in the rock, with a great boulder jammed between its black walls. Below, the flooded plateau was lighted by the smouldering end of a rainbow which spread vibrant colour on the screes where it came to earth.

The rain, reaching us, turned to hail, and was driven into our backs by a fierce wind. We mounted over the shifting blocks of quartzite, testing each hand- and foot-hold before trusting it with our weight.

At length, we attained the summit, and gazed across a group of frightening pinnacles—the "Black Carls" of Beinn Eighe—towards Creag Dhubh, at the end of the range. The descent towards the first looked sheer and dangerous, and, in any case, we had not time to get down and up again if we wished to traverse the remainder of the ridge. We therefore turned back towards Sgùrr Bàn, and began our descent of the now-familiar scree on the west of the Peak of the Black Man. Going down was worse than coming up, and we took care to keep well apart. Over Sgùrr Bàn, we gazed along to where the crumbling edge swept round and up to the pimple marking the big hump on Ruadh Stac Mór, the highest point of the range.

We began a cautious traverse of the broken edge of the ridge, whose narrowness forced us to walk in single file. Over Spidean Coire nan Clach, and past another, unnamed, cairn, following the undulating mountain-top, until we came at last on to the slopes of Cóinneach Mhór, the Big Mossy Place. The soft yellow-green moss underfoot here was a welcome change after the endless white scree. We by-passed the summit of this peak, and descended on to the narrow ridge running above the head of Coire Mhic Fhearchair and up towards Ruadh Stac Mór. This was our last

Beinn Eighe under snow, from Glen Grudie

climb for the day, and I was glad, for the vastness and desolation of Beinn Eighe had long since reduced me to silence. Its utter loneliness pressed like a weight upon the spirit. I felt bleak and empty of all inspiration and strangely depressed, as if the bottom had fallen out of the world, a state akin to what the ancients called the "dark night of the soul". Nowhere was there any longer the life and beauty and friendliness of the earth I knew—only un-ending greyness, and the desolation of the lost world. A different reaction, this, from that occasioned by Liathach, whose air of mystery is always in the nature of a challenge.

My companion, too, was dreich and silent, and we climbed to the summit without so much as a word between us. In the shelter of the cairn, we stood and looked out upon soulless immensity. All about us, the pattern of sombre colour on the hills changed and flowed with the rolling banks of cloud. To the east, across a fearsome corrie sheltering a tiny lochan, Sgùrr Bàn was an ethereal white, with Sgùrr an Fhir Duibhe rising in dark majesty behind. Then the mist purled over, drifting like smoke across the ridge, submerging the summits while, here and there, outlining a ghostly pinnacle against the sky.

Looking northward, we could see the great, shining stretch of Loch Maree, the striped terraces of Beinn a' Chearcaill, the golden sands on the curve of Gairloch Bay. Following the jagged line of the coast, we found Diabaig in shadow, a dark-brown curve of rock dotted with the white of tiny houses. The inward-sweeping gash of Loch Torridon was white with spindrift under a biting wind.

We looked across to Beinn Alligin and the turrets of Beinn Dearg, and saw the narrow pass where "Diana's Cairn" stands guard over the ancient right-of-way to Gairloch. There is a path running from Corrie woods almost to the summit of this pass, and one may have a pleasant and easy day's walking by turning westward at the cairn, climbing a little behind Loch a' Bhealaich, and coming home by Loch Toll na Béiste and along the west side of Beinn Alligin. It is necessary, however, to wait for a long spell of dry weather, as this plateau is waterlogged after even a mild rain.

Today, we could see a thousand silver lochans catching the light on the flat ground between the hills. The wind chilled us, and we huddled into the shelter of the cairn. After a short rest, we returned to the ridge and glissaded down the powdery scree-shoot into Coire Mhic Fhearchair. It was like coming down among the ruins of a long-forgotten world. There was no wind here, and only the loch, lapping over smooth slabs of rock, whispered a tuneless song which found a hollow echo among the listening hills. We saw no living creature apart from one stone-chat which bobbed away among the tumbled boulders at our approach. We heard no voices but our own, and the ghost-music of the water.

It seemed that hours passed before we reached the waterfall at the far end and began the last descent. Far below us, the sunset-fires were trapped in the lochans or spread like a mantle of flame over the feet of the hills.

The light was fading fast as we came around the south curve of Sàil Mhór and looked in awe upon the great, black-toothed mass of Liathach, rising beyond the string of inky lochans in the pass. Walking briskly now, we negotiated the two miles of peat-waste and found the stalkers' path which leads safely down to Corrie. It was dark when we reached the woods—nearly eleven o'clock by the time the Hostel lights came into view; and our one thought was for a cup of tea. We had been out for fourteen hours, done most of the Beinn Eighe ridge, and walked some eighteen miles. We could not pretend that we were not tired.

Yet, it had been a wonderful day—one to be remembered with that joy which the hills always bring in retrospect, after the ache is gone from weary limbs and the weight of desolation has lifted from the heart.

I made my second ascent of Beinn Eighe from Cromasaig, with George Thomas hoping, this time, to do the whole ridge.

It was a doubtful day in late August, with cloud hanging over all the "high tops". However, we had waited for a fortnight for good weather, and had now decided to risk it, and come down again if conditions became impossible.

It was raining as we stepped out of the bus—but, even as we watched from the Cromasaig bridge, a long bar of light trembled over the western landscape, the cloud rolled upwards, and the white screes of Beinn Eighe were silvered over by the sun. We looked up a tree-filled gorge to the shining peak above Coire Domhain, lit by a hundred moving lights and shadows as the cloud peeled away to reveal the pinnacle in all its naked loveliness.

On the advice of "Alec-the-Mail", we began our climb on the right-hand side of the burn. Across the gorge, a long, smooth shoulder ran up towards Sgùrr an Fhir Duibhe, whose sombre crags were still wreathed in cloud. The going was easy, but extremely wet. We splashed along for a while on the lip of the deepening crevasse. Below us, the yellow burn frothed and leapt in the shadow of the tall red pines. Ahead, we could see the shingly hollow where the two branches of the stream met, one fork of it welling out of a gash under Creag Dhubh, the other threading a tortuous way among the white screes of Coire Domhain.

As we climbed, the terrain changed, bog and heather giving place to outcrops of quartzite. Suddenly, ahead of us, a solitary hind appeared on the skyline, gave us one startled glance, and bounded off into the waste land to the north. All about us, the sun lit a million faery lamps among the sparse heather, where crystal drops swung to betray the late rain.

Soon, to our right, unfolded the wild landscape beyond Loch Maree and Kinlochewe. We saw the delicate waterfall pouring down the sheer cliffs of Beinn a' Mhuilinn, the green cleft of Glen Bannisdail, and the great turrets of Slioch, darkly blue under a rolling sky. Above Kinlochewe, the landscape was alive with colour—brown and amber and vivid green, with an overlying mist of mauve to mark the drifts of blooming heather. Darkly green, Glen Dochertie swept away towards Loch a' Chroisg, lightened by the yellow thread of the road. We looked down to the emerald fields around Kinlochewe, through which the silver river danced down to Loch Maree. Eastward, we gazed across Glen Torridon to a wild brown plateau bejewelled with shining hill-lochs, and round to where Loch Clair and Loch Coulin shone like pools of quicksilver, fringed by the dark tangle of their pines.

Before us, the scree-slopes ran up to Creag Dhubh; and there, above the long shoulder running up on the opposite side of the gorge, the "Black Carls" were silhouetted starkly against blue sky, like a company of weird giants clustered on the edge of the ridge to watch and mock at our ascent.

We came well on to the screes now. Following what appeared to be a deer-track beyond the source of the burn, we struggled up on to the ridge. It was strenuous going at this point, steep and loose and incredibly wearying. Frequently, a stone slipped and went rattling down into the great basin of Coire Domhain below. Above us, grotesque knobs of rock blocked out the sky. We climbed on, while the stones shifted under our feet and the great, boulder-filled corrie opened out beneath. Looking back down the scree-drift, we could see the pine-choked gorge carving its way down and down towards the infinitesimal bridge at Cromasaig. Cloud was descending again, and rain struck our perspiring faces as we at length attained the summit of Creag Dhubh. Suddenly, we saw a solitary climber coming up the long shoulder on the opposite side of the corrie, heading for the summit of Sgùrr an Fhir Duibhe. This ridge looked smooth and gradual, and, ascending by this route, one would miss the broken pinnacles. It appeared that our fellow-climber had chosen the better way— but we had a suspicion that ours might prove the more interesting.

The suspicion proved to be well founded. Turning our backs now on the endless grey vista to the north, we tramped along the ridge towards the maze of great peaks rising out of swirling cloud, the grim grey denizens forming the chief pinnacles of Beinn Eighe. For a while, we followed a good path—but, immediately ahead, the "Black Carls" loomed gigantic and sinister to bar our way. In the Scottish Mountaineering Club's guide, the use of a rope is advised here "unless the party are experts". It was our first experience of these pinnacles, and we had no rope. For the benefit of future hill-walkers, I can only echo the S.M.C.'s warning. The ridge breaks up suddenly into a series of perilous escarpments over which one has no choice but to climb. Once started, it is easier to go forward than back. On either side of the pinnacles, the face of the mountain falls away into precipitous gullies and chimneys, littered with sliding scree and steep enough to turn all but the steadiest head. Just before the summit, there is one particularly bad patch with an almost sheer drop below. The whole of this broken part of the ridge should be negotiated slowly and with the greatest care, and we found it expedient to test our holds before trusting them with our weight. Even so, there are places where those who have omitted to bring a rope must make a long reach and trust that the rock will hold. No doubt a seasoned rock-climber would make light of the whole thing; but I write as a hill-*walker*, and it is for such that these warnings are intended.

At intervals, during our climb, we gazed down into the great corrie to the west, where a desolate lochan lay at the foot of Sgùrr Bàn. The whole corrie was in shadow, yet full of weird colour—the loch a vivid jade-green, the cliffs behind a startling red-brown. Northward, Ruadh Stac Beag rose in lonely beauty.

Attaining the summit of Sgùrr an Fhir Duibhe, we began at once the four-hundred-foot descent over the big scree on the opposite side. It was now raining hard, and the whole range ahead was lost in thick cloud. Looking back, we could see nothing of the way we had come except, close at hand, a great, forbidding finger of rock pointing at the sky. To our right, a dungeon-like cleft fell down and down towards the plateau, between the crumbling escarpments of the mountain. Soon, we had completed our descent, and were climbing again, over softer, smaller scree, towards Sgùrr Bàn. We could see nothing at all now, but the way was well defined underfoot, and we attained the summit without difficulty. The wind tore at us, and icy rain battered our faces as we passed the cairn. The ridge narrows again here, the edge of it rising and falling; but it is easy compared to the "Black Carls", and the way is so well marked that one is able to follow it without difficulty. Indeed, it is impossible to leave it, since to step off the right path would be to step out into nothingness!

Several cairns were passed as we tramped westward over grey, pitted rocks that had the appearance of toadskin, among which grew the fir club moss and the crowberry and a tiny starlike creeper. On either side, cleft and gully and scree-slope dropped away into cloud-filled space. We were offered no glimpse of Coire an Laoigh to our left; but, at last, the narrow ridge gave place to another soft slope up which we toiled to what we assumed was the summit of Spidean Coire nan Clach. The cloud flowed all about us; and now, once again, it parted a little to reveal the hump of a pinnacle ahead, the sheer drop of a chimney, or the long shadow of a shoulder leading steeply down into the unknown. But the main ridge was still clearly defined, and we scrambled on, until the going softened and became greener, and we found deer-tracks in the moss.

We had just passed the ninth cairn when a ray of sunlight carved its shining way down to Glen Torridon, transforming the lochs and burns to silver fire. We stood still, in awe, while all about us the great cloud-veils thinned and drifted and parted and swept away to reveal a landscape of numbing immensity, range upon range of white pinnacles and black crags over-scattered with the debris of the ages, the upflung wilderness of ancient beauty which had brooded silently behind the cloud.

There are no words to express the utter desolation of it. We looked across Coire Dubh Mór to Liathach, and saw that she was black and remote, withdrawn into her own dark world of spells and mystery. South-west, we gazed across blue mountains and green glens to the shimmering wastes of the sea, beyond which a jagged wall of smoky blue marked the Cuillin on Skye. Looking back along the ridge of Beinn Eighe, we saw the rock-turrets rising starkly against the sky, and, below them, a shelf of grey rock holding a tiny lochan, from which a lacy waterfall leapt down towards the plateau. Ahead of us, the green slopes of Cóinneach Mhór rose to the dark point of the cairn. North-west, the long ridge swept away and round to the heights of Ruadh Stac Mór, whose scree-covered "pimple" looked no larger than a big cairn.

We were doubly grateful for this glimpse of the landscape, for it gave us our bearings on that part of the Beinn Eighe range where the walker might most easily go astray in a mist. The cloud was down again by the time we reached the green summit of Cóinneach Mhór; but, by following the line of the cliffs, we found the spot where a cairn marks the glissade into Coire Mhic Fhearchair. It was now tea-time, and we had no time to do Sàil Mhór if we wished to be off the hill before darkness fell. We therefore climbed up the long green shoulder of Ruadh Stac Mór, which we surmounted in thick cloud and a fierce westerly wind. At a quarter to five, on the top of this, the main summit, we took refuge behind the cairn and ate our sandwiches. Here, a hail-storm swept over us, stinging our faces and rattling on to our oilskins. We stayed only twenty minutes—but in that time we were chilled to the marrow, our fingers rendered numb and temporarily useless.

As a variation on the glissade from the ridge, and to save re-tracing our steps, we descended into Coire Mhic Fhearchair straight off the north-west end of Ruadh Stac Mór. We could see nothing below, and wriggled cautiously down over big scree, hoping that we were far enough west to miss the dangerous cliffs mentioned in the guide. It was tricky, but not difficult if taken steadily. We were perhaps half-way down when the clouds parted again, to reveal the glorious wilderness to the south-west, with the green cleft of Coire Mhic Nobuil sweeping away to Loch Torridon. For a moment, the whole landscape was suffused with gold, every lochan a dazzling jewel, every rock ashine, every hill alive with blinding colour which was the more enhanced by the pall of black cloud overhead. But, immediately below us, Coire Mhic Fhearchair was dark and desolate, scattered with a million lifeless boulders, its loch like ebony at the foot of sunless cliffs.

The screes underfoot became smaller, the gradient less steep. We found traces of a deer-track, and quickened our pace. Four ptarmigan rose from among the rocks below, and chirred away swiftly with a flash of white-barred wings. It was a quarter past six when we reached the grey lip of the corrie and began the last descent by the waterfall. The sun had gone again now. All the fires were extinguished, all the lights had died, all the colour was withdrawn from the wan faces of the hills. Keeping low, we rounded the foot of Sàil Mhór, and saw that Liathach had gone to bed behind the grey curtains of her clouds.

Only, as we tramped over the peat moss of Coire Mhic Nobuil towards the stalkers' path, a mist of red hung for a brief moment over Loch Torridon, to remind us that the sun was drowning in a sea of flame beyond the isles.

It was dusk when we reached Corrie woods; but our way gleamed faintly, a grey ribbon of a path winding through the sentinel trees towards the bridge.

At nine o'clock we cut down on to the shore path by the manse, and returned to Alligin at a brisk pace in the fast-gathering darkness of the August night. It had been a day of vivid contrasts, of cloud and sunlight and hail and biting wind—a day in which we had flirted with the mist-maidens and met and conquered the sinister Black Man who guards the eastern fastnesses of the Beinn Eighe range. For my own part, I counted it the best climb of the year, a day to dream about, to recall with poignant delight in those nostalgic moments when the exiled hill-lover reaches out in thought beyond the city walls to touch hands with the Spirit of the Hills.

It was during the gramophone recital the following evening that I made an intriguing discovery. One of the audience was the

solitary climber we had seen toiling up the long shoulder above
Coire Domhain on the previous afternoon. He had seen us, too,
and inquired how we had managed to get over the "Black Carls"
without a rope. I could think of no better answer than that we
"just kept on going". In the interval between Chopin and Brahms
we exchanged impressions with our fellow-adventurer concerning
the whole magnificent ridge which, even in cloud, had provided
us with many an unforgettable glimpse of its ancient beauty.

A National Nature Reserve has now been established by the
Nature Conservancy in the Beinn Eighe area, to safeguard the
fragment of aboriginal pine forest—Coille na Glas-Leitire—and
the many varieties of vegetation found among the summits of the
mountain. Experiments in silviculture are taking place, and an
area has been fenced at 1,500 feet to preserve mountain flora
from red deer and mountain hares. Fauna on the Reserve
include the wild cat, pine marten, ptarmigan and Greylag goose,
together with a unique association of insects. A Field Station,
frequently visited by scientists from abroad, has been set up at
Anancaun; the first Warden of the Reserve, Mr James Polson, has
been responsible for the apprehension of many deer-poaching
gangs. In 1958 he was awarded the B.E.M. for his work in the
Beinn Eighe area.

The Chief Warden is Mr R. Balharry, and in recent years the
Reserve has developed a Nature Trail, picnic and tent sites as part
of a programme for public facilities. The rugged mountain trail
begins and ends at the Trail Car Park near Loch Maree, and rises
to 1800 feet, providing a Conservation cabin from which to
study the landscape and glacial geology of this remarkable
region, once the home of wild pig, wolf and bear. A desolate
loch near the summit of the trail was fittingly named Lunar Loch
to commemorate man's first landing on the Moon in 1969.
Conservation Cairn affords, in good visibility, a panoramic view
of thirty-one mountain-tops over 3000 feet high.

CHAPTER XIII

BEINN DEARG

BEINN DEARG is a much-neglected hill, for it seems that there are few who bother to climb it save the shepherds in the course of their work. One reads of people doing it as a continuation of Beinn Alligin, but no one seems to see it as an end in itself. To the collector of "Munro's", no doubt, the fact that its summit is five feet short of the necessary three thousand makes it hardly worth while—but for the hill-walker, who does not worry over-much about such technicalities, it is a particularly attractive little ridge, by many unjustly ignored. Its summit offers views which are surprisingly different from those afforded by Liathach, Beinn Alligin or Beinn Eighe, revealing the Torridon landscape from a new and fascinating angle. In itself, it is a hill of grotesque pan-cake rocks precariously balanced on a crumbling ridge—of broken battlements beyond which the blue glens sweep away in new vistas of beauty—of precipitous gullies which carve deep wrinkles in its western face so that the first glimpse of it from Corrie woods suggests a mountain of almost-perpendicular rock-terraces, so steep as to be beyond the powers of the average climber. Like many another hill, however, it assumes a less forbidding aspect on closer acquaintance, and offers an easy route of ascent via the head of Coire Mhic Nobuil. The top of it is like the ruin of a medieval castle. Those who speak with admiration of the "Horns" of Alligin or the "Teeth" of Liathach should not neglect the "turrets" of Beinn Dearg.

My *Northern Highlands Guide* issued by the S.Y.H.A. made no mention of Beinn Dearg among suggested climbs in the Torridon district, and it fared no better in the Youth Hostels handbook. The Scottish Mountaineering Club's guide, however, described its "precipitous escarpments on the west and south", and the many rock-gullies by which the summit can be reached with more or less difficulty. From Glen Torridon, the view of it is blocked by the great bulk of Liathach, and the visitor usually

gets his first sight of it from the bridge at the beginning of Coire
Mhic Nobuil, beyond which its fierce, riven terraces shut out the
sky to the north.

"Great Scott!" he exclaims, involuntarily, "What a wonderful
hill!"—and, sometimes, he asks if it is Beinn Eighe.

"Oh, no—that's Beinn Dearg, the Red Mountain. Looks fine
from here, doesn't it?"

"Marvellous!" agrees the stranger, enthusiastically. "What
terraces! What gullies! Terrific!" Then, if he is a "pukka
mountaineer" type, he asks the inevitable question: "How high
is it?"—or he takes a closer look at his map.

The result of this is usually a disappointed "Oh! Only 2995
feet? I should have said it was higher than that." And, once more,
Beinn Dearg is deleted from the list of "mountains to be climbed".

A pity, because those who choose to ignore the missing five
feet will have an adequate reward.

I waited for the right day for my first climb, which I did with
two young women who were spending a ten days' holiday at
Wester Alligin. We had already been up to Coire Mhic Fhearchair
together, and knew something of each other's speed and
capabilities.

We left my cottage at ten o' clock, taking tea and sandwiches
for the day. It was a cool morning, with a slight wind drawing
thin wrinkles on the loch. Circlets of fleecy cloud clung to the
high summits and the sun-faeries sewed green patches on to the
garments of the lower hills.

Taking the high road from "Heather Cliff", we turned off
through the woods at Corrie bridge. The little waterfall had been
increased by a week-end of rain. Beyond the woods, the hills
were a cold blue, the terraces of Beinn Dearg dark and lifeless
under a veil of cloud. To our left, the semicircular ridge of Beinn
Alligin was sharp against the sky, save for the cloud-filmed point
of Sgùrr Mór, over which waves of mist poured into the
"Cleft". The replenished Allt Toll a' Mhadaidh sang a deeper song
as it plunged down the hillside to join the main stream. The
path no longer bore the marks of climbing-nails, for the rain had
washed them all away.

We walked along, discussing the soft condition of the ground,
the cloud, the best way up our chosen hill. Finally, we decided to
make the easy ascent from the east end, traverse the ridge, and

descend into the Bealach a' Chòmhla, between Beinn Dearg and Beinn Alligin, a steepish way down, but one which would land us fairly near to our base at the end of the day.

Crossing the wooden bridge, we tramped briskly along the sandy path of Coire Mhic Nobuil. High above, to our left, sunlight began to kindle little fires on the precipitous terraces of the Red Mountain. An odd, crumbling pinnacle which I had nicknamed "The Castle" was jet-black against a patch of blue. Beside it, another smaller excrescence had the appearance of a modern gun-turret or a giant's knobbly cudgel upthrust to hasten the retreating clouds.

Our path meandered beside the river, where a solitary heron rose from a little fall at our approach. Before us, Beinn Eighe was still a dead grey, with cloud hanging over the buttresses above Coire Mhic Fhearchair. To the south-east, the spectacular ridge of Liathach dwarfed everything to a frightening insignificance, so that the colossal boulders strewn over the valley had the appearance of pebbles tossed down by the children of the gods building sand-castles on the deserts of the young world.

We rested for a few minutes where the path came to an end in the peat-moss, and allowed ourselves a biscuit. Then we strode on until we were opposite Lochan a' Chaoruinn, from which point we had planned to make the ascent, following the course of the longer burn on to the ridge west of Càrn na Feòla.

The stream flowed down a steep gully. Keeping to the right of it, we came under grey crags from which we looked behind and down into the desolate valley. Beyond, the dark "Teeth" of Liathach were outlined by the sun. To the east, the blue hills beyond Kinlochewe peeped over the loch-bejewelled pass. Beinn Eighe was a parched and arid grey, as yet unawakened by the moving light. A cold wind had begun to blow from the north, drying the sweat on our faces and chilling us through our clothes.

We climbed on, up the broken rock beside the burn, and came under another buttress whose grey face was striped with white veins of quartz. Above us loomed a wall of rock, slashed by gullies filled with rubble and sparse heather. Below, the debris-littered, water-laden valley was a study in tones of grey, only the lochans giving it life as they trapped for a moment the prying rays of the sun. South-west, the jagged edge of the Black Cuillin rose above bluish cloud.

We were taking our time, anticipating reaching the summit at about two o'clock. The going was steepish, but not difficult. Soon, we stopped on a little ledge where a thin trickle of water poured off the black rock as if out of a tap. Here, we eased off our rucksacks and enjoyed a rest and a drink, gazing in silence at the growing immensity around. There was a hint of colour, now, in the sandy edge of the river below, reflected high up on Liathach where drifts of sand streaked the hanging basin under the Peak of the Horn. Below the "Teeth", Coire na Caime was full of shadows. Eastward, high over the waste of blue hills, cumulus cloud was piled into horizontal furrows, each furrow edged on its upper side with gold.

Around us, milkwort and blooming ling-heather clung among the rocks. We had already crossed several sheep-tracks running along the face of the hill on the line of the terracing. We were so high now that the wrinkled and riven valley below looked like a diagram of the surface of the moon—an apt comparison suggested by one of my friends.

Eastward, we could see far over the weed-patched lochans in Coire Dubh Mór to where thin ranks of trees made olive stripes on the blue mountains beyond Kinlochewe. Beinn Eighe was at last coming to life, as fleeting sunlight touched her cold ridges and turned her ice-blue terraces to palest rose and gold. Most fantastic, though, was the "Grey One", along whose jagged ridge the great gullies slashed down in the form of a series of gigantic spear-heads, each point terminating in a pile of rubble.

Presently, we began climbing again, and came up on to the ridge just east of the tiny lochan we had planned to reach from below. Here, we discovered a whole world of unexpected beauty.

We walked on great grey slabs of sandstone, shaded here and there with the pink which no doubt gave the hill its name. At the end of the ridge, Càrn na Feòla thrust up a hunched shoulder, clad in a green mantle spotted with grey. Following the mounting line of the ridge westward, we saw the derelict "Castle", with its spiky gun-turret hard by.

Beyond lay Loch Torridon and Loch Shieldaig, with their dark promontories and rocky islands, enticing the eye southward to the silver gleam of Loch Carron and Loch Alsh. Northward, we looked away over desolate Loch na h-Oidhche and the sylvan glory of Loch Maree, whose isles were gold under the sun. Near at hand, the south point of Baos Bheinn was like a pyramid, with the ridge sloping away behind. Seen from this new and strange angle, it looked like a completely unfamiliar mountain which had grown up overnight. Between Baos Bheinn and Beinn a' Chearcaill, a blue glen swept away towards the massed isles and the curve of water beyond which Slioch brooded under pearly cloud.

From this point, there remained for us an ascent of some eight hundred feet to the main peak. We took it easily, mounting over springy moss, heather and "pancake" rock, sheltering as much as possible from the icy north wind which swept across the mountain-tops. Some of the boulders around us were most grotesque in shape, like animal-faces peering out of their rocky caverns and leaning over the ridge to see what was going on in the glens below.

Coming up the first rise, we looked back across the striped cliffs of Càrn na Feòla to where Loch a' Chroisg was a silver glare among the hills above Glen Dochertie. Below us, to the north, a grey gash dropped dizzily down to the black, sodden plateau. Sunlight brought colour to the pinkish slabs at the foot of Beinn an Eóin, and set a million diamonds dancing in the pass to Talladale.

Over the rise now—and we gazed away to the fretted coastline of Diabaig and Craig and Gairloch, with the blue islands blurring the wastes of the cold Minch beyond. Nearer, we saw the golden sands at the head of Loch a' Bhealaich, and one outflung limb of the sleeping giantess I had noticed from Beinn Alligin.

Ahead, the ridge led still upward, among scattered boulders— and now we were looking down into the black waters of Loch a' Choire Mhóir, a wind-ruffled pool at the foot of sunless crags, with the knobbly battlements of the summit towering beyond.

Everywhere around us lay the flat rocks, among which we followed a sheep-track along the ridge. But, ahead, the "Castle" blocked our way, rising in a series of formidable steps towards the sky. One of the party remarked that she did not like it at all (and neither, for that matter, did I!) but we had hopes that it would prove easier of access than it appeared.

Our hopes were realised. We found another sheep-track which ran along the south side, under the ruined turrets, and along this we wound our cautious way. We were out of the wind here, and there was complete silence, save for the echo of rushing waters

from the Allt Coire Mhic Nobuil far below. Before us
appeared a great gash filled with scree. Rounding a curve of the
rock-face, however, we discovered that a narrow, slabby ridge
led over it to the last pitch; and, scrambling across this, we found
the sheep-track again, leading up to the main summit. Glancing
back, we were amazed at the wild beauty and seeming difficulty
of the ridge we had traversed—the massive tower of rock, beyond
which a curving plateau reminiscent of the great plateau of
Liathach rolled away and down to the cliffs on the north of
Càrn na Feòla.

The last part of the climb was easy, and we reached the main
summit just after two o'clock. It was too windy to lunch by the
cairn, so we tucked ourselves in among the slabs above the "gun-
turret", and, with gratitude, began on the sandwiches and hot
tea.

When we were a little warmed and refreshed, we gazed in
delight upon this new aspect of the Torridon landscape spread
out before us. Immediately opposite, across the green gash of
Coire Mhic Nobuil, lay the whole of the five-mile ridge of
Liathach, pinnacle and corrie and cleft offering a vision of wild
beauty such as beggars description. We looked right into the
"Grey Hollow", and saw Loch a' Ghlas Thuill turned to a sheet
of quicksilver by the sun, edged with the gold of its sands. Beinn
Eighe was a grey monster hunched against the sky to the east, and
we could see the big ' pimple" on the top of Ruadh Stac Mór,
and the waterfall leaping out of Coire Mhic Fhearchair, with the
steely glint of the loch behind.

But cloud was dimming the landscape to the north, and we
hastened with our meal. The sunlight moved, and touched us,
and slid sideways, gilding the three crumbling turrets of the Beinn
Dearg ridge before slanting down on to the mossy plateau to light
tiny pools among the flat slabs of sandstone, and to dapple, for
the space of a breath, the infinitesimal lochan to which we had
ascended from the valley below. High above Beinn an Eóin, a pair
of buzzards circled, ragged-winged, against the greying sky.

Then we looked south-west, to see rain over the notched ridge
of the Cuillin, while the welter of hills beyond Beinn Damh faded
to a cold blue as the fleeting sun withdrew her gold. Wisps of
cloud brushed the summits of Liathach and spread dark shadows
over her perilous cliffs. Turning northward again, we saw a dense

veil of nimbus cloud advancing with the wind, filming the land-scape with bluish-white, pouring down into cleft and corrie to subdue all colour and tarnish the gold of lochan and stream.

We agreed that it was time to start moving if we were to find without difficulty a suitable place to descend. Cloud was now flowing thickly over all the peaks of Beinn Eighe, and we had no wish to be marooned all night on an unfamiliar mountain, with those sheer gullies lying under us to the west and south.

We came, therefore, with all speed, down the crumbling rock beyond the summit-cairn on to the northern curve of the 'horse-shoe". Before us rose the last shoulder of the ridge, with a little "off-shoot" running out to the west—a point from which we had thought to descend into the bealach between Beinn Dearg and Beinn Alligin. Most magnificent, from this angle, were the fantastic "Horns" of Beinn Alligin, with the sharp point of Sgùrr Mór peering over the top—but we were not afforded many minutes in which to admire. The cloud was suddenly upon us, pouring down like smoke over the entire landscape, drowning known outlines in great waves of smothering white. We could see nothing to the north but mysterious smoke-shadows which might have been hills. The "Horns" of Alligin had entered heaven. Without further debate, we plunged down off the ridge into a green gully which carved its steep and slippery way towards the Bealach a' Chòmhla. It was one of the great gashes which look so formidable from below. Remembering the precipitous escarp-ments on this side of the mountain, we prepared for the worst.

The gully was thick with wet grass, and we slid for a while beside the course of a stream. Then outcrops of rock appeared—the stream cascaded through a deepening chasm, and we ran into a little difficulty which was increased by the unbalancing tendency displayed by our rucksacks. At one point, we looked back up wet rock to where a great boulder had lodged in the dark chimney, so that the water gushed out of a green cave underneath. Then a loose stone started a landslide just in front of us. It went with a terrific roar down the gully, drowning the rush of the waterfall. With one accord, we forsook our chimney and scrambled on to the left-hand spur, where we rested and "re-covered" before completing the last, and easiest, stage of the descent.

Looking up from the bottom, we could hardly believe that we

North-western end of the Beinn Eighe range

had managed it without mishap, for it looked almost perpendicular. There was still cloud on the ridge, and a few spots of rain splashed us as we tramped over a scree-drift into the pass. A tiny white moth rose out of the grasses, the first sign of life we had seen since we left the summit of the Red Mountain. On the other side of the river, however, we found boot-prints and the hoof-marks of a stalkers' pony.

Finding the path, we tramped down towards the wooden bridge spanning the Allt Coire Mhic Nobuil. It was just after six, and we were beginning to think longingly of tea. We made our last stop on the bank of the Allt a' Bhealaich, where two lacy falls purled down into a peat-brown pool and a tiny red-berried rowan nodded in the wind. Above this, another fall cascaded over smooth black rock. Beside the stream, small ferns uncurled among the white-patched boulders, while rowans and silver birches added a sylvan beauty to the already lovely scene. Over tea, we discussed our climb, looking back with appreciation at the almost-sheer terraces on this side of Beinn Dearg. The knobbly ridge was clear of cloud now—but, across the valley, the summits of Liathach were still drowned in smothering vapour. It was no longer raining, and the sunlight had returned to throw a handful of opals on to the ridge of Beinn Eighe.

It was a magnificent scene—but, ever and anon, our gaze stole back and upward to where the dark turrets of Beinn Dearg fretted the brightening sky. A tiny wisp of cloud yet clung over the summit. We were in a hollow, and could not see the "Castle" now, or the great, dark chimney which had afforded us such an exciting descent. Yet they were vivid in our memory; and we returned to Alligin secure in the knowledge that we had that day made a new friend among the Torridon hills.

Beinn Dearg has one feature in common with Beinn Alligin—the sheep are turned loose on it for the summer. Thus, its terraces are scored by the marks of tiny hoofs, worn down here and there into smooth paths along which the climber will tread delicately as he circumvents a crumbling rock-face. At one point on the summit-ridge, we found deer-tracks, but there were no deer visible during our climb—or sheep either, though we had seen plenty on the lower slopes of this hill during our tramp to Coire Mhic Fhearchair.

I did not see my mountain hare. Such wild life as was abroad

129

Beinn Dearg, from Coire Mhic Nobuil

on the hill that day moved in secret under the heather, eluding the prying eyes of human being or bird of prey.

It had been said, recently, that foxes were on the increase again. At one time, apparently, they were very numerous, causing great havoc among the sheep and lambs. Dr Samuel Johnson, in his *Journey to the Western Islands of Scotland*, remarks that the beasts of prey in the West at that time were foxes, otters and weasels, the foxes and otters being larger than those in England. At the time of his visit (1773) the Isle of Skye had been so ravaged that a guinea was offered for each fox destroyed—a "prodigious sum" in those days. The otters are not nearly so plentiful now as formerly; but, according to rumour, a white one occasionally appears, the lovely creature known of old as the King of the Otters. These animals prey on the salmon, and (such being the strange order of things) will take large bites out of several living fish rather than consume one at a time. Of old, the marten was plentiful in the fir plantations of Torridon—but, as this preys upon lambs, it was in turn preyed upon by man, and was extinct in 1880 in the Loch Maree district. The badger is now nearly extinct, as is also the polecat; but occasionally stoats and weasels are caught by the keepers, chiefly by means of the barbarous gin-trap. The weasels were very numerous in Skye in Dr Johnson's time. There are mice, rats and rabbits, and the moles are more plentiful now along Loch Maree, having come from Achnasheen, according to a learned treatise on the *Fauna of the North-West Highlands and Skye* by J. A. Harvie Brown and Rev. H. A. MacPherson, published in 1904. This book also recounts how, in 1873, a live female wild cat was sent from Kinlochewe to Marlow, Bucks. Here, it was mated with a male from Inverness. The kittens were about twice the size of tame ones at birth. The real wild cat is now rare; but sometimes havoc is wrought on hens and chicks by tame cats gone wild, usually as a result of being left behind at the "flitting" of their owners. These poor creatures are fortunate if they meet a merciful end at the crofter's gun. More often, they fight the cruel trap until they die of exhaustion or thirst, or are slaughtered by the keeper on his rounds.

The hedgehog is rare. The first two seen in the district were caught by a stalker in Gairloch in 1902. I was told there are no squirrels, though the pine-marten has returned to the Beinn Eighe area.

With regard to bird-life, the "hoodies" are very plentiful, and these destroy the eggs of the gulls. They will also peck out the eyes of sick sheep and lambs. Several varieties of gull may be seen any day along the shores of Loch Torridon, with a predominance of herring and black-backed gulls. I have not seen the little black-headed gull which is so abundant in Lochalsh. Torridon, too, has fewer solan geese than Gairloch or Applecross; but there are many cormorants, guillemots, razor-bills and an occasional black-throated diver. The greenshank is said to come to Loch Ewe, but I have not so far met it at Torridon. Oyster-catchers, however, abound, flashing along the fringe of the tide, filling the quiet summer days with their shrill "pip-pip-pip" or strutting on the pink Lewisian rock at the narrows, dapper and trim in their spotless black-and-white, with scarlet bill and stockings. The sandpiper, too, haunts these shores, and sometimes the plaintive keening of the curlew may be heard at Fasaig. Most fascinating of the sea-birds is the gentle eider-duck, whose downy broods were hatched among the red rocks beyond my cottage. There are no puffins, but the stately heron fishes among the sea-wrack at evening. At one time, the osprey came to Loch Maree and Fionn Loch; but he was not seen during my visit.

Of the birds of prey, the golden eagle still frequents Beinn Alligin, though there is little enough wild game for her to feed upon. I was told that one hen-bird was known to have killed sixteen lambs in a month to feed her young. There are, of course, the buzzards, merlins and an occasional peregrine falcon. Of the smaller birds, one may find the irrepressible sparrows everywhere. At Loch Maree, the rosy-breasted bullfinch is common, also the chaffinch and the wagtail. Tits may sometimes be seen in the woods of Loch Damh, and the "chink-chink" of the stone-chat echoes among the rocks on all the Torridon hills. The corn-bunting is in the area, and the wheat-ears are often seen, chiefly around Gairloch. It is reported that the redstart used to breed at Inverewe. A swallow coming down into a garden betokens a rainy summer, according to the old traditions.

One of the most common and spectacular of the sea-visitors to Loch Torridon is the porpoise, whose great, gasping breaths may be heard by the fishermen on summer eves. Sharks, too, are not unknown, and one of the crofters told me that he used to shoot them, as a boy, at the narrows. I heard some uncanny stories about their habits—how, for several days, a shark's fin was seen just off Broadford Pier, waiting—until a man was drowned there, when it went away, as silently and secretly as it had come.

There are a few common seals, and the Great Grey Seal has also appeared in Torridon waters. The most common fish are lithe, saith, herring, haddock, cod and whiting—and, of course, the slim silver salmon and sea-trout, the property of the laird, which the law commands the villagers to throw back should they become entangled in their nets. There are brown trout in almost any burn or hill-loch, though many of them are so small as to be hardly worth the catching. Whales—sperm, common beaked or Pilot—have been known to enter the sea-lochs of the West, and one was once caught among the piles of the pier at Strome Ferry. Two, killed by mines, were washed up on the shores of Loch Torridon during the last war.

Of reptiles, the lizard and slow-worm are fairly numerous, and there are said to be a few adders in the woods of Beinn Damh. There are frogs in abundance, and I have seen the road to Fasaig alive with little ones, just out of the tadpole stage and no larger than a thumb-nail.

Loveliest of the hill-creatures is the red deer, everywhere strictly preserved or reserved for the landowner and his guests. However, there is nothing to prevent one from stalking him, out of season, with a camera. . . .

CHAPTER XIV

A LOOK AT THE HOSTELS—CRAIG AND ACHNASHELLACH

IT was during the last days of August that a new arrival at Inver Alligin announced that Craig Hostel was closing at the end of the month, instead of in September as had been anticipated. I made a quick revision of my plans; and, next day, set out to explore this remote moorland outpost between Diabaig and Red Point. Craig had long been on the list as one of the places to be seen.

It felt odd to be "on the road" again, after so many weeks of comfort in the little cottage by the sea. My rucksack, stuffed full of the hundred-and-one small necessities required by the hosteller, felt as heavy as a sack of coal. Yet, I had taken only the essentials for one night—cutlery, an aluminium plate, dry shoes and socks, a change of clothing, and the "approved sleeping sack" demanded by Rule 9 of the S.Y.H.A. handbook. I had been warned that Craig was so cut off that one had to take everything, including milk. This was to be obtained *en route*, at Diabaig.

Having deposited the dogs with kindly neighbours, I set out, muffled up to the ears in waterproofs. There had been a south-westerly gale blowing for three days, driving before it an icy rain. So far, the weather showed no least sign of improving.

But the rain stopped as I climbed the brae towards Lochan Dearg, and my spirits rose. Across the wind-whipped expanse of Loch Torridon, a point of sunlight moved over Beinn Shieldaig, to dance on the yellow waters of a cataract in the flank of the hill. Ahead, the road climbed up between grey, naked rocks among which, for a while, one was sheltered from the gale. A car passed, but it was loaded with camp-equipment, and did not stop.

Beside Upper Loch Diabaig, one looked across wind-furrowed water to the desolate coastline, and back to where the great, cloud-veiled terraces of Beinn Alligin rose to what seemed fantastic heights, enhanced by the mist.

All around, the hills were turning yellow at the first touch of autumn. For a moment, I felt the bitter-sweet nostalgia which

breathes upon the wild places as the year mellows and grows old.
I had come to Torridon while the snows of spring were yet
shimmering on the high hills. Summer had come to hold us in
thrall with her golden beauty, and we had watched the harvest
moon sailing like a galleon across the blue lagoon of the sky. Now
this, too, was passing away. The hay was cut and stacked in the
meadow. The ling was in full flower; the bell-heather browning
on the grey rocks. The butterwort was long dead—the burnished
lances of the bog-asphodel rusting among the peat. The black-
faced lambs that had bleated feebly around the cottage in April
were sturdy and long-coated, the tups ready for the sale. All the
young birds had grown up and flown away—and soon we, also,
would be leaving this ancient land of heart's delight.

But the end was not yet. It was only that the first hint of yellow
in the hills had spoken of the coming change. Before that day,
there was yet much to do, many wild corners to explore.

Ahead, now, across the loch, a weirdly shaped rock had the
appearance of two people standing together on the skyline. The
wind, moving everything round about, created in this, too, an
illusion of movement. One had to look several times to be assured
that these "people" were made of stone.

By this time, I was so buffeted by the wind that my ears were
ringing. By good fortune, I was able to get tea on the fringe of
Diabaig. Scones, fresh butter and crowdie accompanied the heart-
warming drink. A Cairn terrier emerged from under the range
to beg for scraps, and her owner discoursed on dogs while I
warmed my numbed fingers on the tea-cup.

So away again, reluctantly enough, into the gale; and it was
late afternoon, with the hardest part still to go. Ahead, the
shooting-brake was turning along the shore road with the mails
for Lower Diabaig. Before the advent of this "modern improvement", the "Big Post" at Lower Diabaig had walked into Alligin
and back—a total distance of seven undulating miles—every day
except Sunday for forty years! As a neighbour put it, the older
generation were built tough—they had to be!

Beyond the strung-out houses, two fishing-smacks rocked on
the grey waters of the bay. The eye ranged outward and westward, over jagged black rock and foam-tipped sea to where
shafts of light quivered over Rona and the misty table-land of
the Quiraing on Skye.

One tramped on between banks where the yellow tansy created its own sunlight, among the misty hues of scabious, ling and meadow-sweet. At Diabaig, still, they were busy with the hay-making, and great patches of fragrant field had been laid flat by the scythe. Sheep and cattle browsed on the foot-hills behind the white crofts, and hens strutted, clucking, around the little houses.

The wind had turned colder, and the rain was "on" again. A few silver birches wept over the road. Heaps of freshly cut peat were neatly stacked in the ruins of old cottages, or covered by a tarpaulin held down with timbers and sods of turf. The bramble was in flower, the rowans heavy with scarlet berries. Already, the bracken was changing its fringed dress from green to gold.

The road climbed now towards the moor, over softening ground. Past a byre with a thatch of turf—and now the road proper ended at a white farmhouse where a bare-footed child indicated the rough track higher up the brae. Coming on to it, one found traces of a tinkers' camp-fire.

Rough! It was certainly that, and wet, too; in places hardly visible as it meandered on into the unending brown of the moor. Only the toppling cairns built at intervals on wayside boulders guided the wanderer onward over the peat-moss into the bleak unknown.

It was not long before I met a fellow-hosteller going into Diabaig for provisions. We exchanged a greeting above the bluster of the wind. Alone again now, I ploughed along the un-dulating path. Behind, the hills blurred and were dwarfed by the grey, riven rocks sheltering the bay. Ahead, the gale-swept wastes of the Minch began to open out, and the barren coastline revealed itself in brief glimpses through the rain.

There were a variety of boot-prints on the soft parts of the track—the only comfort in a world of wind and rain and utter desolation. The burns were in spate. One of them was crossed by means of a "bridge" made of two slabs of rock laid side by side, like old tombstones. The ghostly obelisks of the cairns loomed at intervals through ever-increasing rain. Wet ferns clung under the crannies of the rocks. A fugitive ray of light picked out two tiny "islands" on the cold sea, Sgeir Dùghaill, where we had fished over the back of a boat for lithe, with the black dot of Sgeir na Trian away beyond, luring the eye towards the long peninsula of Red Point.

The track led up a cleft beside a little stream, which it then crossed to emerge into a waste of marshland, a yellow-green "valley" which seemed to invite unsuspecting feet. Keeping west of this, one jumped from tussock to tussock over black peat-bog, heading towards a cairn on the skyline. This part proved to be the worst of the whole tramp, and, despite my care, I finally lost the track. For some half-hour, then, I wallowed through the bog, bearing slightly east, until, at length, on a knoll ahead, rose another cairn marking the errant course of the path.

By this time, the rain was driving viciously through every crack in my oilskins, and I was weary from battling against the merciless wind. The pack-straps were cutting my shoulders, and my soaked feet were beginning to feel as if they had had enough.

But now a welcome green gash opened out in the moorland ahead, marking the valley of the Craig River. There were frequent cairns again now, leading over the last rise, from which one looked down a steep brae to the desolate and stony glen below.

There, set in the midst of the wilderness, beside the fierce yellow torrent, was a grey house with S.Y.H.A. painted in enormous letters on its side wall. A blue plume of smoke curled up from the chimney. With joy, I followed the steep path down the hillside. It was then seven-thirty—and, already, the light was dying, drowned in fresh waves of rain.

To many a weary wanderer through the peat-bog, Craig Hostel must have seemed like some lonely outpost on the edge of beyond. Its isolation and difficulty of access for supplies have been vividly described by the well-known Scottish writer, Miss Elizabeth Orr Boyd, who spent a season as Warden there. A sign on the notice-board informing all and sundry that ladies wash in the shed outside, men wash in the river, is a sample of what the hosteller must expect to find. One learns with concern that all coal required has to be carried up from the seashore on the Warden's back—a distance of about a mile over sodden peat-bog. All food is perforce brought, or fetched from Diabaig, which is four miles away. There is no road of any kind, and the Hostel is the only house in the glen save for two derelict cottages on the seashore. One of these is known officially as "The Warden's Cottage"—but the Warden (at that time an Aberdeen University medical student) was living in the Hostel, as, to put it in his own words, the cottage had running water in every room!

Coal necessitating such hard labour in the obtaining, the Craig Hostel cooking-range runs chiefly on wood, and everyone is expected to add a little to the woodpile before leaving. The lovely fragrance of burning pine meets the latecomer as he crosses the threshold.

There is a warning on the notice-board against crossing the Craig River any other way than by the bridge when it is in spate, together with a variety of postcards and photographs taken by visitors. The common-room is warm and clean, with the usual scrubbed tables and benches and a good range. At the time of my visit, the mantelshelf (as a quaint reminder of the Warden's profession) was adorned with an array of animal skulls, sheep, deer, collie, goat, and even two cooked lobster-faces as colourful end-pieces! In the scullery, a neat row of tin-openers and bread-knives suggested surgical instruments laid out for an operation.

I have yet to meet a hosteller who did not like Craig. Despite the bleakness of its surroundings, it is the sort of place one remembers with affection.

After the oil-lamps were lit, we sat down to a typical "hostel supper"—spaghetti, cod's roe paste on toast, "Pom" and coffee. My companions included two who had been stranded at Shieldaig the preceding day by bad weather, and had spent the night in a disused church. Outside, the day died in a weird red glow, and the wind, veering round to north-west, howled on a deep, hollow note about the lonely house. Above the range steamed an array of wet socks, while the boots were piled underneath. There were seven of us including the Warden; but, at around nine-thirty the hosteller I had met on the moor returned with the news that seven more, all girls, were at Diabaig and were planning to walk on to Craig tonight. Our Warden, Robin Williams, debated as to whether he should go out with a lantern to guide them, as it was now quite dark and still raining hard. Finally, he was persuaded that they must have stayed at Diabaig for the night.

At ten-thirty, he made a good-night pot of tea which was shared by all. We talked for a while of ghost-stories, the Second Sight and past hostel "céilidhs". As we went to our dormitories, we could hear a fresh torrent of rain swishing against the windows.

There were only two of us in the women's dormitory, and we

helped ourselves liberally to the blankets. I slept well, and awoke at daylight to a strange silence. The wind had dropped at last! Through the skylight gleamed the blue firmament, flecked with tufts of fleecy cloud. Already, someone was astir downstairs, chopping wood for the fire.

Outside, in the cold, bright morning, the whole sombre landscape of the Craig valley had taken on life and colour. The river was lower, and only faint, chilly breaths of air stirred the red marsh-grasses around the house. Beyond mauve and green braes, the sea was an ethereal blue, unbroken by so much as a hint of spray. Eastward, the green flank of Tom Buidhe ran up into pale-gold cloud.

The fire was already alight in the common-room, the resinous tang of it bringing a tingle to the nostrils and a sting to the eyes. A kettle was boiling for tea.

After breakfast, there was sweeping to be done, the table scrubbed, waterproofs packed and boots oiled. Then I bade farewell to the Warden, picked up my stick and stepped out on to the moor.

A very boggy track led down to the "Warden's Cottage" on the seashore. It was a small building, whitewashed and red-roofed, on the edge of a little birch-wood, with beyond it the grey curve of a shingly bay. The garden was over-grown with currant-bushes, fuchsias, nettles and roses, the house itself fast falling to dilapidation, with potatoes growing up through broken floor-boards. In one of the downstairs rooms, redecoration had been started but never completed; and the new panelling and blue paint looked lost and forlorn above the rotting floor. Up the broken staircase were two rooms in fairly good condition, one containing an improvised couch for anyone who could not be fitted in at the Hostel. Emerging, one noticed "Home Sweet Home" daubed in paint on the front door!

I mounted the brae in the bright morning. The sea danced under the sun. A few sheep grazed around another derelict house farther along the beach. Behind the cottage, grey cliffs thick with heather and birch-trees, with an occasional tendril of wild honey-suckle, rose against the sky. A good path meandered up beside a stone dyke, among moss-cushioned boulders and under green hazels, until it emerged at the top of the cliff on to the open moor. Here, tramping once more southwards, I gazed across blue water to the winking cottages of Àird, and westward to the dazzling white lighthouse on the Isle of Rona. The wind was strengthening again, and the strong waves of the Minch broke in showers of spindrift on the Trotternish peninsula. White cloud gathered and hung over Staffin and the Quiraing. Behind me, golden sand gleamed on the curve of Red Point, and the desolate moors swept away beside the blue sea.

Soon came a sign which marked the division of the paths, the point to which I should have proceeded before bearing east the day before. Approaching from beyond the peat-bog were the seven ladies who had arrived at Diabaig the previous night. We exchanged greetings, and they said they had spent a comfortable night at Diabaig in the mail-driver's barn.

The sun was high on the big brae beyond Upper Loch Diabaig. Cloud still clung over Beinn Alligin; but it was gold cloud now, and the whole landscape was a symphony of gold and green, with patches of mauve where the heather raised its delicate bells to the sun.

By Lochan Dearg, the Beinn Damh hills peeped over beyond the pale gleam of Loch Torridon. Beinn Alligin was demure behind her cloudy veil; but, looking eastward, one saw that the last shred of mist had peeled off Liathach, revealing her enchanted pinnacles and corries to bring a memory of past climbs.

I came back to Inver Alligin with two pictures clamouring to be painted on the canvas of remembrance—the sun on the naked ridges of "The Grey One"; and the pine-smoke rising from the desolate hollow of the Craig valley, where the lonely Hostel and its friendly Warden waited for all the young in heart who tramp the hills.

★　　★　　★　　★　　★

The ancient route from Kinlochewe to Achnashellach goes over the Coulin Pass, and walkers may now (thanks to the Scottish Rights of Way Society) join the "private" motor-road just beyond Loch Coulin and follow it through magnificent hill-scenery. One may not, however, use a wheeled vehicle without permission, and the Rev. A. E. Robertson's valuable *Old Tracks* ... *and "Coffin Roads"*★ warns cyclists that they may have to push

* *Old Tracks, Cross-country Routes and "Coffin Roads" in the North-West Highlands,* by the Rev. A. E. Robertson, B.D., Chairman, Scottish Rights of Way Society (The Darien Press, Edinburgh).

their machines beyond Tòrran-cuilinn. Among notable people who have used this route are Principal Forbes during the retreat following Culloden, and James Hogg, the Ettrick Shepherd. In a subsequent letter to Sir Walter Scott, Hogg records his journey from Loch Carron to Kinlochewe:

". . . Shortly after I lost sight of the valley, my path divided into twain, equally well frequented. I hesitated long which to take, having no directions saving what I had from the map, but following the left hand one it led me at length into the Vale of Colar, a curious, sequestered place, in the midst of the mountains to the east of Sir Hector Mackenzie's forest. The haughs are of considerable extent, of a deep sandy soil, with a clear stream winding through them; and some of the haughs were very good for such a country. The hills around it were very black, and mostly covered with strong heather.

"I spoke to no person here, nor all this way, but again took to the muir, being resolved if possible to reach the house of Letterewe that night, but ere I got into the next valley I was quite exhausted by hunger and fatigue, having travelled an unconscionable length of way, and a slated house appearing on a plain beyond the river I made toward it.

"I was obliged to wade through the river once, which being in a swelled state was very deep, and getting to the house asked if it was an inn, and was answered in the affirmative, at which I was very well satisfied. At this place I lodged. It is called Kinlochewe; was built by Sir Hector Mackenzie, in order to accommodate himself and others travelling from Dingwall into his country of Gairloch, or toward the ferry of Poolewe, where there is a packet once each week to Lewis, and though he hath annexed several advantages to it, it is very ill kept and in very bad order. . . . The floor was well sanded, as is the custom in that country. The windows were broken, and the bed was as hard as a stone. They had however plenty of whisky, oat-meal cakes, tea, and sugar, with some eggs, and stinking fish, on which I fared sumptuously. . . ." *

Just beyond the policies of Coulin Lodge, one comes upon a notice which mentions a "footpath" to Achnashellach, indicated

* "Unpublished Letters of James Hogg", *Scottish Review*, vol. 12, July, 1888.

by an arrow to the right. This path branches off at the stone bridge over the Easan Dorcha, and leads through wild and majestic country. It is not permissible, however, to follow this track during the stalking-season—as a friend and I discovered to our cost!

(I still think the sign should have made this clear. Its wording was most confusing, giving the impression that pedestrians might use the "private" road as a means of reaching the footpath. Unless one had previously read the directions of the Scottish Rights of Way Society adorning the wall of the Youth Hostel, one was apt to walk, innocently enough, into trouble.)

But to recount our adventure from the beginning:

The rain was falling in sheets as we left Alligin and began to climb the brae to catch the mail-bus. The burn by Heather Cliff was so high that we had to find a fresh crossing-place. Reaching the high road, we stood for some fifteen minutes watching the rain-drops exploding like shooting stars in muddy puddles. Finally, the shooting-brake came swishing along, and we piled into the back.

At Fasaig, we piled out again to make room for three people who had previously reserved seats. The rain was still falling mercilessly. Above us, however, a break in the dense cloud brought a faint hope of better things to come.

The Torridon–Kinlochewe bus agreed to take us as far as Loch Clair, though this small vehicle, too, was full of steaming humanity. Splashing along Glen Torridon, we gazed in awe at the smoking mountains towering up on either side, their every revealed cleft and corrie magnified and outlined by the waves of cloud. Liathach was dead-black, her pinnacle-ridges like the battlements of some nightmare fortress, the habitation of the Powers of Evil. Across the glen, Sgùrr Dubh, also, lived up to its sombre-sounding name. Everywhere, the mad yellow burns careered and roared and leapt down the rubble-strewn hills, singing their wild song of the elemental forces unleashed by the demons of the storm. Most awesome was the great, yawning cleft of Coire Dubh Mór looming behind a skeleton bothy, slashing its way up between the sheer terraces of Liathach and Beinn Eighe, echoing weirdly the surge of falling waters.

It was ten-fifteen when we left the bus at Loch Clair. A grey shooting-brake immediately offered us a lift down to the second bridge, where the footpath follows the north side of Loch Coulin, to join with the road again just beyond Tòrran-cuilinn.

Just by the junction, we found the misleading sign *re* the footpath to Achnashellach; and, in consequence of this, branched innocently to the right at the stone bridge over the Easan Dorcha. We were out of the wind here, sheltered by weeping birches, and we tramped happily beside a series of wild yellow waterfalls, up and up into the smoking grey hills. Ahead, Beinn Liath Mhór loomed through downpouring cloud, with just east of it the sharper pinnacle of Beinn Liath Bheag. Beside us, the stream leapt down black steps of rock and poured over smooth grey slabs on its wild journey down to the stone bridge built by Lord Leeds at the meeting of the waters. Looking back, we could see a hint of Beinn Eighe, a shadowy blur behind dense vapour.

The path led us on among the grey rocks, past banks of blooming heather and ferny hollows where the tall bracken rusted in the rain. Close by, the amber burn fell and swirled into dark whirlpools of mystery. Presently, we reached another "watersmeet" where the Allt Coire Beinne Leithe cascaded from the heights to join the Allt nan Dearcag at the foot of roaring falls. Here, we found a timber bothy; and, the door being open, in we went for shelter from a fresh deluge. The hut had benches and a scrubbed table. In our innocence, and still thinking that we were on the public footpath to Achnashellach, we assumed it to have been erected for the use of stranded mountaineers! After a rest, we ate our sandwiches, not forgetting to sweep the floor afterwards with the broom provided. We spent an hour and a half resting, watching the rain flattening scabious and heather, and taking photographs of the falls from the window. Apparently, we were not the only wanderers who had taken refuge here under such circumstances, as was revealed by an "Ode to a Wet Day" scrawled in pencil on the door:

> "To whomsoever owns this shack,
> We say that you may ask us back.
> Although not quite a home from home,
> 'Tis not too bad for those who roam
> The bens and glens and craggy ridges
> Abounding here, despite the midges.
> And, finally, what e'er your ranks,
> We say to you 'a million thanks'."

I see now that this poem should have served as a warning—but, at the time, while agreeing heartily with the sentiment expressed, we failed to realise its implications. It was almost three o'clock when we collected up our packs, crossed the wooden bridge over the falls, and departed into the rain on the last stages of our journey.

Up again now over the wild braes, beyond the last red pine, into the desolate upper reaches of the pass. Here, the track climbed over wet marshland, through rushing burns, among a waste of boulders, and so into the treeless wilderness bounded by the misty slopes of Càrn Eite and the great grey cliffs on the east side of Beinn Liath Mhór, down which a hill-burn poured in three lacy falls, to lose itself among the countless little amber lochans by the path.

At the top of the rise, we saw a blue mountain hare. At the sight of us, he swerved with a flicker of long hind legs and darted off among the boulders littering the pass. Soon, we looked down and westward to the great basin of Coire Lair, where the wild river flowed down from cloud-capped pinnacles, sheltered on the south by the steep cliffs of Sgùrr Ruadh. We were walking in cloud now, and the great, soft waves of it soaked us through and drew a veil of clammy mist across our perspiring faces.

Our feet began to squelch dismally in our boots. Down and down went our path now, shelving over wet rock and through water-laden shingle, until the black crags fumed up behind us to obliterate the sky, and we looked down the great gash worn by the river to the tree-line.

Far below, a grey gleam marked Loch Dhùghaill, beyond Achnashellach, a desolate stretch of water set in the midst of close-clustered hills. We plunged on, ever downward, and at last emerged from wet woods to cross the railway. Swinging north-north-east, we passed the telephone-kiosk and came, at half-past four, to the lumbermen's huts which had been opened as a Youth Hostel. It was raining harder than ever as we plodded up to the open door.

I had been told that Achnashellach Hostel was a primitive place with little or no comfort. I was greeted by the fragrance of wood-smoke and an apology from an earlier hosteller because the kettles were off the boil! The common-room proved to be large and warm, with lines to dry wet clothes and a big range. True, one had to go outside to reach the dormitories, and, at the time of our arrival, there was no water in the taps. Still, there were pails and a pump outside, plenty of coal, paraffin in the lamps; and the Warden, who lived a short distance up the road, had a cow to provide us with fresh milk, so we had little of which to complain. Off came sodden boots and socks, scarves and jackets, and before long we were toasting ourselves before the range, exchanging small-talk with the five other wanderers (all cyclists) who would be our companions for the evening. My soaked companion accepted the loan of some dry shorts.

The bunks proved to be very comfortable apart from the pillows. These being, apparently, stuffed with some of the lumbermen's left-over sawdust and wood-chippings, we solved the problem by discarding them altogether and substituting a rolled-up blanket.

Outside, the rain stopped, and pale clouds floated over Sgùrr na Fiantaig. To the south-west, the lovely valley of Glen Carron swept away among tree-girt hills. A single star sailed dreamily into the deepening indigo of the sky.

But, in the early hours of the following morning, the rain came on again, and it was pouring by the time we were ready to leave. Our clothes were not quite dry, so we put some of them into the oven while we were eating breakfast. The next thing we knew, my friend's trousers were on fire, and we were held up for another half-hour while I did an urgent job of mending! Apparently, there was a hole in the side of the oven.

Starting off again up the path to Coire Lair, we climbed laboriously over wet rock into the mist, having planned, as a variation, to return to Torridon via Coire Lair and the Bealach na Lice to Annat. Above the woods, the grim buttresses of Fuar Tholl loomed through gathering cloud. The path became steep; but we were fresh from our rest, and plodded on at a good speed, ignoring the hammering of our hearts.

But alas for our ignorance! At the junction of the paths, on the cloud-swept plateau, after a dogged slog up some 1250 feet, we met with a stalking-party whose ghillie unceremoniously ordered us to return the way we had come! Useless to argue, or point out that we had no intention of leaving the marked path— the entire party had obviously set their minds on accomplishing our immediate retreat. We therefore shrugged, turned, and

144

The peak of Fuar Tholl, above Achnashellach

plunged, a little wearily, down again, having become soaked and breathless to no purpose, for it was now too late to follow either of the alternative routes (i.e. the Coulin Pass proper or the path by Coulags) if we hoped to reach Alligin by nightfall.

It was at this point that my companion had a brainwave. If we hurried, we might *just* get the train to Achnasheen! Ploughing recklessly down through mud and water and long heather, we reached Achnashellach station with five minutes to spare. In the train, we sat drinking scalding tea out of our flasks, recounting our woes to sympathetic listeners. At Achnasheen, we emptied a good pint of water out of our boots into the fire-buckets!

Spectators registered amusement—but a kindly railway employee took pity on our dejected state and suggested that we might like to dry off and make some fresh tea in "the van" while waiting for the mail-bus to Alligin. The train from Inverness was over an hour late, and the bus could not leave, anyway, until it arrived.

We accepted joyfully. Seated before a roaring fire in a railway carriage converted into living quarters for the linesmen, we drank steaming coffee and ate what was left of our food. My boots went into the oven, and were almost dry by the time the train arrived. Finally, feeling warm and cheerful, we boarded the shooting-brake for Alligin. The morning's misfortunes were forgotten. After all, we had achieved our object and spent a pleasant night at Achnashellach Hostel. The fragrance of the pine-logs and the friendliness of fellow-wanderers would be remembered long after the abruptness of the stalkers on the hill.

Returning home on the mail-bus, we met three sleek black cars driven by imperturbable chauffeurs. The Secretary of State for Scotland had that day visited Alligin and Diabaig, to discuss with the inhabitants the long-awaited project of the new road.

"I passed him coming up," said the mail-driver, "and I knew he was somebody special by the nice smile and salute he gave me. ... There's many will pass you without so much as a nod, these days. . . ."

We looked for a repetition of the salutation, but the three cars were empty. The Secretary of State had embarked on the Fisheries cruiser at Diabaig, after an amicable discussion, resulting in nothing definite.

The three chauffeurs showed no interest in the project, one way

The coast at Diabaig

or the other. Serene, aloof, dignified to a degree, they swept past us with as much aplomb as if they had been driving along Princes Street, instead of over what must surely have been one of the wildest, narrowest and steepest roads they had yet encountered!

Achnashellach Hostel was closed in 1965, but the lonely outpost Craig still provides a haven for those prepared to follow the wild route over the bleak moor north of Diabaig.

CHAPTER XV

NORTH STROME AND KISHORN

DURING the first week in September, the coal-boat arrived from
Glasgow. For the next few days, the men of Inver Alligin were
busy unloading the supply for the coming six months. The
coal-boat, an orange-funnelled tanker, came only twice a year
to Loch Torridon, and the unloading depended on the tide. There
were usually two such boats on the loch at this time, one dealing
with the village of Alligin, the other with Diabaig, Fasaig and
Annat. The coal-merchant at Alligin was the Postmaster; but all
the local men who were young enough and strong enough
assisted with the unloading. Clad in dungarees or oilskins, they
rowed their boats out to the sturdy Glasgow vessel and covered
themselves with sweat and coal-dust, working steadily until pre-
vented by darkness or the tide. The load was dumped in piles by
the shore, to be later taken up on barrows to the houses or collected by the villagers as needed. Most people filled their own
sacks from the appropriate pile. I knew of one lady, living alone,
who had ordered three tons, and quite cheerfully faced the
prospect of filling sixty one-hundredweight bags by herself.

It was this same lady who nonchalantly proposed sweeping her
own chimney, as there was no chimney-sweep then in Torridon
or Alligin, though there used to be one before the war.

The arrival of the coal-boat was the more welcome as, already,
at evening, the tang of winter was in the air. The last of the hay
had been dried and stacked, and the local women were bringing
out their knitting to while away the lengthening evenings. The
shepherds and crofters looked forward to the approaching sales
of livestock. Later, the remaining sheep would be brought down
again from the hill to winter around the village—a task at which
my young collie would have been a willing assistant. She was
growing up fast now, developing in mind and body, and she
was the keenest creature I had ever seen; having what Duncan
called "a look of the sheep-dog trials" about her. I had assumed

that it was necessary, in the first place, to arouse a young dog's interest in its future work. I was the more astonished, therefore, when Bridie demonstrated otherwise. From the age of four months, while there were sheep on the horizon she had no other interest. Tense in every nerve, she would freeze at sight of them, tiptoe a few cat-like steps, then, unbidden, drop into a crouching position, taking advantage of every boulder or tuft of heather to creep upon them unobserved. As practice, at home, she would round up my neighbour's hens—all, of course, without a word of command from me! I have never seen so startling a proof of the theory of inherited consciousness. Shepherding was in her blood, and the joy of her existence. I felt a pang of regret, often, at the thought of taking her away from this lovely land of hills and heather, of whose life she was an integral part and yet separate— a little exile whose heart was for ever Highland, to whom the chance bleat of a sheep would always bring a surge of love, but no understanding. . . . Poor Bridie! No doubt the two of us would be wanting the hills again at the turn of the year—and it might be that the good Father would be merciful and grant us another sight of Torridon before her wild beauty had faded from the heart. . . .

On September 20th, the first snow fell on Liathach. It was hail in the glens; but, looking up, towards evening, we saw that the lonely pinnacles above were capped in shimmering white. Later, a full moon shone coldly on the ice-crusted shoulder of Beinn Alligin. The night sky had a blue-green transparency against which the big clouds floated like icebergs adrift on an Arctic sea. We realised, with a pang, how truly the year was growing old.

My gramophone recitals came to an end, as I was to be away hostelling myself for the last few days of the month. On the last night, my Cambridge friend took some indoor photographs. We played Mozart's "Linz" Symphony, and Jascha Heifetz's lovely rendering of the Beethoven Violin Concerto in D, which I can never hear without visions of Yehudi Menuhin playing it so superbly during a wartime performance in the Albert Hall as to bring the people, cheering, to their feet at its conclusion.

At the close of this recital, I found the following comment written in my "Visitors' Book" by a member of the Y.H.A. Staff from Sheffield:

"An unlooked-for musical treat in this most remote and lovely corner of Great Britain. The Beethoven Concerto was aptly chosen; its most stormy passages being reminiscent of the weather that has accompanied us through Affric to Kintail, the length and breadth of Skye, and now to Scotland's finest sea-loch in the heart of the Torridons. The calmer, more serene melodies were akin to pleasant evenings at rest after days well-spent, and, yes, to the occasional sunlit intervals. We shall long remember this evening as something 'different' in a holiday so full of enjoyable surprises."

. . . For my own part, I knew that I would long remember the recitals, and the rich reward they had yielded, not only as an intellectual stimulus, but as a means of forming delightful friendships. Second only to the music had been our discussions over coffee in the intervals, when we had exchanged views on everything from crofting and trout-fishing to history, religion and the poems of Rabindranath Tagore.

On September 21st, I awoke to an orange dawn over cold white hills. The air had the keen smell of ice. After a cup of tea, I shouldered my pack and trudged down to the beach to cross by boat to Shieldaig, having deposited the dogs with kind friends the preceding afternoon. The launch left the pier before my cottage at around eight o'clock, tide permitting, in time to connect with the mail-bus at Shieldaig.

Cloud was filming the snow-powdered corries of Liathach as we pushed off. The loch was dead-calm, the colour of cold steel as the dawn-flame died in the eastern sky. There were three cyclists beside me in the launch, their machines packed in the bows.

Faint yellow lights awoke in the western heavens. A plume of smoke curled up from the schoolhouse chimney. My neighbour emerged from the door to wave good-bye. Ahead, the hills over Shieldaig were dark-blue under grey cloud.

The delight of being on the water in the early morning has to be experienced to be understood. About us, the cormorants dived in the ice-calm deeps. Behind, Beinn Eighe and Liathach loomed ethereally through their mists, and the pale hills around the head of Loch Torridon were mysterious and aloof, garlanded with cold blue snow.

We chugged under the pink and grey rock towards the

149

narrows. Even the little hump of Ruadh Mheallan behind Wester Alligin was sprinkled with the new snow.

The wind freshened, and the grey ripples broke from the prow. We sat in the stern, muffled up in waterproofs to keep out the wind. The morning was brightening again, patches of pale green and gold giving life to the snow.

An Ruadh-stac was ghostly blue behind the white hills of Beinn Damh forest. Cloud flowed like smoke over the farther-off peaks, giving an illusion of great height and distance.

Gradually, the light brightened. Beinn Alligin and Liathach were clear of mist now; but the sea was still cold and colourless, the sombre coast relieved only by the outcrops of pink quartzite at the narrows and the yellow-green turf of Camas an Lèana. But the growing radiance was adding a burnish to the copper-coloured bracken on the foothills.

Now the sun broke through over Fuar Tholl and Sgùrr Ruadh, turning the snowfields to crystal. Now Beinn Eighe cast off her clouds to reveal terraces striped in a striking contrast of black and white. Beyond Shieldaig, Beinn Bhàn rose savagely above tufts of cloud, belying her name of "White Mountain" with a black knife-edge on which the snow clung only thinly, like opalescent dust.

Shafts of light struck gold spears into the water to the east. A guillemot dived near the boat. Along the shore, tendrils of smoke from cottage chimneys turned the mind to the homely thought of porridge and hot tea.

Beinn Shieldaig was still dark; but everywhere was a feeling of awakening colour, a tenseness at the rebirth of light, a sense of imminent beauty.

We passed the fishing-trawler, *Maggie Devie*, moored in the narrows. Her new blue, buff and white paint shone above the pitched hull. Beyond the rocks, the heavy swell of the sea caught and bore us up. On the western horizon, the blue mountains of Harris loomed under rosy cloud.

Entering Shieldaig Bay, we looked back over the low headland to see Beinn Alligin a great, silver hump like a grizzled old whale, with Baos Bheinn white and sharp behind. Eastward, Beinn Dearg led the eye round to the hunched shoulders of Beinn Eighe and the lovely, weird pinnacle-ridge of Liathach, all robed in silver sequins and clear of cloud.

Shieldaig village was still drowsy in the brightening sunlight, but the friendly smoke curled up from the chimneys, and the cattle and hens wandered along the single street. We landed, inhaling the fragrance of the sea-tangle—and, slowly, the village came to life, and people with parcels gathered outside the Post Office and at the bus-stop. The crossing from Inver Alligin had taken us thirty-five minutes. We were early, and I had a quarter of an hour to wait for the bus to emerge from its garage. I went into the Post Office and bought some canned baked beans and sardines to while away the time.

The only other passenger on the bus was a sad-eyed collie dog with a muzzle tied to his collar and a label for Lairg. The driver was ready for a chat, and proved to be a mine of information. We talked while the vehicle bounced up a narrow road whose wildness was only matched by that from Kinlochewe to Alligin. The collie cried plaintively at leaving his home and master. I sat with him for a while, in a vain attempt to comfort him, wondering how he would fare in strange hands and new surroundings.

We sped through lovely woods with the river purling below. Past Loch Dhùghaill (much smaller than the loch of the same name at Achnashellach) whose face was mirror-still under red pines. Out into craggy hills now, slashed by cascading burns. Round the back of Beinn Damh and Beinn na h-Eaglaisse (how different they looked from this angle!) and down to Loch Coultrie, where they and Sgùrr Ruadh peered at their snow-garlanded reflections in the dead-calm, reed-fringed water—a sight to stir the soul. To our right, Beinn Bhàn was still ink-black, a massive ridge of dark corries and turrets looming over the road. Above the white lodge of Culldoran, her two weird, distinct rock-towers brooded in Stygian gloom, backed by sheer cliffs of dark and sinister beauty.

Ahead, now, we glimpsed the pure-white mountains beyond Glen Carron, and the shining expanse of Loch Kishorn, pale silver among navy-blue hills. From Tornapress, the driver pointed out the Plockton peninsula, the patch of woods that hid Duncraig, the wild road to Applecross swinging westward over a stone bridge. There was no bus then, I was told, over the Bealach nam Bó—only a merchant's van once a week. On any other day, one walked, or took the Stornoway boat from Kyle of Lochalsh.

Indeed, at that time the outpost of Applecross was more remote than Alligin. Yet I knew that I must get there somehow,
when the appropriate time arrived.

A sight, now, of Broadford, on Skye, with Beinn na Caillich
rising behind, clear of cloud and mantled in the rosy glow of the
morning, luring the gaze away westward to the blue-shadowed
Cuillin range beyond. Looking back, we saw Beinn Bhàn rising
in a series of great, close-packed towers behind Seaford Farm.

A young fisherman boarded the bus here—later, a lady whose
destination was Jeantown. We passed the little lane to Kishorn
Hostel, and saw Achintraid on the blue curve at the head of the
loch. Away down Loch Kishorn, beyond the trees, past the dark
islands, the blue-patched peaks of the Cuillin, all untouched by
snow, were a dream of unbelievable beauty.

We sped on through russet woods and up Glenmore. The road
had a good surface now, though it wound and climbed "more
than somewhat". Swiftly we drew nearer to the wild white hills
ahead—Beinn Dronnaig and the high peaks beyond Attadale—
Móruisg and Sgùrr na Ceannaichean to the east. Fuar Tholl,
one of whose promontories is known locally as "Wellington's
Nose". Below, Loch Carron was calm and silvery-blue. In a few
minutes, we were sweeping into Jeantown.

It is a gay little town, built in the usual west-coast style, with
one long street running beside the loch, and clean white shops
and houses. Beside the Post Office, I found a cottage advertising
luncheons and teas and accommodation. Having left Alligin
without breakfast, I was attracted. The name decided me—it was
called "Shangri-La".

I went in, and requested a cup of tea, apologising for being so
early. The artistic atmosphere enfolded me at once. There were
bowls of bright flowers on window-sill and table, Eastern wood-
carvings, and etchings on the walls. A ginger-and-white kitten
bounced in to purr around my feet. Beyond the peach curtains,
the wings of swooping gulls were mirrored in the loch, behind
which Beinn Dronnaig rose like a faery mountain robed in rose
and crystal by the sun.

The tea was brought in, with homemade cakes and bread and
cheese. My hostess sat and talked to me, and the conversation was
as refreshing as the meal. The ginger kitten purred an appreciative
accompaniment. I felt that the little house lived up to its name—a

sanctuary of peace and friendliness where the wanderer could find his "Lost Horizon".

As we talked, the sunlight grew and strengthened outside, tossing gems into the loch. Presently, I went out to buy my meat ration on an emergency card—and saw that the mountains beyond Achnashellach were a blinding white, like a vision of the remote ranges of Tibet, a sight to awaken the artist in us all, to lift the mind to an awed contemplation of the infinite wisdom of the Creator.

And, now, I was away on the road again, tramping steadily towards Strome. At Slumbay (lovely name!) one gazed across Loch Carron to see the Kyle train puffing along under dark braes which dwarfed it to the size of a clockwork toy.

The road was excellent here, and led between fragrant woods where an occasional grotesque oak added a touch of rust to the dark glory of the pines. I had lunch on a bridge, beside the timber buildings which housed the "Loch Carron Hand-Loom Weavers", and, afterwards, studied the lovely goods and materials in their display-windows. Beyond here, I was offered a lift, and rode for a mile in a grocer's van. At five minutes to three, I reached North Strome Youth Hostel (closed in 1964).

It proved to be the usual, fair-sized, grey-stone house, over-looking the narrows on the north side of Strome Ferry, with the ruin of Strome Castle on the little headland beyond. It was so shut in by brown braes that there was little or no view from any of the windows, and nothing to distinguish it save comfortable beds and a very friendly Warden who lived in a cottage down the road. There were oil-lamps, and a water-tap outside the Hostel door.

I was the first arrival that day, and lit the fire. Gradually the others drifted in—a young geologist, a soldier in the Catering Corps, a girl, and a young man who had attended one of my gramophone recitals in June. Speedily, we made ourselves comfortable, cooked our various suppers, and exchanged reminis-cences of past travels with the easy familiarity soon cultivated by the habitual hosteller.

Milk was obtained from the Warden's house, and a black-and-white kitten came in to share it with us. As darkness fell, we started story-telling, exchanging views about psychic phenomena and Priestley's theory of the inherited consciousness. At eleven o'clock, we put some newly chopped firewood into the oven and went off to bed.

I was first up—and found the firewood reduced to powder by what was left of the fire. There was no more to be found anywhere, so the range was eventually lighted with dry heather and minute scraps of coal from the heap outside.

It was an average morning of grey sky and grey hills, with a hint of pearl behind the clouds. We had slept well on the wire-bottomed bunks. The kitten, which had spent the night on the mantelshelf, shared our first meal. By the time breakfast was over, the day had begun to wake up. Scrubbing to be done then, and the re-packing of the rucksack. As always, one marvelled at the weight of it when finished.

As I tramped down the road again towards Slumbay, the sun came out; and, suddenly, it was a blue-and-gold morning, full of colour and beauty, with gilded cloud veiling the snows on the high hills.

A car pulled up beside me.

"Going far, lassie?"

"Kishorn."

"Get in."

I laughed. This was a luxurious way of hostelling, and no mistake! The car proved to be the school bus, a neat shooting-brake upholstered in striped cloth hand-woven by the Lochcarron weavers. I told the driver I wanted to break my journey at Jeantown and get the bus down to Kishorn after lunch. We chatted as the brake rolled along. He was a much-travelled man, and told me of his adventures, and how he had visited almost every port in South America. Being full of enterprise, he was now growing his own tobacco-plants at Kishorn.

At the cross-roads, I left him, and tramped on to Jeantown for lunch at "Shangri-La", where I was presently joined by two of the hostellers who had been at North Strome.

The day increased in warmth and brightness. The snow had melted now on all save the highest of the mountains. After lunch, I trudged along to the Post Office to await the mail-bus which ran from Strathcarron station to Shieldaig. The Kyle train warned us when it was due. For some twenty minutes, then—so unpredictable is this west-coast weather—we drove through teeming rain!

But the storm was short-lived. At three o'clock, as I tramped down to Kishorn Hostel, the cloud was already blowing away, revealing a landscape of wild beauty.

As a hostel, I think Kishorn—which opened in July, 1948—took "a lot of beating". It was a disused schoolhouse,* situated almost on the beach, in excellent condition, with a brightly decorated common-room, water indoors and a good, though small, range. To my surprise, the young lady Warden had laid the fire, and it needed no more than a match to start it. The dormitories were light and airy, with large windows; and one looked westward down the whole sparkling length of Loch Kishorn, beyond a dark island to the majestic panorama of the Cuillin on Skye. There were Bibles on the windowsills.

After tea, I sat for a long time on the lichened rocks of the beach, watching the light dapple the water, the colours change over that fantastic range rising pinnacle on pinnacle under cotton-wool cloud—and I felt, anew, the ineffectuality of man's gifts in the face of so much beauty. . . .

The tide was out at the head of Loch Kishorn, leaving wet grey sand ruffled by worm-turrets, patched with shiny brown sea-tangle. A child paddled far out in the shallow water, and gulls and oyster-catchers dabbled at the edge of the tide. The Cuillin faded to an ethereal blue, backed by gold cloud—but near at hand, to the north, the corries of Beinn Bhàn were dark and full of shadows, and the great flat steps of Sgùrr a' Chaorachain loomed through the fading light.

I had now made my plans for the morrow, and it was up there, under the shadow of those wild turrets, that I would be tramping, following the wild Bealach nam Bó over to Applecross. The Bealach nam Bó, or Pass of the Cattle, is the second highest hill-pass in Scotland, and goes up to 2053 feet. Remembering the weight of my pack, I prayed for an early start and fine weather. Surely, September had given us enough rain to last for the time being? . . .

---

* The schoolhouse was subsequently sold, and the Youth Hostel is now a villa at Achintraid.

CHAPTER XVI

AFOOT IN APPLECROSS

KISHORN is a fine "base" from which to make the tramp over the famous "bealach" to romantic-sounding Applecross. If it is a calm day, the Cuillin will be pale blue and silver on the western skyline. You trudge through Kishorn village, past Courthill house with its fern-thick walls and stone arch bearing a Gaelic motto—its massive, studded door adorned with an ornate brass knocker. Through the woods, then, and round the head of Loch Kishorn, where, if the tide is out, the sheep will be browsing on the yellow-green machair.

Swinging left at Tornapress, one leaves behind the bird-haunted shallows, the grey croft with its sleepy hens and bleating sheep. The road begins to climb into the desolate hills where, often, a buzzard will sail up from the bracken at your approach. Above, tower the great, grim buttresses of Sgùrr a' Chaorachain, like a giant's fortress. Beyond, Meall Gorm is dark and forbidding, untouched, as yet, by the sun.

On a windless day, there is not so much as a ripple on the tranquil surface of Loch Kishorn. One hears, sometimes, of calm water being compared to silk. The waters of Loch Kishorn are like chenille where the little tufts of grass break the surface at the ebbing of the tide.

The sun is gaining strength, melting the snow on the high hills. Forsaking the russet valley backed by the long, jagged vertebrae of Beinn Damh, you follow the white road which winds up and up, as yet gently, into the wild folds of the moors.

Soon, you sight the Russel Burn, foaming out of the green basin between Beinn Bhàn and Sgùrr a' Chaorachain, ducking under the road, to leap down wide steps of black rock to join the loch at the little outpost of Russel. From here, one could make an easy ascent of the long ridge of Beinn Bhàn, which rises temptingly above, curving round in a graceful horseshoe to meet wild Sgùrr a' Chaorachain. But you press on, ever upward, over the strongly built bridges, following the hill-road over to Applecross.

The gradient of the pass is still easy, the road flanked by great rock-steps on the north and shadowed on the south by the gully-slashed face of Meall Gorm. Across shining water, the blue hills of Skye loom under fluffy cloud. You round a bend, to see the road going on and up into a great basin out of which the Allt a' Chumhaing foams in a series of thin trickles to the dark valley under the cliffs of Meall Gorm.

You are coming under the shadow of the hills now. You have seen no house since leaving Tornapress, apart from the little cottages of Russel away down by the shore. Nowhere is there any sign of life, save for the striped caterpillars crawling across the sunlit road. There is no wind, and no sound except the song of the burns as they dash under the road, their tumultuous waters imprisoned and directed by artificial gullies made at the building of the road over the Bealach. These gullies, it may be noted in passing, are a stonemason's triumph, built by the fine workmen who fashioned the bridges. Each gully is deep enough to hold the burn when in spate, and is bounded on both sides of the road by some fifty paces of stone wall, to prevent overflow. An old man of the district informed me that the stonemasons who designed and built these bridges were paid ninepence per day. The labourers working on the road received fourpence halfpenny. Plans had been drawn up for the road to follow the shore, but three elderly ladies who owned the land at that time used their influence and wealth to get it put over the hills.

At the head of the Allt a' Chumhaing, the road has risen to a height of 1400 feet. The air is cooler here. Close above, to the right, the red terraces and cliffs of Sgùrr a' Chaorachain have a smooth, scorched appearance, though they are crumbling at the top. The fine black terraces of Meall Gorm are slashed by great arrow-heads which cut up the mountain into a series of close-packed towers.

It was at the beginning of the famous series of sharp curves marking the steep part of the Bealach that a car came up behind me, hooted, and went on to a convenient stopping-place on a bend. I caught up, and accepted the offer of a lift from this, the first vehicle I had seen or was likely to see in the pass that day. The gradient now became one-in-three, and we toiled up in low gear, zigzagging, double-locking to take sharp corners, looking down at intervals to the wonderful valley behind, where the sheer cliffs of Meall Gorm cast weird shadows over the snaking river.

Across the deep cleft, the screes of Sgùrr a' Chaorachain shimmered under the sun. Far below, the silver "V" of the loch gleamed in the moving light. Then we were over the summit of the pass, and the vision gave place to a waste-land of boulder-strewn desolation, where the brown braes were relieved only by the glint of a hill-loch. To the west, the weird blue isle of Raasay formed a fantastic silhouette, the 'dead crater' of Dun Ca'an dark against the sky.

Down we went now, and down, into the brown valley. Two deer-stalkers' ponies eyed us curiously from the side of the road, awaiting the return of their master.

Below, the landscape opened out, revealing dark trees, a large white house, a river winding away into a green glen to the north. At two o'clock, we came down to the village of Applecross.

The sun was twinkling now on blue water. After the barrenness of the moors, the bay had the appearance of a sanctuary—as, indeed, it once was.

Of old, the whole district of Applecross, within a six-mile radius of the ancient monastery, was holy ground, and any fugitive entering the charmed circle was safe from capture for as long as he cared to remain within its precincts. The monastery was founded in A.D. 672 by St Maelrubha, who also built the old church. When the saint died, he was laid to rest in the sanctuary he himself had founded. At one time, it was customary for travellers to carry with them a handful of earth from his grave to ensure protection against danger on their journey. For many centuries after the old monastery had fallen to ruin, an alternative name for Applecross was "A' Chomaraich", or "The Sanctuary".

Despite the ravages wrought by later, more "enlightened" ages who identified the Celtic relics with ignorance and superstition, the ancient peace of the sanctuary yet lingers. Around Eilean nan Naomh, the Saints' Island, the wet wind sings softly, blowing from the Isles. Even now, in this chaotic age, it seems that the serenity of the gentle saint and his followers remains in this blessed spot, to provide a place of rest and refreshment for all who come here seeking "the peace that passeth understanding".

"Aporcrossain", as it was known of old, was the sort of place which wove a subtle enchantment over the heart of the wanderer. Yet, during my visit, I could not help thinking that it would hardly do to be taken with acute appendicitis in such a place during the winter months! The Bealach nam Bó rises to such a height that it is sometimes blocked by snowdrifts at the summit from November to March, and, at this time of the year, the sea is often too rough to remove an emergency case by boat! The village was even more cut off from civilisation than Inver Alligin, where, at least, there was then a bus running every day except Sunday to Kinlochewe and Achnasheen.

Yet the beauty of the village, in summer and autumn, caused one to forget the lack of such amenities. One took away a memory of one long street of sun-dappled, white-washed cottages with tiny gardens full of marigolds, and tabby cats drowsing on grey-stone walls. The houses faced the sea, and opposite each was a pile of coal, the winter ration. The hens pecked and cackled along the street, and I found a rabbit in a sunny hutch by the sea-wall. There were many small, solemn, bare-footed children—and I did not pass a single adult of either sex who forbore to smile and give me good day. I was told that there are seventeen villages in the parish of Applecross, all scattered along the coast, some so small as to comprise only a few houses.

Beyond the grey beaches, the heron and gull and curlew fish undisturbed, and the solan goose flips over and dives like a meteor, causing a small explosion as he hits the water, filling the air with his strange, creaking flight as he takes off for a fresh attempt.

It did my heart good to walk along the ragged coast to Camusteel, to watch the sea-pinks blowing in the salt wind, to inhale the fragrance of mown hay, and see the women lifting potatoes, with their perambulators "parked" beside them in the field. There were thatched byres at Camusteel, and, beyond the Holy Island, the blue Sound swept away toward Eilean a' Cheò.

At tea-time, I turned back towards the little hotel—the Stornoway boat was in, the mellowing sun shining on her red funnel and white paint, the ripples from her passing lifting the rowboat that waited to bear passengers ashore. Soon, she steamed away again towards Rona and the Minch, leaving a black plume of smoke on the sky—and, in her wake, the sea darkened, and the lights died among the "far Coolins". Then, beyond Scalpay, Beinn na Caillich was a soft dove-grey, while "King Blaabheinn" and his attendant princes dreamt under their crowns of gold cloud. A faint shaft of light quivered and died over the far cleft of Sgùrr nan Gillean. The pinnacle of Bruach na Frìthe was remote and unreal, devoid of colour. Only, over Glamaig and the Red Hills, a mist of rose yet lingered, recalling the warm hues of a perfect day.

In the dusk, I came back to Applecross—to where the peace of the old Celtic saints waited to enfold me, and the lights of the little hotel called the wanderer to supper and rest.

Few will leave without stopping for a while to browse among the lichened stones of the cemetery. It is here, in the north-east corner of all that remains of the ancient burial-ground, that St Maelrubha sleeps under a green mound in an unmarked grave identified only by two big stones which lie nearby. The grave is said to be lined with stone slabs, and is thought by some authorities to have been a cell of the old monastery.

Despite the inroads made on traditional beliefs, there are still people who secretly hold that a handful of earth from the saint's grave brings a blessing. During my brief stay in Applecross, I was told of an American of Scottish ancestry who comes to this spot each time he visits Britain, for the sole purpose of collecting a fresh handful of St Maelrubha's dust to take back with him across the Atlantic.

The saint had a wide influence in his day, and many places in the surrounding district are named after him. He established one of his churches at Askig (Strath) in Skye, and it was here, so the old histories tell us, that he hung in a tree a bell which, for centuries, rang of its own accord on a Sunday morning to call the faithful to worship. Eventually, it was moved to a new church at Kilchrist, where it became dumb. Thereafter, the tree at Askig withered away.

One does not have to delve very deeply into the ancient records to realise that St Maelrubha was at one time known and loved throughout most of the north-west of Scotland.

In the latter part of the eighth century, the west was ravaged by Vikings, who violated the sanctuary, burned the old church, and plundered the monastery. The abbot of those times, Ruaridh Mór MacAogan, fled to Bangor.

Many stories are also told of the last of the "lay abbots", the Sagart Ruadh, or Red Priest, of Applecross. He is thought to

Sun and cloud from Courthill, Kishorn

have been either a MacDonald or a MacKenzie, and owned lands in the Isle of Lewis. Being a warrior as well as an ecclesiastic, the Sagart Ruadh served in the wars, and was killed at the Battle of Harlaw in 1411. He was carried back to Applecross on the shoulders of four red-headed men, and was buried in the sanctuary, near to Maelrubha; but his grave lies outside the limits of the present cemetery, and is no longer marked or known.

History records that the cemetery of Applecross was once of considerable extent, and contained many ancient and curious slabs and obelisks and Celtic crosses. Most of these, however, were destroyed by the misguided zeal of the extreme Reformers, who saw them as a means of encouraging the continuance of "idolatry" and primitive superstition. Other wonderful monuments were broken up in the sacred name of Progress to make way for cultivated land, and the old stone with its strange carvings was used to build drains. A holy water font discovered in 1874 served incumbents at the manse as a drinking-trough for their hens.

One beautiful relic, however, yet stands in memory of the ancient culture—a nine-foot-high slab on which is carved a Celtic collared cross. It was on this stone, so tradition says, that the body of Ruaridh Mór MacAogan floated back from Bangor, Ireland, to his last resting-place in Aporcrossain. The slab now stands in a commanding situation just inside the present limits of the cemetery. Ruaridh Mór (or Big Rory) is said to have been as tall as the stone in its original position, but this cannot now be ascertained, for it was moved about one hundred and fifty years ago.

I found no traces of St Maelrubha's monastery, though it is believed to have risen on the site of the old cemetery. The roofless chapel at the east end is not the original church in which he and his brethren worshipped. It has been pronounced, however, as pre-Reformation, possibly belonging to the eighth century. The walls, in which there are niches for crucifixes, are now bare, the stone slabs that formed the floor are pathetically overgrown with nettles. At one time, much of the land around the present cemetery was under cultivation; but it, too, is now a morass of weeds under which, no doubt, the treasures of a forgotten age of faith and culture lie broken and buried in the peat-bog.

There is one tombstone in the churchyard bearing a skull and

The Applecross ferry-boat with passenger and mail for the steamer

crossbones, but I was unable to discover in whose honour this strange memorial was erected.

A modern church now stands among the few monuments that remain, and new gravestones mingle with the old. At the time of my visit, the old manse close by was unoccupied and derelict, with broken windows and moss growing on the roof. Above and around it, the grey ash-trees cast their browning leaves and shivered in the chilling winds of autumn. I found a sheep's skull lying in the long grass, among red fungi and all the "trappings of decay".

Saddened by the whole scene, I at last turned away. Behind me, the rain was falling into the little roofless chapel. The bleak thought struck me that it would make the nettles grow. Beside the west wall, the lonely, moss-crusted Celtic slab was leaning over a little, as if weary from its long vigil for "the days that are no more".

In the cold, withdrawn light of the evening, I trudged back to the hotel. After dinner, I found a new Maurice Walsh novel in the bookcase, and could ask no more.

There was little point in going to bed, as I was catching the steamer at four a.m. on her return from Stornoway. I tried to persuade the kindly manageress not to get up and call me—but to no avail. At a quarter to three, as I was dozing, fully clothed, over my book, her light knock came at the bedroom door.

"There's a flask of tea for you in the dining-room," she said softly. I became suddenly aware of the buffeting wind outside. Bleakly, I rose, and began to pack my rucksack.

It was a strange and somehow weird experience to walk through the village in the pitch-dark and down to Milton pier. In two cottages only—those of the boatmen—a lamp flickered to warm the gusty night and cheer the heart of the voyager.

The tame rabbit loped around its hutch as I passed, its large eyes mesmerised by my torch. I trudged on down to the stone ramp which serves as a pier, where a shadowy figure in waders loomed through the dark.

Presently, the second boatman arrived, and we sat in the hut chatting and jesting while waiting for the steamer. Our cigarettes made points of red fire against the soft glow of a hurricane-lamp. I learned that the tame rabbit belonged to the younger of the two boatmen, and that his cat and dog would eat out of the same dish with it. Beyond the tiny window, the black sea burst in clouds of spume on to the primitive "pier".

The boatmen told me that they did not have anything other than a row-boat at Applecross because of the rough seas, which would smash an outboard or propeller against the jetty. I remembered how, two years before, on a voyage from Kyle to Lewis, it had, in fact, been a motor-launch which met the steamer at Applecross. I subsequently discovered that, oddly enough, this was the only day a motor-launch (borrowed) had been used. Before and after that occasion, it was always the big rowboat.

At last, the two lights of the steamer *Loch Ness* crept around the distant point. We gathered up the mail-bags and went out into the wind. I carried the big hurricane-lamp over wet slabs and slippery weed to the dim edge of the jetty. The black waves creamed and broke over my feet. One of the boatmen took the lamp and we scrambled into the rowboat. The other, in waders, pushed off.

"Whoosh!" we went through the dark breakers; and "Ssswish . . ." hissed the undertow as it drew us out into blackness. The hurricane-lamp leapt and bobbed on the prow, spilling gold on to the lurching waters. Above, the cold stars jazzed and the indigo arch of the sky tilted as we wallowed in a great trough of heaving ocean.

The steamer was away out in the mouth of the bay, like a floating palace with her rows of faery lights. Soon, we realised with dismay that she was drifting, and we were not getting any nearer. The boatmen pulled mightily, and the spray shot up in clouds from the prow. For three miles, we cut the heaving billows in pursuit of that phantom ship. Had it not been for the presence of a passenger, the weary oarsmen would long since have abandoned the chase. Finally, by flashing our torches, we succeeded in making the steamer aware that she was on the move. The order was rung to heave-to; and, a few moments later, the faery palace loomed gigantic overhead.

Hands reached out to help me aboard. Two passengers disembarked and took my seat in the rowboat. Immediately, the bells rang again, and the *Loch Ness* was under way, churning up the black waters of the Inner Sound.

At five-thirty I went down to the dining-saloon and had a

breakfast of grilled kippers and strong tea. I was wide awake—but all over the ship were little groups of sleeping figures, huddled pathetically out of the wind in attitudes poignantly reminiscent of Henry Moore's air-raid shelter drawings.

We docked at Kyle of Lochalsh at a quarter to six—and I knew, somewhat sadly, that the "Applecross adventure" had come to an end.

Yet, for many days, the atmosphere of the sanctuary lingered —as it lingers with all who choose to visit this remote corner of the north-west Highlands, following the footprints of the old Celtic saints in search of a lost world of peace and enchantment.

In recent years, a number of developments have taken place in Applecross, making the area considerably less remote. Electricity and telephone-communication have been installed, and improved transport facilities, tarred roads and water supplies have been carried to most of the adjoining villages. A pier has been built at Toscaig, with a good car-park, and a daily mail and passenger service operates from Kyle of Lochalsh. Training-centres for boys and girls have been opened by the West Highland School of Adventure, offering courses in boating, canoeing and mountain-climbing. The long-awaited motor-road to link Applecross with Shieldaig and Torridon is still under construction each section being completed as funds become available.

Applecross is a crofting community and most of the residents have Gaelic as their native tongue. The visitor may find excellent accommodation at the hotel or with the hospitable families of the five small townships listed in the brochure issued by the Crofters' Commission. There are good facilities for caravans, and both caravans and houses may be rented during the summer months. Sea-trips are available, and boats may be hired for the sea-fishing, when one may occasionally observe seals off the Crowlin Islands. Hill-walking and rock-climbing are restricted only during the stalking-season from September to mid-October. The burns and hill-lochs are inhabited by brown trout, and bird watchers may glimpse the golden eagle sailing majestically over the cloud-brushed crags above the ancient Pass.

Chapter XVII

CARN DEARG, OPINAN, KYLE

THE day following my return from Applecross was perfect—but, on the Sunday, the eider-duck crossed to the north side of Loch Torridon.

"The wind will be changing again," said my landlord. "It's queer how they know."

The gale started just after dark. During the night, it seemed that the entire cottage would be lifted off the point, so great was the force of the wind. In the small hours of the morning came a crash and the sound of tinkling glass. The tide was at the full, and one could hear the huge rollers thundering on to the beach just outside the window, to retreat with a savage hiss and the long-drawn roar of rolling pebbles. I lay there in the dark, listening—and slowly came the feeling of the merciless sea surging closer, rearing itself up to engulf the cottage. . . .

Scolding myself for these too-vivid imaginings, I lit the candle and rose to make tea.

The gale continued to rage, and daylight brought no relief. The path outside the cottage was littered with the broken glass and lead framework of a skylight which, being left an inch open, had been torn out bodily by the wind. I blocked it up as well as possible with a piece of linoleum.

At eight-thirty I crossed the wild burn by "Heather Cliff" and climbed the brae to catch the mail-bus to Kinlochewe, on the first stage of a further expedition in search of the surrounding hostels. I was the only passenger. Along Glen Torridon, we saw no one save a solitary cyclist battling with the fierce wind.

The mountains were shrouded in gale-driven cloud. The surface of the road was soft and loose after torrential rains. Even sheltered Loch Clair was alive with "white horses". But wildest of all was the river, for here wind and current conflicted, so that the whole surface seemed to steam and boil, while great sheets of spindrift were lifted and swept along under the tormented trees.

I waited at Kinlochewe for the afternoon bus to Gairloch. The wind accompanied us all the way. At Strath, I shouldered my pack and began the tramp to Càrn Dearg Youth Hostel.

The gale seemed to be increasing now. Several times, along that two and a half miles of open road, I was nearly blown off my feet. Below, gigantic seas lashed the grey rocks and leapt up in clouds of flying spray. Only the grey gull and the cormorant and the solan goose were at home on the heaving waters, the latter spreading snowy, black-tipped pinions to ride on the wind. Away out across the wild Minch, a faint grey shadow marked the distant Isle of Lewis, looming dimly through the storm. Foam lifted in great white gobbets from the crests of the inshore breakers and blew like rolling snowballs up the brae and across the road. The drab beaches below were one seething mass of up-flung spume, and fine clouds of spray fell like salt rain upon the face and lips and stung the wind-sore eyes.

At four o'clock, I reached Càrn Dearg Hostel, a large, red-roofed house in a particularly exposed position on the headland above Big Sand.

If Kishorn Hostel afforded the most superb view hereabouts, then Càrn Dearg certainly provided the most comfort. The house is spacious, and warm inside despite its unprotected situation. The big cream-enamelled kitchen range is the "last word", and always hot. There is actually a bathroom with a bath in it, and running hot water, and a fine, cosy "lounge" whose windows overlook the sea. The walls are decorated with maps, photographs and paintings, and, on the day I arrived, there was a pewter mug of cornflowers on the mantelpiece. These, together with the cretonne-covered furniture and friendly bookshelves, gave the room a home-like atmosphere which dispelled all weariness.

The Warden and his wife greeted me with a friendliness which was like a balm to the wind-battered spirit. I was the first arrival that day, and was allowed to rest by their fire for a while, to pet the black spaniel, Roguie, and admire the sleek tabby cat. Outside, the gale roared incessantly; but one no longer cared. . . .

The grey day died with only a flicker of rose in the smouldering sky. The voice of the storm had changed from a deep-throated roar to a thin, eerie piping which vibrated strangely around the lonely house. The sea was an engulfing waste of heaving white broken by dark and desolate headlands whose sombre tones were lightened only by a patch of cornfield at Badachrò. The tireless gulls sailed high above the grey sea; but the solan goose spread his strong pinions and swooped low to churn the foam-filled air above the breakers, his spotless plumage matching the wind-whipped spray.

Another hosteller arrived, the cyclist I had passed that morning in Glen Torridon. We made tea, and sat for a while exchanging small-talk about mountains and photography.

Outside, the red-gold bracken grew sombre as night came down the hills. Long shadows fell upon the face of the waters. In the west, a gleam of palest gold marked the path of the departing day.

We lit the lamps, and made more tea. The merciless gale rattled the windows, and the black sea roared upon the rocks below. More hostellers arrived, and the kitchen became filled with various savoury aromas as we each cooked supper. The comfort and friendliness of Càrn Dearg enfolded us until we forgot the wind, or no longer worried.

It was hard to leave next day—but finally, just after eleven, I emerged once more into "the wind and the rain". The day started well, however. A moment later, I had "thumbed" a lift on a lorry, and was rattling down to Gairloch, sandwiched between the driver and his mate. From Gairloch, as it was still deluging with rain, I took the afternoon bus for Port Henderson.

The wind howled as we swept out of Gairloch. The retreating town looked drab and grey. Even the lovely sands below the golf-course had lost some of their gold. The big fish-lorries stood idle on the gale-swept pier, for there had been no boats out for two days. Far ahead, over brown moors, the dim hump of Beinn Alligin scowled through grey cloud.

The rain eased up a little as we ran through the dripping woods of Kerrysdale. Down to the little bay now, which bears the name of Shieldaig—as does the one on the south side of Loch Torridon. Here, however, the resemblance ended. There was no real village of Shieldaig at Kerrysdale—just one or two cottages and the hotel, beyond which grey, island-dotted waters swept out towards the open sea. There were two big drifters lying in the shallow bay, each wrecked and yawing over with half of its decaying hull rising grotesquely out of the water. The bus-driver told me that both had gone down while at anchor, one breaking her keel.

They made a weird and sinister picture—two derelict shells of what were once good ships, lying helpless and forsaken at the mercy of the tide.

On, now, along the ragged coast; through Badachrò, where we hooted long and loudly outside the school, awaiting the scholars whose homes were at Port Henderson. At last, they piled in, some half-dozen of them, carefree and hilarious. One small boy had received the strap for talking in class; but he took the grown-ups' teasing good-humouredly enough, his merry face all smiles. The bus rumbled on, past cold Loch Bad na h-Achlais, finally discharging its passengers at the little village of Port Henderson, on the edge of the sea. I made inquiries, and learned that it set off from the garage at eight-fifty next morning. Shouldering my pack, I then started off along the moorland road for Opinan.

The wind blew as hard as ever. To the east, the brown braes rolled away into the mist, broken by desolate lochans, with the blue folds of high hills beyond. To the west, the moors sloped down to the white-flecked sea.

Fighting the persistent gale, I tramped over the rise—and there, below, lay Opinan, a little community of scattered houses lying around the curve of a wild bay where, beyond the pale stubble-fields, a great sweep of yellow sand ran down to the sea.

Those sands were the loveliest surprise of all—the wind-ruffled, tufted dunes whose gold was enhanced by the brilliant green of the machair. One imagined Opinan on a summer's day, with the sea a vivid turquoise-blue and the houses white in the sun—a vision of burning colour which must have brought many a hosteller to a halt on the edge of the sands.

Past the big house and another smaller one; and then there came the red-and-white sign marking the Hostel.* The building was grey and fairly large, and had obviously been a schoolhouse. It seemed that I was the first arrival.

Before long, I had found the coal-pile and the firewood and had a kettle steaming on the old-fashioned range. The women's dormitories were upstairs at Opinan, the men's on the ground floor. There was a sink in the scullery, with running water. The common-room window looked out on to those wonderful sand-dunes—but, on the afternoon of my arrival, one could get only

* Now closed

a glimpse through the driving rain. Above the gale, a shepherd was whistling to his dogs across the machair—a desolate, plaintive sound which was well suited to the wild landscape.

Dusk fell early—and still no one else had come to the Hostel. I filled another coal-pail from the heap outside, cooked and ate my solitary supper of fried eggs and black pudding, and lit the paraffin lamps.

Before it was quite dark, I went out to find the Warden's house. It lay behind the Hostel, well back, and only the chimneys were visible from the common-room window. I was told that the Warden, who was also the local schoolmistress, would be in later and would come down to the Hostel to stamp my card. Walking back over the corn-stubble, I looked south-west across the wild sea to the grey tip of Rona, and along the coast to where the narrow road ran on for three miles to Red Point. Beyond this, a footpath straggled past the old Fishing Station and on for some four wet miles along the wild north coast of Outer Loch Torridon, crossing eight fast-flowing streams on its way down to the lonely outpost of Craig.

Buffeted by the wind, I came back to Opinan Hostel and stoked up the range. Soon, it was pitch-dark outside; and still the wind roared without ceasing. I had chosen the dormitory on the leeward side of the house, and was quite reconciled, now, to the solitude.

I turned up the lamps, and sat reading for a while at one of the scrubbed tables in the common-room. For company, I had the hoarse voice of the wind outside, the tap of rain on the window, and the friendly bubble of the kettle on the fire. Presently, the Warden called. We made tea, and she told me of the days when she was the schoolmistress at Alligin, and inquired after her erstwhile pupils. I suggested that this hostel, too, had been a school. Oh, yes—at least, the next-door half had. What was now the Youth Hostel had been the masters' house, and was once occupied by three teachers, while there were over one hundred pupils attending the school. Now, of course, things were different. No one had such large families—and, indeed, the schoolhouses of Opinan and Badachrò had only about thirty pupils between them. . . .

We discussed west-coast roads then, and the joys of auto-cycling—but the conversation soon veered back to education,

American versus British, the old-fashioned methods as compared to the "progressive". My companion favoured the latter, and believed in teaching children at an early age to be self-reliant. She loved her own little co-educational school, and experienced no difficulty in handling several different age-groups all at once.

"It's so interesting," she said, "like bringing up a family. . . . But the Highland children are so shy. The greatest problem is to get them to express themselves. When they move to city schools, they're bewildered at first because they're not used to competition. . . . They're usually very intelligent, but it takes them a long time to learn that one has to be a little bold to be noticed in a big class. . . ."

Before she left, the Warden asked if I were nervous of being in the Hostel alone. If so, I could spend the night at her home.

Grateful for this further instance of Highland hospitality, I assured her that I would be all right. After she had gone, I banked up the fire, in the hope that it would make a cup of tea for me in the morning. The lamps were running out of oil now, and I had no choice but to go to bed.

I locked up carefully and clattered up to the empty dormitory. By the flickering light of a candle, I read myself to sleep.

Of course, I awoke in the "dead of night" to hear something moving downstairs—a stealthy, rustling thing which set every nerve at once a-tingle. Switching on the torch, I tip-toed down— and came face to face with a very thin and startled cat. The surprise was mutual—but while I just stood and stared, the nocturnal visitor vanished like a wraith in the direction of the men's dormitory. Remembering how thin she was, and her wild, pinched face, I put some stale cake on a saucer under the table, in the hope that she would come back.

It was not until the morning that I discovered that she had already found my locker, drunk all the milk, and eaten large chunks out of the black pudding I had saved for an early breakfast!

I was fortunate in catching the mail-car up to the garage at Port Henderson. The wind was still strong, but sunlight dappled the moors and the big peat-heaps and turned the sea to a shimmering blue. The smoke of a steamer made a black smudge on the far horizon, like a shell-burst suspended over the sea.

The bus emerged from its garage and absorbed its crowd of

laughing children, who were duly discharged at the school at Badachrò. We went first to Strath, in Gairloch, to collect mails and passengers, then back and down beside Loch Maree to Kinlochewe. The faery towers of Slioch were looming through wreaths of bluish cloud. We had dropped two stalkers by Loch Bad na Sgalaig, and watched the moor swallow them up. Nimbus cloud was now descending over the russet braes. At Kinlochewe, it was raining, and a veil was drawn across the wan face of Beinn Eighe.

On the "last lap" of the Hostel tour, now, I continued by bus down to Achnasheen, and caught the mid-day train to Kyle of Lochalsh. It was over an hour late coming in, so I paced the platform with a hosteller from Càrn Dearg, and the two of us discussed religion above the rush of the icy wind.

In the train at last, we basked in the warmth, looking out over the windswept, sun-washed landscape. Most impressive was the unfolding tapestry of high hills across Loch Carron—Beinn Bhàn, the turrets of Sgùrr a' Chaorachain, the sheer cliffs of Meall Gorm, with the tiny ribbon of the now-familiar road to Applecross climbing dizzily up the wild "bealach" between.

At Plockton, the choppy loch danced around lichened islands thick with trees. Ahead, now, the Red Cuillin of Skye grew up out of the mist.

Kyle Hostel proved to be a cluster of Army buildings of the Nissen type,* set on the headland to the north of the harbour, some half-mile out of the town. One looked down on to the lighthouse of Eilean Bàn, and across to the white houses of Kyleakin. Military signs still abounded on the buildings, and, on the night I arrived, to add to the wartime atmosphere, there was a slim grey corvette in the bay, like a leashed hound in its streamlined grace and air of watchfulness.

The common-room at Kyle Hostel was large and somewhat draughty, and each dormitory was a separate hut. The bunks were narrow and looked extremely hard—but I was assured that they were not, though they were occasionally damp as a result of a leaking roof.

I had plenty of company that night—a party of seven walkers from England, a French couple, a motor-cyclist and two girls who had arrived by bicycle. Water, we found, was indoors, and

* The present hostel was formerly a school.

171

the range good. "Conveniences", however, were at the other end of the camp. The Warden had her own Nissen hut, and stamped cards in a tiny office while a baby chortled from behind a blanket serving as a screen.

It was a friendly crowd that evening. After supper, we discussed tramps and cycle-rides we had made, and the party of seven invited me to join them for a good-night cup of tea. The wind was "on" again, and howled round the camp, surging in with a mad swirl as soon as a door was opened. Rain pattered on the windows. The French couple sat apart, conversing in their own soft, musical tongue. The rest of us read, studied maps, smoked and discussed everything from climbing to the "news".

In the night, the gale raged with increased force, rattling doors and roaring among the hutments. Rain drummed on the corrugated-iron roofs, and the whole camp was a bedlam of noise. But the bunks were surprisingly cosy, the blankets thick, and nobody was unduly disturbed.

Chapter XVIII

FACT AND FANCY

THE day following my return to Inver Alligin was a Saturday—of old, it would have been a special Saturday, during which the Highlander would watch the weather with more than usual interest.

Tonight was the night of the new moon—"Sòlus Di-Sathuirne foghair, 'na rìgh air seachd sòluis", or, "the Saturday moon of autumn, king of the seven moons". At one time, it was believed in the Highlands that when the new moon came on a Saturday in the autumn, it would determine the weather for the next seven months, or "moons".

The day dawned brightly enough; but with a strong wind and a promise of rain over Liathach. I sat by the window, looking out on to the sun-splashed loch, the sombre hills beyond. The eider-duck had come back to the green pools among the rocks. Somewhere in the grey sky, above the curtains of the clouds, the infant "King of the Seven Moons" waited to reveal himself to the world.

I sat and meditated on this, and such-like of the old beliefs, now fast being driven into the void of things forgotten. Of old, the Highlander, living close to nature, completely cut off from the outside world, had had his own answer for everything. When sickness fell upon him, he used his own quaint and time-honoured methods to relieve it. It was long believed that warts could be cured by a touch from a hand on which a living mole had died; and the "King's evil", also, was an affliction most commonly treated by the "laying on of hands". In this case, however, the physician had to be a seventh son in a family containing one daughter who was born either before or after all the sons. It was also imperative that this seventh son should lead a blameless life, as any sin on his part would destroy the miraculous powers of healing that were his heritage.

For epilepsy, the Torridon patient had to drink in secret from

173

a special skull which was believed to have powers of healing. It was kept buried in a place known only to those who could be trusted, and was dug up when required. The sufferer must on no account tell anyone of the method used to cure him, nor must he at any time thereafter have any dealings whatever with corpses or funerals. If these conditions were not observed, the disease would surely return.

Bleeding, of course, was widely used to relieve all kinds of fevers and kindred ailments; and there was hardly one among the "old folk" who was ignorant of the uses of various herbs gathered from the hill. It was long thought that the Highlander's knowledge of herbal medicines was obtained originally from the "Leannan Sìthe", or faery women who had become the mistresses of mortal men.

Much has been written of the physical hardiness of the ancient clansman—how he would lie down to sleep in the open air, having previously soaked his plaid in water to keep out the wind. These plaids were made of home-spun wool. Of old, most of the people went bare-footed, and it is on record that rheumatism was almost unknown in the Highlands until the adoption of linen shirts.

For consumption and wasting illnesses, the Highlanders used at one time to pare the nails of the patient, put the parings into a bag made from a fragment of his clothing, and bury them, after repeating a Gaelic incantation. This is a very ancient belief which is thought by some authorities to have come from the Romans. It was also thought possible to inflict such a disease on an enemy by making a "corp creadha" or clay-body, of him, and putting it into a stream for the waters to waste away. As the clay image melted, so its living prototype would decline in health.

Sick cattle were cured by burning juniper in their stalls—but it had to be kindled with "forced fire" made by the rubbing together of two sticks. After the juniper was burned, all the fires in the village were re-kindled from the "forced fire".

It was long believed that a vindictive neighbour could abstract the goodness from a cow's milk by employing the "Evil Eye" to put a charm upon the cow. As an antidote for this, the animal's owner would go out early in the morning and take some water from a running stream beside which had passed both the dead and the living. Into the water was put a piece of gold, silver and copper, and the whole stirred up. The cow was sprinkled with the water in the name of the Father, the Son and the Holy Ghost, and given the rest to drink. This treatment was carried out for three mornings in succession, and was the customary way of removing the "Evil Eye" from animals, children or any living thing which had fallen under its malignant influence.

In the Torridon and Diabaig district, at the time of the illegal whisky-distilling, there was known to the people a Gaelic rune—now long forgotten—which was supposed to have the power of making those who repeated it invisible to the "gaugers". It was vital, however, that you should see the Revenue officers before they saw you. This condition fulfilled, you could stand quite still, repeat the magic words, and they would pass you by as if you were not there! (If you had your doubts about the efficacy of this method, you might emulate a quick-witted Torridon lady who, it is recounted, pulled the pins out of her hair, rolled her eyes and burst into a flood of insane gibbering, so that the "gaugers" betook themselves off with all speed—leaving her sitting on the keg of whisky!)

The old beliefs died hard. In Mr J. M. McPherson's *Primitive Beliefs in the North-East of Scotland* (Longmans, Green & Co.) one reads that, on August 6th, 1678, the Minister of Gairloch reported to the Presbytery of Dingwall a certain Hector Mackenzie, his three sons and grandson, for "sacrificing a bull in a heathenish manner (i.e. with the fire-ritual) in the island of St Rufus, commonly called Ellan Moury in Lochew, for the recovery of the health of Cirstane Mackenzie, spouse to the said Hector".

Other odd tales are centred near Gairloch, and many have already found their way into print. One such, with a modern and rather sardonic "twist in the tail", is the story of Uisdean, (or Hugh), as told by Mr J. F. Campbell in his *Popular Tales of the West Highlands* (Alexander Gardner). This story was originally handed down orally, and was translated from the Gaelic of Hector Urquhart. It recounts how Uisdean, a servant of the Laird of Gairloch, was one day out hunting. Suddenly, he heard exquisite music and saw a wreath of mist hovering above him. He fired his gun into the mist, and a beautiful maiden fell at his side. She appeared to be dumb; so, at last, unable to converse with her, he took her home.

A year later, he was "slaying bogles" on the hills. Night fell, and he saw a light ahead. Soon, he came to an open door, beyond which the Wee Folk were dancing and drinking from a cup. Uisdean got into conversation with one of their servants, who confided that last year at this time they had lost the Earl of Antrim's daughter, and she would be unable to speak to anyone until she had drunk from the cup. Watching his opportunity, Uisdean snatched the cup and made off at top speed. The Wee Folk pursued him—until the crowing of the cocks sent them back to their hollow hill. Uisdean reached home safely, and gave the maiden a drink from the cup. She at once began to speak, revealing that she was, indeed, the daughter of the Earl of Antrim, whom the faeries had stolen in childbed. Uisdean asked the maiden to choose where she would reside, and she chose to go home. They put the magic cup by the faery knoll, and went over to Erin. Here, they stayed at a little house where they learned that the Earl of Antrim's daughter was very ill. Uisdean posed as a great doctor, and gained access to the palace. Entering the sick-room, he approached the bed with his drawn sword in his hand—and the changeling "daughter" went out of the house like a flame! The grateful Earl offered Uisdean the choice of staying on at the palace or departing thence with a bag of gold.

And (here comes the surprise ending)—the canny Highlander took the bag of gold, bade a courteous farewell to the Earl and his restored daughter, and went back to his own simple life and the absorbing business of "slaying bogles" on the hills.

Another story is told about Uisdean and his bogles, and this was said to have happened some time after his adventure with the Earl of Antrim's daughter. It appears that Tom-buidhe, in Gairloch, had become the haunt of a monster which frightened or killed so many people that none would go out after dark.

Uisdean resolved to slay this creature, and, while making his plans, stayed for a while at the house of a "yellow-footed weaver" who lived at the foot of the knoll.

One day, the weaver asked him how he intended to kill the "goat of Maol-bhuidhe". He replied that he would do it with his gun, his sword and his mother's sister. The weaver laid a spell on the first two, but could make no sense of the third. Uisdean went out, met the monster, and stabbed it with his dirk, which he had nicknamed his "mother's sister". Returning, he found the weaver

The landscape of Kerrysdale, on the edge of Gairloch

bleeding under the loom. He killed him; and no man was slain or frightened by any monster at the knoll thereafter.

I have given only a brief summary of these two "old tales", which are told in all their full and charming detail in Mr J. F. Campbell's valuable book, with which I have spent many a happy interlude.

Other popular traditions of Gairloch include several of the famous "Prophecies" of the Brahan Seer, who foretold that "A bald black girl will be born at the back of the Church of Gairloch", "A white cow will give birth to a calf in the garden behind Gairloch House", and, at Flowerdale, "A black hornless cow will give birth to a calf with two heads" (*The Prophecies of the Brahan Seer*, by Alexander Mackenzie, F.S.A.Scot. Eneas Mackay, Stirling.). All these prophecies have been fulfilled, two within living memory. Another prophecy, as yet unfulfilled, says that "a dun, hornless cow will appear in the Minch, and make a bellow which will knock the six chimneys off Gairloch House". It is thought that this may refer to a steamer . . . or could it be a warship?

Second in importance to the Brahan Seer in this district is the "Wizard of the North", a MacLeod from Skye who, I was told, lived as recently as the last century and who was believed to have obtained his knowledge of the "black art" from an Egyptian woman. Many are the tales yet told about him—how, on one occasion, a young lady who was trying to "take a rise out of him" found an egg on her chair when she herself rose! Another story describes how the "Wizard" (who was obviously addicted to practical jokes) was making a sea-voyage, as a member of the crew. One of the ship's officers, who was leaning out of a porthole, flung insults at this "extra-ordinary seaman" over his shoulder. The officer suddenly discovered that he was unable to get his head back through the porthole. Finally, when assisted to do so by several of the crew, it was found that he had grown horns! It is also said that the "Wizard", desirous of travelling on a certain ship, once compelled the captain, by witchcraft, to sign him on as one of the crew.

Some of his tricks, however, seem to have taken the form of mischievous pranks enacted for the sheer fun of the thing. One hears how, on one occasion, his mother was broiling a cockerel for dinner and went to the fire to see how it was progressing.

177

The crofter's enemy, bracken, on the Torridon hills

The lid of the pot thereupon shot up, and the cockerel crowed at her from the saucepan! Another tale describes how this much-to-be-pitied lady was once remonstrating with her son for capering and dancing about on the Sabbath day. As he remained deaf to her entreaties, she finally went and fetched the minister to deal with him. But the wicked "Wizard" put a spell on the two of them, so that they, also, commenced to caper and to dance together around the house, to the undoubted horror of themselves and the neighbours!

The "Wizard" died in America, within living memory. At one time, his escapades were often recounted in Alligin; but they are dying with the older generation, and much is already forgotten.

A quaint tale used to be told in Strath, Gairloch, about a mythical village called "Foolstown". This was handed down orally from father to son, until translated by Mr J. F. Campbell and published in his *Popular Tales of the West Highlands*. Mr Campbell's version concludes with a quotation from the verses of Iain Lòm Macdonald of Lochaber, a celebrated Gaelic poet who died in 1710. Another version of "Foolstown" appears in *Tales from the Moors and Mountains*, by Donald A. Mackenzie, a book whose great charm I have already described.

The story, a masterpiece of humour, tells of a village where the men were so stupid that they believed anything that their wives told them! (A bad start, you may say—but there it is!) That the men were stupid, there can be no doubt. A traveller, returning to this village after many years' absence, found things in a fine state of chaos. By the side of the road, two men were lying with their legs entangled, unable to decide which limbs were their own. The traveller "sorted" this by scratching them with a bramble. Going on through the village, he saw one man racing a big cheese down a hill, and another trying to put a cow up to eat the turf growing on a thatched roof. A third male inhabitant of "Foolstown" was hauling a big eel down to the shore to drown it for stealing the fish!

The traveller was quite disgusted with all this. Presently, he met three women, and had a sudden idea which might succeed in bringing the men back to their senses. He offered a gold ring to the woman who could make the biggest fool of her husband—a challenge which was, of course, delightedly accepted.

Without more ado, the women got busy. One wife told her

husband that he was sick; and he immediately went and lay groaning on his bed. She told him he was worse—then dead. He lay motionless with his eyes closed, and she went out and ordered a coffin for him!

The second wife told her husband that he was not himself— and he thereupon went out and hid himself in a wood until he could find out who he was!

The third husband was away at the fair; but his wife "put on her thinking-cap" and had her plan of campaign ready. When he returned, he was told that his friend had died, and he had arrived home just in time to attend the funeral. He undressed, and went to the cupboard to get out his black clothes. But his wife, coming in at that moment, assured him that he had them on already. So off he went, stark naked, to the funeral, where the mourners, taking him for a lunatic, fled at his approach! He was left alone with the "corpse"—but presently, the man who was "not himself" stole out of the wood to join him. The two of them sat down and talked things over—and came to the belated conclusion that they had been made fools of by their wives.

The traveller, however, gave the ring to the wife of the "corpse", for *he* would not stir a limb, despite his friends' entreaties, until she had come to assure him that he was alive!

Though the two published versions of this story to which I have referred differ substantially in parts, they are easily recognisable as being the same tale.

Passing from legend to history, we find that the moral code was rigorous of old in the Highlands, and punishments for offences severe. In a *History of the Scottish Highlands* edited by John S. Keltie, F.S.A.Scot., and published by A. Fullarton in 1877, one reads that for·disloyalty to the marriage-vow the offending party was at one time obliged to stand in a barrel of cold water at the church door—presumably to cool his or her ardour! When the congregation were all assembled, the culprit was brought into the church clad in a wet canvas shirt. After the service, the minister explained the nature of the offence.

Toleration, here as elsewhere, was unknown, particularly on the subject of religion. Those who (very rightly, from modern standards) condemn the persecutions of Mary Tudor or the Spanish Inquisition should also remember that in Scotland, during the seventeenth century, a man could be deprived of all civil rights, imprisoned and even put to death on suspicion of being a Roman Catholic, should he refuse to declare publicly his allegiance to the Reformed Church. The old histories reveal that there were serious riots in Gairloch when attempts were first made to abolish the Episcopalian religion in favour of the Presbyterian. Perhaps it is only in this later age, with all its faults, that we have come to understand that "in My Father's house are many mansions . . .".

The "Saturday moon of autumn" came and went, and the weather continued fine. In Alligin, the potatoes were ready for "lifting". Of late, boats had been out after the herring, and the women of the village were busy salting them down for the winter. Salt herring and "tatties" are a popular winter dish in the Highlands, and it is still customary with many people to eat them with the fingers.

The livestock sales were over, but the shepherds and their willing dogs had no respite. The Highland crofter or shepherd may keep two working-dogs without a licence—and, indeed, he needs them. New sheep acquired at the sales were driven into the fank to be branded and ear-marked and injected against "louping ill". The potatoes were then lifted, so that the remaining sheep could come down from the hills to winter on the field.

Almost without exception, now, the mornings were cold. The frosty pink dawns of autumn were upon us. The loch was often windless under a rose-dappled sky. Beyond, the tranquil mountains raised their heads among blue veils of mist, awaiting the snows.

The rowans shed their leaves. The apples turned yellow and crinkly on the trees. The rose-hips were scarlet flambeaux lighting the way along the shore-path. In my tiny garden, the montbretia was drooping among the long grass. Even the persistent tansy had felt the icy fingers of "Jack Frost" upon her golden hair. The "season of mists and mellow fruitfulness" was upon us—with ever in the air, at the back of all flamboyant beauty, the lurking sadness of approaching death. . . .

The crops in, life was keyed to a slower tempo. The stubble grew yellow. The swallows flew away—but the eider-duck stayed to dream on the loch.

On a dead-calm morning, when the pale sun kissed the wan

hills and the breath was like steam on the frosty air, Bridie and I set out in a last attempt to find the elusive "Golden Cave" of Liathach. (Jeannie, who was growing old, and feeling the finger of autumn on her bones, was relieved to spend the day at Baldarroch.)

The mountains wore a chaplet of mist under mother-of-pearl cloud. Enchantment laid her fingers on the landscape, and the nostalgic melancholy of the year's end took possession of the heart.

We walked along the shore path. The sun strengthened, the mist melted, the dew dried on the bent grasses. Before long, we became hot and a little weary, and it was pleasant to call for lunch at Annat.

The meal refreshed us, and presently we tramped back again to the high road, and set about looking for the cave in the wilderness of tumbled boulders at the foot of the "Grey One". We found nothing but cracks and crevices and ferny shelters formed by one great boulder leaning over on to another. After an hour of vain searching, we had to come away to meet the mail-bus back to Alligin. Again, we had failed, so well is the entrance concealed.

Later, I was told that there are two caves known to the local people. One is situated a short distance up the hillside, just beyond the last cottage, almost opposite the Annat turning. This one is known as the "Whisky Cave", having at one time provided a haunt for smugglers. The other, the "Golden Cave" proper, is also near the Annat road, and it is this one which was once supposed to go through to Gairloch. It also knows the fate of the two pipers who entered its recesses, never to return. It is now blocked by a fall of rock, and its site known only to a few. There are people who dismiss it altogether, believing that the "Whisky Cave" and the "Golden Cave" are one and the same. Around the head of Loch Torridon, beyond Annat, there is said to be another cave which opens once in every seven years. Tradition has it that if one happened to be there when it opened, and dropped in a pin or anything metal, it would stay open. It is believed that this cave provides a hiding-place for "Prince Charlie's gold".

My informant also told me a story about Annat itself, where there was said at one time to have been a holy well which had been blessed by St Maelrubha. In ancient times, three floating stones used to revolve in its waters, which had miraculous powers of healing. Now, however, the well is dried up and the site all but forgotten.

Many of the old legends, of course, deal with the "Second Sight", a faculty which is, even now, believed by some to be occasionally inherited by the Highlander. When belief in the Second Sight was general, it was thought that the time of day at which visions were seen was of great significance. For instance, an event foretold in the early morning would come to pass within a few hours. If the vision appeared around noon, it would become a reality that day. If, however, it were seen at night, by candle-light, it would not be fulfilled until the passing of several weeks, months or even years.

Many of these visions dealt with death, which was heralded by phantom funerals, shrouds, empty chairs or rappings on the window. It was also possible for a seer to behold in advance the arrival of a stranger or visitor or bringer of good or bad news. If a man and woman were beheld standing together, the woman on the man's left hand, it betokened that they would be husband and wife, whatever their circumstances or commitments at the time of the vision. The seer, while in a trance, appeared to lose all awareness of the visible world around him, and could only stare, without so much as blinking, at the vision for as long as it lasted.

At one time, it was a widespread practice among the High-landers to leave a saucer of milk each night for the household faeries who were believed to perform certain tasks about the croft overnight. Respect for the "Daoine Sìthe" was, however, mingled with fear, for they were thought to be evil at heart, fallen angels living in a tinsel world of artificial pleasures, envying mortals their way of life and liking nothing better than to make captive one of the superior race and subdue him or her to their will. Women in childbirth were closely watched, and the child was never left unattended until it had been baptised, for fear it should be stolen away and a changeling substituted in its place. No washing belonging to the child was ever left out after sunset.

Despite the "debunking" influence of present-day education, I have known a modern Highlander to shudder and hastily bid me "hush" when I expressed a mischievous wish to meet the Wee Folk.

There is a hill at Wester Alligin called Cnoc nan Sìth, or the Knoll of the Faeries, where it is said that unearthly music used to be heard. It was also heard along the Alligin Burn, near the gorge which forms a great gash in the hill just behind Inver Alligin.

Being fallen angels, the Faery Folk are said to have no power against the Bible or the Sign of the Cross, and are enraged and impotent at the Name of the Almighty. The rowan is traditionally a powerful charm against them, as is also the root of the groundsel which used to be put into milk to prevent its being stolen away. It is known that the faeries cannot cross running water. Regardless of whatever attractive shape they have assumed to charm the unwary, they will be seen in their true colours should they come to a stream, and will be unable to follow their quarry to the opposite bank. (The kelpie, or water-horse, was, of course, an exception to this rule—but he was more monster than faery, and made his abode in certain lakes or burns which were known and avoided like the plague.) Burns, in his famous "Tam o'Shanter", recounts how Tam and his mare, Meg, were pursued by witches until they came to the "Brig", when, unable to follow Meg across the river:

> "The carlin caught her by the rump
> And left poor Maggie scarce a stump".

This belief in the saving grace of running water is also recounted by Scott in his story of young Buccleuch and Lord Cranstoun's goblin page in "The Lay of the Last Minstrel".

It is still customary in the Highlands to keep Hallow-e'en—though the "celebrations" are much tamer now, and confined chiefly to the children. Gone are the glorious days when young men and maidens tied up the doors and scaled the house-roofs to drop a turnip down a neighbour's chimney into a pot of soup bubbling on the fire! Now, the local schoolchildren do little more than put on "false faces" and go rather self-consciously from door to door collecting pennies.

At one time, there were many quaint beliefs connected with Hallow-e'en. It was on this eve that the Highland maidens used to perform certain rites to determine their future husbands. One way of finding the "lucky man" was to let down a ball of wool into the "àth" or kiln where the grain was dried. The wool was then wound up again, almost to the end. Then the maiden would ask: "Có th'aig ceann mo shnàithne?" (Who is at the end of my thread?), and it was believed that the bridegroom-to-be would reply.

Another method was for the maiden to enter a dark room so that she faced a mirror. Before this, she stood still and passed half an apple on a fork three times around her head. Her future husband would appear in the mirror, and take the apple off the fork.

If neither of these ways appealed to her, she could eat a raw salt herring before going to bed, and her bridegroom would come and offer her a drink in the night!

Christmas is also celebrated in Torridon, to the extent of sending cards and small presents and having a Christmas-tree and party for the children—with sometimes a "céilidh" afterwards for the adults. One gets the feeling, however, that there are those who still view it with suspicion as originally a "pagan festival", and the chief occasion for rejoicing in the Highlands remains unquestionably Hogmanay, or the New Year. On this wonderful night, the young men—and, for that matter, many of the older ones—form up into large parties and go from house to house, singing and making merry—and at every house they are welcomed and offered a "wee sruabag". It is a waste of time to go to bed—one is speedily roused and made to come down and join in the fun. The singing may go on all night—for several nights, if the Sabbath does not intervene. And often the loudest and merriest singers are those who are too shy, or too dour, to exchange more than a casual greeting with you for the rest of the year!

Everyone rejoices at Hogmanay—though a woman who is in mourning is not supposed to attend parties or céilidhs or participate in any form of enjoyment for the twelve months following an immediate relative's death. During this period, also, black must be worn, or local sentiment would be outraged. There is no shortage of kind hearts, though, and the neighbours will all take turns at sitting with a sick person to relieve members of the family.

Family feeling is extremely strong in the Highlands, as is the love of the locality in which one was born and reared. The Highlander, when his work is done, is buried in the same little cemetery as his ancestors. The usual question put to a stranger is not "Where do you come from?", but "Where do you belong to?"

Children are almost invariably named after relatives, so that the same names recur in each generation.

Towards the end of October, I was fortunate in at last finding a guide to show me the smugglers' cave at the foot of Liathach—and, indeed, I do not think I would ever have found it otherwise. It is much lower down the hillside than I had thought, only a few feet above the track which runs along from the gravel-pit opposite the turning to Annat. The entrance is just an almost-horizontal crack among the rocks, overgrown with bracken and brambles. One could pass it a dozen times without realising that it is anything more than a crack. Inside, however, the cave runs back for some twenty feet into the hill, and is perhaps ten feet high near the entrance. It is the perfect "hide-out", warm, spacious and completely invisible until one is almost upon it. It would comfortably accommodate a dozen people, and has the advantage of being reasonably dry, as caves go. The far end is now blocked by smaller rocks and rubble. It is almost pitch-dark, due to the tiny entrance, and a torch is essential to the would-be explorer. It is so well hidden that it is almost impossible to direct anyone to the spot. It is no use looking for the entrance at eye-level. It is under the heather and bracken at your feet—a deep, narrow crack between big boulders, leading down into impenetrable darkness. It is the ideal haunt for smugglers—or the ideal bivouac for a weary mountaineer. If this and the "Golden Cave" are one and the same, it is the cave spoken of in an old Gaelic song known to several of the people of the Torridon district:

> "Bi na searraich òige
> Cuir am mach an òtraich
> Mu ruig mise, s'mu pill thusa
> Á uaigh a n-òir."

Which means, quite simply and literally, that "the young ponies will be putting out manure before I'll come or you'll return from the Golden Cave".

CHAPTER XIX

THE "PEAT-FIRE FLAME"

THE "Communion-time" had come and gone. From the cottage windows, one could watch the little boats bringing visitors from up the coast, and taking them away again after the services.

For a while, the village had been a hive of activity, full of intending worshippers in their best and rather sombre dress. As is the Highland custom, every house had opened its doors to the incomers, providing them with meals and rest during the periods away from the church. In this part of the Highlands, the Communion is held once in six months. The Sacraments are partaken of only by "members" of the Kirk, or those who live their lives in complete accordance with its rules. This involves forgoing dances, cinemas or any place of amusement. Those who attend the Kirk regularly, but cannot pledge themselves to this rigid code of conduct, are called "adherents", and are judged (by themselves as well as others) to be unworthy to partake of the Supper of the Lord. Solemn services of preparation are held before the great moment when the communicants seat themselves around the Lord's Table, to be served by the minister with the Bread and Wine. On the following day comes a service of thanksgiving, after which the remainder of the boats go away, the life of the village resumes its usual tempo, and the visiting ministers depart by bus or boat, perhaps to conduct identical services at Gairloch or Lochcarron. All the main services are in Gaelic, but an English prayer-meeting is often held for the benefit of strangers and holidaymakers. It is quite usual for the Communion to be held in the open air, the better to accommodate the large congregations.

In the Highland homes, the Communion-time is preceded by a great day of baking, when the housewife prepares large piles of scones, oatcakes, shortbread and pancakes for the expected influx of relatives, friends and visitors from neighbouring villages.

Special buses are run for those wishing to attend the Communion at other villages and towns within reasonable distance. For the Highlander, it is a solemn and sober time, lightened by the renewal of old friendships, the reunion of relatives who would not otherwise see each other from one year's end to the next.

And now, it was all over for another six months; and the life of the village went its quiet way as before. The last batch of potatoes was lifted and the cows were allowed on to the field. The evenings were drawing in now, the "season of storms" approaching to chill the blood and light the "peat-fire flame".

I suddenly knew that there was one thing I must do before leaving Inver Alligin. I must hold a "ceilidh" at the cottage, a little intimate gathering of the friends and neighbours who had contributed in so great a measure towards my enjoyment of a memorable summer.

Informal invitations were delivered without further ado. The response was immediate and enthusiastic. On the day of the party, I was overwhelmed with gifts of scones, Scotch pancakes, biscuits and home-made cakes, contributed by the lady guests "because you have no convenience for baking". The owner of an Ayrshire cow brought milk and fresh butter. We had port-wine and sherry, purchased from the grocer's van. (Unfortunately, I was unable to provide the classic drink of the Highlands, as the "pot dubh" in my shed lacked a piece of vital equipment!)

The guests arrived at around eight o'clock, and there were fifteen of us in all, arranged on various improvised seats around the little low-ceilinged room. The light from the two paraffin-lamps fell on friendly faces, all a trifle shy and stiff, but as good-humoured as a school-treat. The local crofters had come in their "Sunday best", and looked very correct and formal, sitting on straight-backed chairs. One made the surprising discovery that the Highlanders, on such occasions, are more shy of each other than they are of the host or hostess. However, once the wine had circulated, everyone was less reserved.

After supper—and the table literally creaked with food—there were a few conventional party games and prizes. Then—the high-light of the evening—came the Gaelic songs, without which no Highland "ceilidh" is complete.

These, above all, linger nostalgically in the memory. The heart-searching melodies of "An t-Alltann Dubh" (The Black

Burn), finely sung by a young crofter. "The Fair Maid of Barra",
tender and sad and holding all the romance of the Isles—a song I
had already heard sung as a test-piece at the Gaelic Mod. "Màiri
Baile Chrò", and the rhythmic lilt of "Tiugainn Leam" (Come
With Me), led by the Postmaster, with the rest of the company
joining in the choruses. In English, we had "Down by the Green
Bushes". Then, a young fisherman from Wester Alligin sang
"Tìr nam Beann s'na Gleann s'na Gaisgeach", an unpublished
song by Mr Duncan MacLennan, a local bard then living at
Achanalt. With the composer's permission, I reprint the following
verses:

> "Tìr nam beann s'na gleann s'na gaisgeach,
>   Tìr na breacan uaine,
> Tìr mo ghràidh's am fearann bòidheach
>   Far biodh an òigridh uallach.
>
> Se tìr mo dhùthcas is mo ghràidh,
>   Tìr na sàr dhuin-uasal,
> Far am bithidh na botuil làn,
>   Gach tràghadh anns na cuachan.
>
> Tìr nam beann, etc. . . .
>
> Far bithidh na gillean dol s'na righil
>   S'na nigheanagan ri guaillean,
> S'iad dhannsadh grinn air ùrlar bòrd
>   N'uair shéideadh ceòl ri'n cluasan.
>
> Tìr nam beann, etc. . . ."

My Highland friends helped me to work out the following
translation of this charming song:

> "Land of bens and glens and heroes,
>   Land of the green plaidie,
> Beloved land and bonnie land
>   Where all the young are merry.
>
> My native country and my love,
>   Land of thorough gentlemen,
> Where the bottles will be filled
>   And emptied into 'cuachan' *

* "cuachan"—Highland drinking-cups.

Land of bens, etc. . . .

Where the young men dance the reel
  With maidens at their shoulder,
Lightly dance on wooden floors
  When blows the tuneful piper.

Land of bens, etc. . . ."

One has, however, to hear it sung in the original tongue to appreciate its haunting beauty.

At one time, no "céilidh" would be complete without its legends—often of so fearsome a nature as to make the visitors afraid of walking home alone. But such story-telling is a habit which (except in some remote corners of the Outer Isles) is dying out with the older generation. There are few among the Highland youth of today who either know or care for the tales of their grandparents, and, despite the efforts of an enlightened minority to preserve it, this ancient Highland custom is fast passing into oblivion.

One of the tales which used to be told in Alligin is the story of the Jew's Harp. This instrument was at one time played by many a solitary shepherd on the hill, and was considered blessed through its association with God's chosen people.

The story recounts how three lads were once away at the shieling, caring for the cattle which had been turned out on the hill for the summer. As was the custom, they were spending the night in a little hut up in the mountains, where two lazed on improvised beds while the other sat at the primitive table and entertained them by playing airs on his Jew's harp.

Presently, feeling at a "loose end", they audibly wished that three handsome lassies might join them and help to while away the night. No sooner was the wish expressed than in walked three tall damsels of startling and sinister beauty. Two of the visitants went and lay beside the lads who were resting, while the third sat down at the table and sombrely watched the boy who was playing the Jew's harp. Each time he would have stopped playing, he saw her long-nailed fingers curving to tear him. Out of the corner of his eye, he could see blood streaming across the floor from the two beds. All through that terrible night, he kept playing the harp, tune after tune, while the wild-eyed maiden narrowly watched him, waiting for him to stop. At last, in desperation, he flung his "breacan" and staff on to the table and made for the door. Looking back, he saw her tearing the tough plaid to shreds with nails and teeth. A few moments later, he heard the rustle of her gown as she came swiftly after him.

Still playing the Jew's harp, he ran headlong across the hill to a park where he knew that horses were kept. The patient creatures were standing about sleepily in the mysterious half-light which comes before the dawn. Groping around, the lad found a colt, and scrambled on to its back. Here, he was protected without need of the harp, for the colt was of old counted a sacred animal due to its association with Our Lord's triumphal entry into Jerusalem. As the exhausted shepherd-boy clung to the colt's mane, panting to regain his breath, a streak of flame in the east heralded the birth of the new day. A moment later, the cock crew. With a weird screech, the vampire vanished, leaving the lad shivering but safe in the cold light of the mountain dawn.

At one time, of course, a score of such tales were told around the peat-fire flame on winter nights in the Highlands, some traditional, some invented on impulse by local bards who had achieved renown as story-tellers. Many were blood-curdling in character, and one hears how two friends would be returning home together after such an evening, and how one would keep glancing covertly at the other to see if he had grown a cloven hoof! If you went home alone, you would be almost too scared to look round at all—in a state of mind reminiscent of that described by Coleridge in "The Rime of the Ancient Mariner":

> "Like one that on a lonesome road
> Doth walk in fear and dread,
> And having once turn'd round, walks on,
> And turns no more his head;
> Because he knows a frightful fiend
> Doth close behind him tread. . . ."

And now, the "old tales" are all but vanished. Particularly is this evident in communities which are entirely Protestant in faith and outlook, for many of these ancient traditions have been felt to have their roots in ignorance and credulous superstition. Yet, there are tales concerning ministers of the Reformed Churches which are, to say the least of it, "passing strange". Of old, according to Alligin tradition, there was a famous minister in the parish of Lochcarron who was also a prophet and a seer. At his passing, a green branch grew out of the pulpit from which he used to preach. This same learned man was one day conducting a Communion, and when he came down from the pulpit to perform the customary rite of drawing a "gàrradh" or spiritual wall around the Lord's Table to bar the unworthy, he found himself unable to say a word. Twice he returned to the pulpit and prayed. The third time, he said, "I'll serve this Table, if the Devil himself is sitting there!" When he came down again, he walked briskly round the Table, tapped a man on the shoulder, and told him to get up at once, as he was an adulterer and unworthy to partake of the Supper of the Lord. This minister also converted Ceit Mhór, or Big Kate, a great sinner who literally wept herself blind on realising the state of depravity into which she had fallen. Afterwards, the minister was wont to say that there had been a devil at every Communion Table he had served, except the one he had once served especially for Blind Kate.

There is also told a story of two young men who were talking lightly and frivolously about death and the various beliefs concerning the hereafter.

"Well," finished one of them, jokingly, "if I die first, I'll come back and tell you what it's like!"

"Yes, do!" laughed the other.

. . . And, in a short time, the first lad fell ill and died. Thereafter, his friend was haunted by a vision of him which met him every night and made signs for him to follow. In distress, the young man went to the minister and poured out the whole tale. He was advised to go with the apparition, but to take with him the Bible and a piece of iron. This last he was to hold out if the ghost wished to shake hands. The next night, he followed the phantom to a desolate spot, where it said that it wished to deliver the promised message concerning the next world.

"And where I am," it finished, sombrely, "I hope that you will never come!"

It then held out its hand. The lad extended the piece of iron—and, at the contact, the metal crumbled to powder and the apparition vanished for ever.

Such are the stories yet told, on occasion, of a winter's night among intimate groups of friends or neighbours. But of the

ancient faery-lore indigenous to these wild glens of the west,
little is heard now that the Wee Folk have been driven from the
hollow hills. Only sometimes, somewhere, a chord of memory
will be stirred and a tale told which surprises this utilitarian age
with a vision of

"... magic casements opening on the foam
    Of perilous seas, in faery lands forlorn. . . ."

Of this enchanting nature is the following legend, which used
to be recounted in the little crofts around Loch Torridon:

At one time, there lived in the district a young fisherman, who
diligently pursued his craft on the grey waters of the loch. One
day, to his amazement, he caught in his nets a mermaid of a quite
astonishing beauty. So lovely was she that he could not find it in
his heart to lose sight of her—so he took her home, and, as an
experiment, cut off her tail.

In a short time, to his joy, she grew human legs, and lost all
memory of the sea. The young fisherman hid the tail among the
rafters of the barn, and, in due course, he and the ex-mermaid
were married. His strange bride bore him several fair human
children, and, for some years, they lived happily together in their
neat little house by the shore.

But one day, when the fisherman was away at sea, the inevitable
happened. His fair wife was, as usual, carrying on happily with
the work of the croft—and perhaps she was singing, for she was
very contented. Going into the barn for some fresh hay for the
cattle, she suddenly noticed what looked like a big dried fish
tucked up in the rafters. For a while, she stood and looked at it in
surprise . . . and, slowly, crept upon her the strange desire to get
it down and examine it more closely. With some little difficulty,
she achieved her object, and was presently holding the tail
wonderingly in her hands.

. . . And, all at once, the tang of the blown spray was in her
nostrils—not alien now, but remembered, and bitterly sweet.
Shaken with an irrepressible yearning, she stood trembling in the
dark barn, her sad heart aching for the cold caress of the sea.

In secret, like the wild and strange creature she had suddenly
become, she slipped down to the shore. Behind a rock, she cast
off her clothes and drew the dried and crinkled tail over the human
legs. Slowly, exquisitely, life flowed into the dull scales, and they

Turf-thatched byres on the fringe of Alligin

began to shine and glitter in the sun. With a powerful flick and a flash of blinding silver, the mermaid dived off the rock, and was gone down and down into the green billows of the embracing sea.

She did not forget her husband, however, or her earth-born children—though she had become far too wise to allow anyone to catch her again. But, for many years afterwards, their nets would be full of fish, even while their neighbours caught nothing at all. The sea, however, had completely reclaimed its own, and the mermaid herself was never seen again.

. . . But no doubt the ageing fisherman would often fancy that he saw the glint of her green-gold hair in a sunlit swirl of the tide; and when the seals sang at night along the grey beaches it would be for him the voice of his lost love, crooning strange lullabies to the children she had borne him.

Among the Highland legends, it is such tales that put a spell upon the heart.

During a cold, moonlit night in the second week of October, more snow fell on the high hills. In the dawn, the pinnacle of Mullach an Rathain was an icy blue, backed by rose-edged cloud. All day, the loch was dead-calm, lighted by a frost-haloed sun. Night came again, and all the quiet hills were mirrored in the motionless waters, silvered by the unearthly radiance of the full moon. All over the high arch of the heavens floated delicate stipplings of grey-gold cloud, between which a few wan stars peered down on a spell-bound world. There was no sound but the far-off roaring of stags, vibrating eerily among the moon-washed hills. The cottages were a ghostly white, backed by shadowy braes and fronted by the silver sea.

That night, we sat around a neighbour's fire and discussed crofting. My cottage, sub-let to me, was almost the only one in the village which belonged to the laird. Under the Crofting Act which followed the bad old days of the evictions, each of the modern crofters owns his house and cannot be ejected; but he pays a rent to the laird for the land, including that on which the house stands. Each croft has so much arable land and so much common pasture. The crofter buys his ewes and cows, but rents rams and bulls from the Ministry of Agriculture. The rams stay for only one winter; but the bull stays two years. Any rented animals which die must be paid for. At clipping-time, the sheep

193

Sunlight on snow—Beinn Eighe from Coulin

are all driven down to the fank, and each person clips his own. Even old ladies who own only three or four sheep sally forth in a business-like manner, each armed with her shears.

In Torridon, all crops must be harvested by November 1st, when the cattle and sheep are turned loose to winter on the fields. I discovered from experience that people with young dogs must keep a vigilant eye on them at this time of the year. Several times Bridie eluded me, or chewed through her tether, to entice Jeannie away for a glorious unofficial round-up! The Highlander believes that a collie and a terrier are the worst possible combination, and there is a danger that such escapades may end in sheep-worrying. Once embarked on this, a dog, it is said, can be cured by nothing short of the gun.

During my last week in Inver Alligin, we had the first heavy snowfall at sea-level. Most of my packing was done now. Among the souvenirs which had gone down to Corrie by boat to await transport to Achnasheen was an old Highland spinning-wheel, carefully crated and the subject of amused comment from my Alligin friends.

On the Monday, I went into Achnasheen to register the luggage. Snow had been falling all night, and all along Glen Torridon the mountains were robed in dazzling white. Snow-cornices edged the ditches along the road and sparkled on the peat-heaps beyond. Every pool was an icy mirror, blurred by the reflections of the frozen grasses. Towering over the glen, the great, shining pinnacles of Liathach and Beinn Eighe brooded remotely over the wintry landscape.

The wheels of the shooting-brake crunched over a thin crust of ice on the road. The sheep nuzzling the brittle grass-blades were a dirty grey against the purity of the snows. The river, grown old, flowed calmly beside us, as if it had never known the rush of wild brown waters in the spring. The white-robed mountains towered coldly up into the pale firmament, aloof and un-awakened—until the sun pierced once more through the clouds and turned their chaste peaks to shimmering gold. Then, for a few brief moments, we feasted our eyes on a beauty beyond all telling—a picture destined to remain as a vivid memory of this wild land of heart's delight.

The road has come to Inver Alligin now—and a number of

noticeable changes have inevitably occurred in the little hamlet and in its surroundings since my sojourn there. The once-rough road through the glen has been tarred all the way from Kinlochewe to the hamlets on the north side of Upper Loch Torridon, and a road now runs along the opposite side of the loch, linking Annat with Shieldaig. A daily bus runs to and from Strathcarron Station, on the direct Inverness line, and a new road around Loch Carron by-passes Strome Ferry. Beinn Damh Lodge has become the luxurious Loch Torridon Hotel, offering every Highland amenity, including water-skiing, salmon-fishing and deer-stalking. Those of more modest means may find homely accommodation with the hospitable crofters, listed by the Wester Ross Tourist Organisation, who also arrange lectures, rambles and boat-trips to places of interest.

In May, 1967, following the death of the 4th Earl of Lovelace, the 14,000-acre estate of Torridon passed to the National Trust for Scotland. A few months later was added the 2000-acre estate of Alligin Shuas, presented to the Trust by the sons of the late Sir Charles Blair Gordon. Every year shows a large increase in the number of visitors to the Glen Cottage Hostel and the Trust's comprehensive Information Centre at Loch Torridon, where one can study colour-slides and exhibits of wild life, and see live animals of the area in an enclosure at the house of the present Warden, author Mr. Lea McNally. The Trust and the Nature Conservancy between them now administer an area over twelve miles long, in close co-operation with the Highlands and Islands Development Board and the County Council of Ross and Cromarty. The aim is to balance the growing demand for facilities for visitors against the need to maintain the unspoiled character of this unique and beautiful region—and right well is this aim being achieved.

Remote among their clouds, the "grey gaunt heights" of which Swinburne wrote—these "stern hill-ranges that hardly may change their gloom"—brood in their ancient wisdom over strath and stream. And it is to such hills as these that the City-weary wanderer, seeking a God-given grandeur to sustain him amid the stresses of Twentieth Century Living, will continue to lift up his eyes.

GLOSSARY

In compiling this Glossary, I have been assisted by James B. Johnston's *Place-Names of Scotland* (John Murray, London) and MacAlpine's *Pronouncing Gaelic Dictionary* (Alex. MacLaren & Sons, Glasgow). Spoken Gaelic, however, varies in different localities, and, to save the visitor embarrassment, I have endeavoured to give the names, as nearly as possible, as they are pronounced *in Torridon*.

In Gaelic, broadly speaking, "mh" and "bh" are pronounced as "v"; "d" before "ia", "ea" or "iu" as an English "j" (a Highland "j" being much softer) and "ch" throughout as in "loch". "S" before "e" or "i" is pronounced as "sh"; "fh" is silent, and "dh" takes the sound of a gutteral "g" or a "y". Adjectives agree with the nouns they describe, as "Sgùrr Mór" (masculine), "Big Peak"; but "Beinn Mhór" (feminine), "Big Mountain".

I am indebted to my friend A. MacD. for advice concerning the meaning and pronunciation of the more obscure words.

B. G. M.

Achanalt (*ach'analt'*), G. Achadh an uillt, the field of the stream.

Achnasheen (*ach'nashe'en*), G. Achadh na sìne, the field of the rain or storm (sian).

Achnashellach (*ach'nashell'och*), G. Achadh nan seileach, the field of the willows.

Àird (*airrd*), a height or promontory.

Àird na h-Eighamh (*airrd na hay'uv*), doubtful; possibly G. Aird na h-Éigheach, the height of the outcry or proclaiming.

Alligin (*all'igin*), possibly G. Ailleag, a jewel, a pretty woman (Johnston).

Alligin Suas (*all'igin su'as*), Alligin Height.

Allt a' Bhealaich (*allt a vallich*), the stream of the pass.

Allt a' Chumhaing (*allt a choo'ung*), the stream of the strait, or the narrow stream.

Allt Coire Mhic Nobuil (*allt corrie vic no'bul*), the stream of the corrie of the son of Nobul.

Allt Coire Beinne Leithe (*allt corrie ben'y lay*), the stream of the corrie of the grey mountain.

Allt nan Dearcag (*allt nan jerr'acag*), the stream of the berries.

Allt Toll a' Mhadaidh (*allt toll a vah'thi*), the stream of the hollow of the wolf, or stream of the fox hole.

Am Fasarinen (*am fas'ranan*), the teeth; G. also Fiaclan, teeth, prongs.

An Teallach (*an tyall'och*), the forge.

Applecross, G. Apor Crossain, mouth of the Crossan (Johnston); also known as A' Chomaraich (*a chom'rich*), The Sanctuary.

Badachrò (*bad'acro'*), the plain of the cattle-fold.

Baos Bheinn (*boosh'ven*), the mad mountain.

Bealach a' Chòmhla (*byall'och a cho'la*), G. còmhla, in company, together, or còmhlaich, to meet or intercept. Could mean "Pass of the obstacle".

Bealach na Lice (*byall'och na leey'k*), the pass of the flat stone or flagstone.

Bealach nam Bó (*byall'och nam bo*), the pass of the cattle.

Beinn a' Chearcaill (*ben a chairr'kil*), the mountain of the girdle.

Beinn a' Mhuillinn (*ben a vu'lin*), the mountain of the mill.

Beinn an Eóin (*ben an yoen*), the mountain of the bird.

Beinn Bhàn (*ben vahn*), the white mountain.

Beinn Damh (*ben dahv*), from Beinn an Daimh or Beinn nan Damh, the mountain of the stag or stags.

Beinn Dearg (*ben jerr'ag*), the red mountain.

Beinn Dronnaig (*ben dron'aig*), the hunched mountain.

Beinn Eighe (*ben eh*), the mountain of the file (?), the mountain of ice.

Beinn Liath Bheag (*ben leah vek*), the little grey mountain.

Beinn Liath Mhór (*ben leah vorr*), the big grey mountain.

Beinn Liath Mhór Fannaich (*ben leah vorr fan'ich*), the big grey mountain of Fannich.

Beinn na Caillich (*ben na ky'lich*), the mountain of the old woman.

Beinn na h-Eaglaisse (*ben na hay'glesh*), the mountain of the church.

Blaven (*blah'ven*), G. Blabheinn, the blue mountain (Norse "blà", blue) (Johnston).

Bràigh (*bry*), top or summit.

Bruach na Frìthe (*broo'ach na free*), the bank of the deer-forest.

Camas a' Chlàrsair (*cam'as a chlarr'sarr*), the bay of the harper.

Camas an Lèana (*cam'as an lyen'a*), the bay of the lawn or meadow.

Càrn Dearg (*carrn jerr'ag*), the red cairn.

Càrn Eige (*carrn aig*), G. Càrn na h-Eige, the cairn of the notch.

Càrn Eite (*carrn aitj*), the cairn of the unhusked corn, or quartz.

Càrn na Feòla (*carrn na fyo'la*), the cairn of the flesh.

Cas chrom (*cass crowm*), crooked spade.

Céilidh (*kay'ly*), a visit, social, sing-song.

Cnoc nan Sìth (*croc nan shee*), the knoll of the faeries.

Cóigach (*koy'gach*), a fifth part.

Coille na Glas-Leitire (*koly na glosh laychter*), wood of the grey slope.

Cóinneach Mhór (*koen'yoch vorr*), big moss.

Coire Mhic Fhearchair (*corrie vic err'aker*), the corrie of the son of Farquhar, i.e. Farquharson's Corrie.

Coire Mhic Nobuil (*corrie vic no'bul*), the corrie of the son of Nobul.

Coire na Caime (*corrie na kae'ma*), the crooked corrie.

Coire an Laoigh (*corrie an lao'ih*), the corrie of the calf.

Coire Dubh Mór (*corrie doo mor*), the big black corrie.

Coire Domhain (*corrie do'an*), the deep corrie.

Coire nan Clach (*corrie nan clach*), the corrie of the stones.

Creag a' Ghrianan (*crag a hre'anan*), the crag of the sun.

Creag Dhubh (*crag goo*), the black crag.

Creag Sgòrach (*crag sgor'ach*), G. Sgòrrach, conical or peaked crag.

Diabaig (*je'abeg*), deep bay.

Dùn Ca'an (*dun kahn*), G. dùn, a fort or hill; Ca'an possibly from Cathan, battles or conquests.

Duncraig, hill or fort of the crag.

Dundonnell, G. Dòhmnull, hill or fort of Donald.

Eag Dhubh na h-Éigheach (*ek goo na hay'och*), the black notch of the outcry.

Easan Dorcha (*aiss'an dorr'cha*), dark waterfalls.

Eilean a' Chaoil (*ee'lan a chao'il*), the isle of the strait.

Eilean a' Cheò (*ee'lan a cheaw'*), the isle of mist, poetic name for Skye.

Eilean Bàn (*ee'lan bahn*), the white isle.

Eilean a Dà Uillt (*ee'lan a dah ooilt*), the isle of two streams.

Eilean Dubh na Sròine (*ee'lan doo na srone*), the black isle of the promontory or headland.

Eilean Eachainn (*ee'lan yo'chan*), Hector's Isle.

Eilean Gruididh (*ee'lan gru'dy*), Grudie Isle. Doubtful, G. Gruid, lees, dregs.

Eilean nan Naomh (*ee-lan nan noov*), the isle of the saints.

Eilean Ruaraidh Mór (*ee'lan roory morr*), Big Rory's Isle.

Eilean Sùbhainn (*ee'lan su'van*), the isle of berries.

Fasaig (*fass'ag*), G. Fasadh, a little dwelling or stance.

Fuar Tholl (*foo'ar hole*), cold hollow.

Garbh Eilean (*gar'av ee'lan*), rough isle.

Inver Alligin, G. inbhir, mouth of a creek or river—mouth of the Alligin.

Inverness, mouth of the Ness.

Isle Maree (*maree'*), from St Maelrubha.

Killiecrankie (*kil'icrank'ie*), G. coille chreitheannich, wood of the aspens (Johnston).

Kinlochewe (*kin'lochew'*), G. ceann, head—head of Loch Ewe.

Kintail (*kintail'*), G. Ceann an t-sàile, the head of the salt water.

Kyle, G. caol; a strait, narrows.

Kyleakin (*kyle ak'in*), Hakon's Strait.

Làirig Ghru (*lar'ig gru*), G. Làirig ghruamach, gloomy defile or pass, or làirig ruadh, red defile or pass.

Liathach (*le'agich*), grey one, or hoary place.

Loch a' Bhealaich (*loch a vallich*), the loch of the pass.

Loch a' Bhealaich Mhóir (*loch a vallich vorr*), the loch of the big pass.

Loch a' Chaoruinn (*loch a chaor'un*), the loch of the rowan tree.

Loch a' Choire Mhóir (*loch a horrie vorr*), the loch of the big corrie.

Loch a' Chroisg (*loch a rosk*), Loch Rosque; the loch of the cross.

Loch a' Ghlas Thuill (*loch a hlas hule*), the loch of the grey hollow.

Loch a' Ghobhainn (*loch a yo'van*), the loch of the blacksmith.

Loch a' Mhullaich (*loch a vul'ich*), the loch of the summit.

Loch an Eóin (*loch an yoen*), the loch of the bird.

Loch Bad na Sgalaig (*loch bahd na skal'ag*), the loch of the plain of the workman.

Loch Broom, G. Loch a' Bhraoin, the loch of drizzle, light rain.

Lochan Dearg (*loch'an jerr'ag*), small red loch.

Loch Damh (loch dahv), Loch an Daimh or Loch nan Damh, the loch of the stag or stags.

Loch Dubh (*loch doo*), black loch.

Loch Dùghaill or Dhùghaill (*loch doule*), Dugald's loch.

Loch Grobaig (*loch grob'ag*), Loch na Grobaig, the loch of the broken tooth.

Loch na Fideil (*loch na fe'jil*), the twisted loch.

Loch na h-Oidhche (*loch na hoo'icha*), the loch of night.

Loch nan Cabar (*loch nan kab'ar*), the loch of the antlers or rafters.

Loch Toll na Béiste (*loch toll na bay'istj*), the loch of the hollow of the beast.

Maelrubha (*mulro'va*), Saint, founder of monastery at Applecross, A.D. 672.

Màm Sodhail (*mam soul*), Màm Sabhail, the rounded hill of the barn.

Maol Chean-dearg (*Mowl heownd jerrik*) the bald red head.

Meall a' Ghiubhais (*myall' a yu'vis*), the hump of the fir-tree.

Meall an Laoigh (*myall' an lao'ih*), the hump of the calf.

Meall an Tairbh (*myall' an tar'av*), the hump of the bull.

Meall Dearg (*myall' jerr'ag*), the red hump.

Meall Gorm (*myall' gor'um*), the blue hump.

Móruisg (*mor'usk*), big water.

Mullach an Rathain (*mooll'ach an ra'an*). Known among mountaineers as the summit of the horn, or horns; but properly translated as the ridge of the pulley.

Mullach Coire Mhic Fhearchair (*mooll'ach corrie vic erraker*), the summit of the corrie of the son of Farquhar (i.e. Farquharson's Corrie).

Òb Gorm Beag (*ob gor'um bek*), the little blue bay.

Òb Gorm Mór (*ob gor'um morr*), the big blue bay.

Òb Mheallaidh (*ob vyall'i*), deceitful bay. So called because it appears a safe haven, but gives no real protection in a storm.

Portree, capital of Skye, G. Port an Rìghe, the harbour of the king.

Quiraing, O. Norse, crooked enclosure (Johnston).

Ruadh Mheallan (*roo'a vellan*), the red knoll.

Ruadh-stac (*roo'a stack*), the red cliff or steep. Properly An Ruadh-stac.

Ruadh Stac Beag (*roo'a stack bek*), the little red cliff.

Ruadh Stac Mór (*roo'a stack morr*), the big red cliff.

Sagart Ruadh (*sack'ert roo'a*), red priest.

Sàil Mhór (*sahl vorr*), the big heel.

Seann Mheallan (*shen vellan*), the old knoll.

Sgeir Dùghaill (*sgairr doule*), Dugald's rock.

Sgeir na Trian (*sgairr na tree'an*), the rock of the third part.

Sgùrr a' Chadail (*sgoor a hat'al*), the peak of sleep.

Sgùrr a' Chaorachain (*sgoor a choor'achan*), the peak of the cataract or waterfall.

Sgùrr an Fhir Duibhe (*sgoor an ir dooe'a*), the peak of the black man.

Sgùrr Thormaid (*sgoor orr'mid*), Norman's peak (ref. Prof. Norman Collie).

Sgùrr Bàn (*sgoorr bahn*), the white peak.

Sgùrr Dubh (*sgoorr doo*), the black peak.

Sgùrr Fiona (*sgoor fio'na*), the peak of wine, or white peak.

Sgùrr Mór (*sgoorr morr*), the big peak.

Sgùrr na Bana Mhoraire (*voorar*), the peaks of the wife of the Lord (i.e. Beinn Damh).

Sgùrr na Ceannaichean (*sgoor na kyan'achan*), possibly Sgùrr nan Ceannaiche, the peak of the merchants.

Sgùrr na Fiantaig (*sgoor na fian'tag*), the peak of the black heath-berry.

Sgùrr nan Gillean (*sgoor nan gill'ean*), the peak of the young men.

Sgùrr Ruadh (*sgoor roo'a*), the red peak.

Shieldaig (*shield'aig*), herring-bay.

Slioch (*slee'och*), G. Sleagh, a spear (Johnston).

Spidean a' Choire Leith (*speet'jan a horrie lay*), the pinnacle of the grey corrie.

Spidean Coire an Laoigh (*speet'jan corrie an lao'ih*), the pinnacle of the corrie of the calf.

Spidean Coire nan Clach (*speet'jan corrie nan clach*), the pinnacle of the corrie of the stones.

Staffin (*staff'in*), a place of basalt or columnar rock (Johnston).

Stùc a' Choire Dhuibh Bhig (*stuchg a horrie gooi veek*), the point of the little black corrie.

Toll a' Mhadaidh (*toll a vah'thi*), the hollow of the wolf.

Toll na Béiste (*toll na bay'istj*), the hollow of the beast.

Tom Buidhe (*tom boo'i*), the yellow knoll.

Tom na Gruagaich (*tom na gru'agich*), the knoll of the maiden or faery-woman.

Torridon, G. Toirbheartan, a place of transference or portage.

Vugie, properly Badan Mhugaidh, the gloomy clump.

Winged Isle, or Eilean Sgiathanach (*ee'lan sgee'anach*), poetic name for Skye.

BIBLIOGRAPHY

A Fauna of the North-West Highlands and Skye
  J. Harvie Brown and Rev. H. A. MacPherson (David Douglas, Edinburgh 1904).
A History of the Scottish Highlands
  Edited by John S. Keltie (A. Fullarton, 1877).
A Journey to the Western Islands of Scotland in 1773
  Samuel Johnson, LL.D. (Alexander Gardner, Paisley).
British Hills and Mountains
  Peter Bicknell. "Britain in Pictures" Series (Collins, London).
Glen Dessaray and Other Poems
  John Campbell Shairp (Macmillan, 1888).
Hills and Glens
  Brenda G. Macrow and Robert M. Adam (Oliver & Boyd, Ltd., Edinburgh).
Northern Highlands Guide
  Scottish Youth Hostels Association, Edinburgh.
Old Tracks, Cross-Country Routes and "Coffin-roads" in the North-West Highlands
  Rev. A. E. Robertson, B.D., (Darien Press, Edinburgh).
Place-names of Scotland
  James B. Johnston, B.D., F.R.Hist.S., (J. Murray, London).
Popular Tales of the West Highlands
  J. F. Campbell (Alexander Gardner, Paisley).
Primitive Beliefs in the North-East of Scotland
  J. M. McPherson (Longmans, Green & Co., 1929).
Scottish Youth Hostels Association Handbook
Smuggling in the Highlands
  Ian MacDonald, I.S.O. (Eneas Mackay, Stirling).
Tales from the Moors and Mountains
  Donald A. Mackenzie (Blackie & Son).
The Northern Highlands
  Second Edition. W. N. Ling and John Rooke Corbett. Scottish Mountaineering Club Guide (printed by Oliver & Boyd, Ltd., Edinburgh).
The Prophecies of the Brahan Seer
  Alexander Mackenzie, F.S.A.Scot. (Eneas Mackay, Stirling).
The Poems of Algernon Charles Swinburne
  Volume VI (Chatto & Windus, 1904.)

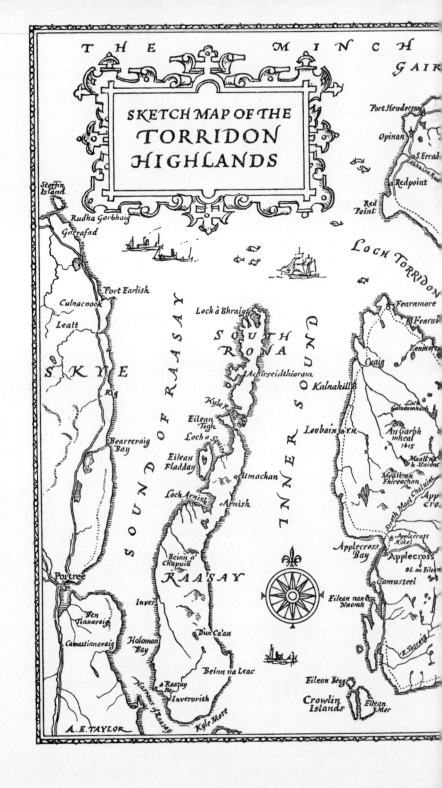

THE   MINCH
                                        GAIR

SKETCH MAP OF THE
TORRIDON
HIGHLANDS

Port Henderson
Opinan
S. Errad
Abhuinn Ruad
Redpoint

Staffin
Island

Red
Point

Rudha Garbhaig
Gairafad

LOCH TORRIDON

Port Earlish

Loch à Bhraig

Fearnmore
Fearub

Culnacnock
Lealt

SOUTH
RONA

Cuaig

Kenmore

SKYE

Acharseidthioram

Kalnakills

Loch
Gaineamhach

Rig

An Garbh
mheal
1615

Bearreraig
Bay

Kyle R.

Eilean
Tigh
Loch a Sguirr

Eilean
Fladday

Loubain zo Y.H.

Mealt na
h-uaidne

Mealt an
Fhireachan

Umachan

Loch Arnish
Arnish

Strath Maol Chaluim

App
cro

Applecross
Hotel

Beinn a'
Chapuill

RAASAY

Applecross
Bay

Applecross

Portree

Eilean na
Eilean

Inver

Camusteel

Ben
Tianavaig

Dun Ca'an

Eilean nan
Naomh

R. Toscaig

Camastianavaig

Holoman
Bay

Beinn na Leac

Raasay
Ra
Inverurish

Eilean Beag

Narrows Raasay

Crowlin
Islands

Eilean
Mor

A. E. TAYLOR

Kyle More

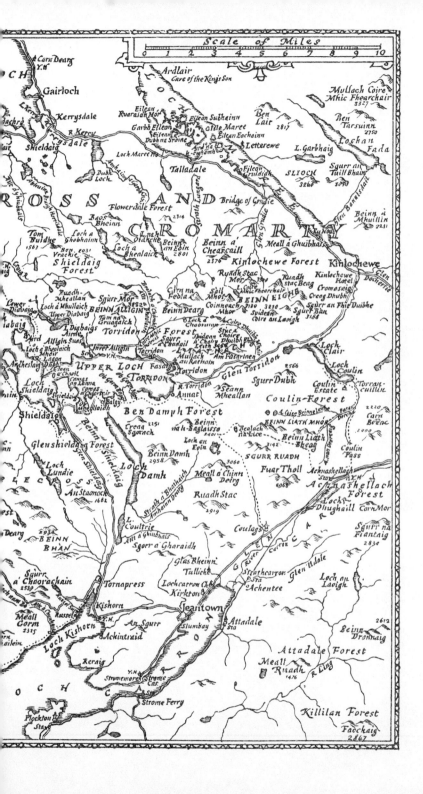

INDEX

INDEX

INDEX

209

INDEX